Protecting Your Proprietary Rights
in the Computer and High Technology Industries

Tobey B. Marzouk, Esq.

The Computer Society Order Number 754
Library of Congress Number 88-70782
IEEE Catalog Number EH0265-9
ISBN 0-8186-8754-1

THE COMPUTER SOCIETY OF THE IEEE

IEEE THE INSTITUTE OF ELECTRICAL AND ELECTRONICS ENGINEERS, INC.

COMPUTER SOCIETY PRESS

PROTECTING YOUR PROPRIETARY RIGHTS

IN THE COMPUTER AND HIGH TECHNOLOGY INDUSTRIES

TOBEY B. MARZOUK, ESQ.

Marzouk & Parry

Published by Computer Society Press
1730 Massachusetts Avenue, N.W.
Washington, D.C. 20036–1903

Cover designed by Jack I. Ballestero

Computer Society Order Number 754
Library of Congress Number 88-70782
IEEE Catalog Number EH0265-9
ISBN 0-8186-8754-1 (casebound)
ISBN 0-8186-4754-X (microfiche)
SAN 264-620X

Order from:

Computer Society	IEEE Service Center	Computer Society
Terminal Annex	445 Hoes Lane	13, Avenue de l'Aquilon
P.O. Box 4699	P.O. Box 1331	B-1200 Brussels
Los Angeles, CA 90080	Pisataway, NJ 08855–1331	BELGIUM

THE INSTITUTE OF ELECTRICAL AND ELECTRONICS ENGINEERS, INC.

Table of Contents

Appendix D

Appendix E

Appendix F

Appendix G

PROTECTING YOUR PROPRIETARY RIGHTS
IN THE COMPUTER AND HIGH TECHNOLOGY INDUSTRIES

SECTION 1
INTRODUCTION

Section 1: Introduction

The computer and high technology industries have undergone revolutionary changes in recent years. These changes, in turn, have resulted in significant developments in the rapidly growing field of computer law. Among the most important questions facing computer and high technology firms is how they can best protect their proprietary rights in software and hardware without unduly hampering their business development and competitive abilities.

This monograph is an attempt to acquaint the reader with the fundamental elements of proprietary rights protection in the computer and high technology industries and begins with a discussion of three basic methods of asserting proprietary rights in software and hardware: trade secret, copyright, and patent. The scope and application of each method are summarized and applied to computer firms.

Second, a discussion is given of how high technology employment contracts can be used to maintain computer trade secrets and confidential information, as well as employee allegiance and support. Specifically, the reader is provided with suggestions in negotiating, drafting, executing, and enforcing employment contracts.

The next section of this monograph discusses how computer firms can protect their proprietary rights when they market their products. Among the topics discussed are: (1) licensing agreements for software authors, as well as publishers and manufacturers of mass-produced and custom software; (2) trademark protection; (3) trade name and trade dress protection; and (4) antitrust considerations in computer marketing activities.

Next, import and export protection for computer products are discussed. The reader will learn how to avail himself of international protection afforded by the International Trade Commission, U.S. Customs Service, federal courts, and international treaties.

Proprietary rights protection in the highly lucrative and growing field of federal government contract procurement of computer products and services is then discussed. Finally, the problem of computer crime is discussed, and the reader is introduced to a sample statute aimed at stemming the growing tide of criminal activities in the computer industry.

The following material does not pretend to be a substitute for competent legal counsel. Rather, the material merely summarizes the basic legal principles underlying computer and high technology proprietary rights. The summary will allow the computer/high technology firm to appreciate the high stakes involved in protecting its intellectual property rights and to take appropriate legal steps in acquiring such protection.

PROTECTING YOUR PROPRIETARY RIGHTS
IN THE COMPUTER AND HIGH TECHNOLOGY INDUSTRIES

SECTION 2
TRADE SECRET PROTECTION FOR SOFTWARE AND HARDWARE

Section 2: Trade Secret Protection for Software and Hardware

Trade secret protection, if properly maintained, represents an effective means of safeguarding proprietary rights in software and hardware. A computer firm seeking such protection, however, must first understand the basis and purpose of trade secret protection as well as its attendant requirements and limitations. The following section discusses the elements of a trade secret, the means of establishing trade secret protection for software and hardware, and the advantages and disadvantages of such protection. (For additional information regarding trade secret protection, the reader is referred to Appendix A.)

A: Definition of "Trade Secret"

A trade secret is defined as:

> any formula, pattern, device or compilation of information that is used in one's business, and that gives [one] an opportunity to obtain an advantage over competitors who do not know or use it.

Restatement of Torts, Sect. 757, Comment b at 5 (1939).

Trade secret law assures the trade secret owner that no one else will be able to use or otherwise benefit from this proprietary information. Before acquiring trade secret protection, however, a computer firm must demonstrate that its trade secrets meet three requirements: (1) novelty, (2) secrecy, and (3) value to business.

1: Novelty

a: General principles of novelty under trade secret law: Novelty is defined as an innovation, something unique, or not commonly known. Thus, "matters of public knowledge or of general knowledge in industry cannot be appropriated by one as his secret." *Sperry Rand Corp. v. Pentronix, Inc.*, 311 F. Supp. 910, 913 (E.D. Pa. 1970). *See also Kewanee Oil Co. v. Bicron,* 416 U.S. 470, 475 (1973) ("subject of trade secret must be secret, and must not be of public knowledge or of a general knowledge in the trade or business"). For software, novelty requires the application of "new principles and concepts with unique engineering logic and coherence," and the expenditure of time and money for the development of new software features that provide the employer a competitive advantage. *Com-Share, Inc. v. Computer Complex, Inc.,* 338 F. Supp. 1229, 1234 (E.D. Mich. 1971), *aff'd,* 458 F.2d 1341 (6th Cir. 1972). With respect to hardware, a trade secret may arise from the unique combination of hardware features that are neither new nor innovative. *See Telex Corp. v. International Business Machines Corp.,* 367 F. Supp. 258 (N.D. Ok. 1973), *modified,* 510 F.2d 1382 (10th Cir.), *cert. dismissed,* 423 U.S. 802 (1975).

Sufficient novelty exists when the information is not common knowledge to the computer industry. As a practical matter, most software will be treated as unique, since any given program will involve numerous algorithms and programming decisions that vary with each programmer and result in differences in "speed, accuracy, cost, and commercial feasibility . . . from system to system." *Com-Share, Inc. v. Computer Complex, Inc., supra* at 1234.

One case will help exemplify how the courts evaluate novelty in the context of the computer industry. In *Sperry Rand Corp. v. Pentronix, Inc.,* 311 F. Supp. 910 (E.D. Pa. 1970), Sperry Rand developed a secret process for manufacturing magnetic memory cores. Three of Sperry Rand's employees, who had signed employee confidentiality agreements and who had access to confidential documents that discussed the manufacturing process, left Sperry Rand to work for a competitor, Pentronix, Inc. Within two months, Pentronix announced its intention to manufacture a complete line of magnetic memory cores. Sperry Rand immediately sued to enjoin permanently Pentronix and sued the former employees.

At trial, Sperry Rand submitted expert testimony that the process for manufacturing the memory cores required seven to 12 months to develop. The evidence further showed that one former employee gained all of his knowledge about the magnetic memory cores from Sperry Rand. Sperry Rand, therefore, argued that its former employees had used its proprietary information to manufacture the memory cores for Pentronix.

Because of the time required to develop the memory core manufacturing process, the court concluded that the process was sufficiently novel to be a trade secret and that Sperry Rand's confidential information concerning the process gave it an advantage over its competitors. The court recognized that the fact that portions of the manufacturing process were matters of general knowledge did not "conclusively negate the existence of a legally protectable trade secret." *Id.* at 913.

The court further held that Sperry Rand's former employees had a duty not to disclose the confidential information. The collusion between Pentronix and the former employees to duplicate the memory core manufacturing process constituted a breach of that duty and an unlawful misappropriation of Sperry Rand's trade secrets. The court, therefore, enjoined Pentronix from further using Sperry Rand's confidential information and held Pentronix liable to Sperry Rand for lost profits arising from its misappropriation of the trade secrets.

b: Trade secret novelty applied to software: In evaluating the novelty of computer software, one must look at the unique logic and coherence of the program. The following three factors should be considered: (1) whether the software represents a unique combination of generally known information, (2) whether the computer firm spent substantial time and expense on the software to create a competitive advantage, and (3) whether the application of the program is in some way unique.

1. *Whether the software represents a unique combination of generally known information:* While most software programs are based on general information in the computer industry, programmers can apply such information in new ways to create unique programs that give rise to trade secrets. For example, in *ComShare, Inc. v. Computer Complex, Inc., supra,* Com-Share and Computer Complex entered into a Technical Exchange Agreement, whereby the companies agreed to exchange all information relating to the SDS 940 Time Sharing Computer System. The agreement also provided that, for 24 months after the termination or expiration of the agreement, neither company would divulge any information it received from the other company regarding software

development without the other company's express consent. During the course of their business relationship, Com-Share provided Computer Complex with a time-sharing operating system that had cost Com-Share nearly $2 million to develop.

After the companies terminated their agreement, Computer Complex announced its plans to enter into an agreement with Tym-Share, Inc. Com-Share, thereupon, sought to prevent Computer Complex from disclosing to Tym-Share the software developments Computer Complex had received from Com-Share during the course of their agreement.

Computer Complex argued that the software developments in question were public knowledge. The court acknowledged that all time-sharing software systems "contain certain elements which perform similar functions and many utilize certain similar fundamental concepts of a general nature." *Id.* at 1234. The court declared, however, that "[t]he specific engineering of these software systems, and their particular underlying technologies and design, together with what has been referred to as their 'logic and coherence,' as well as their speed, accuracy, cost and commercial feasibility may differ greatly from system to system." *Id.* The court concluded that even though the time-sharing software was based on general information in the computer industry, Com-Share had applied "new principles and concepts with unique engineering, logic, and coherence" to develop the program and that Computer Complex had breached its agreement with Com-Share by disclosing the program to a third party. *Id.*

Another case involving trade secret protection for a unique combination of generally known information is *Nichelson v. General Motors Corp.*, 361 F.2d 196 (7th Cir. 1966). Unlike the Com-Share case, however, the court denied trade secret protection. In *Nichelson,* a firm sued one of its employees for misappropriating a trade secret pertaining to a chrome plating process. The firm claimed that the "steps in the process [of vapor blasting chrome plating] had never previously been combined in such a manner, and that the combination resulted in a superior product and a trade secret." *Id.* at 199. The court recognized that a combination of common elements may constitute a trade secret, but noted that the new combination must differ substantially from other combinations and must represent a valuable contribution to the industry. Under the facts of the case, the court found that vapor blasting was a relatively common practice in the chrome plating industry and that the new steps in the process did not represent a sufficiently valuable contribution to the industry to warrant trade secret protection.

Generally speaking, most software involves the application of commonly known information and programming skills. If a computer firm applies the information and skills in a unique or novel manner, it will likely receive trade secret protection for its newly-developed programs.

2. *Whether the computer firm expended substantial time and expense on the software to create a competitive advantage:* Another factor used to evaluate trade secret novelty is the amount of effort that the developer expends to create a competitive product. A computer firm will usually spend substantial time and money to develop a new program. Even though a software developer may have

applied only general information in developing a program, a trade secret exists if the program is sufficiently innovative or represents a valuable contribution to the industry. A business that has dedicated time and expense to develop a new program that provides it with a competitive advantage, therefore, will have its efforts protected under trade secret law.

3. *Whether the application of the software is unique:* The courts also have granted trade secret protection to generally known computer programs that are applied to functions not previously automated. An example of this is found in *Structural Dynamics Research Corp. v. Engineering Mechanics Research Corp.,* 401 F. Supp. 1102 (E.D. Mich. 1975). There, Structural Dynamics had developed a general purpose program that used isoparametric elements in structural analysis. Given the unique application of the program, the court granted trade secret protection to the software.

c: Problems in determining trade secret novelty: Determining whether a particular process or information is sufficiently novel to warrant trade secret protection raises some questions in the context of employer-employee relations. If a data processing employee or programmer could have acquired the same or similar experience and knowledge at another firm, then the information that the employee learns during the course of his employment will not be protected as a trade secret.

In *Wilson Certified Foods, Inc. v. Fairbury Food Products,* 370 F. Supp. 1081 (D. Neb. 1974), for example, Wilson Foods developed a drip-rendering process for manufacturing cooked bacon bits. Wilson Foods' foreman subsequently left Wilson Foods and became President of Fairbury Food Products. Soon after, Fairbury Food began to produce a product similar to Wilson Foods' bacon bits. Wilson Foods claimed that the former employee unlawfully appropriated its trade secret manufacturing process. The court, however, found that Wilson Foods' dry-rendering process was a matter of general knowledge in the cooked-food industry. Because Wilson Foods had not made any significant adaptations to the process, the process was not a trade secret, even though the former employee may have gained all of his knowledge about the process from Wilson Foods. Furthermore, because the former employee had not signed any agreement not to compete with Wilson Foods, he was free to leave his former employer at any time and engage in any type of business activity he chose.

The question of novelty, then, is mainly one of degree. Generally speaking, computer software and hardware will be sufficiently novel for purposes of trade secret protection depending upon the extent to which general knowledge has been creatively combined to create a new idea or process.

2: Secrecy

Perhaps the most important aspect of maintaining a trade secret is actually keeping the program or proprietary information secret. (The various internal and external measures that a computer firm can use to protect its trade secrets from disclosure will be discussed later in Section 2.B.)

Despite the importance of maintaining secrecy, absolute secrecy may not be required. For example, in *E.W. Bliss Company v. Struthers-Dunn, Inc.,* 291 F. Supp. 390, 400 (S.D. Iowa 1968), *rev'd on other grounds,* 408 F.2d 1108 (8th Cir.

1969), the court stated that "[i]t is not necessary that a trade secret be absolutely secret; qualified secrecy is sufficient." (Emphasis added.) The standard of "qualified secrecy" may allow a computer firm to divulge its trade secrets without fear of losing trade secret protection. To maintain this protection, however, the firm should inform those to whom it divulges its trade secrets that the information is confidential. Specifically, the computer firm should notify them (and obtain their prior approval) that theirs is a confidential relationship with certain duties and responsibilities. Thus the firm has a right to protect its trade secrets from those who have obtained possession of proprietary information in confidence, and seek to use or divulge such information.

The courts may protect a firm's trade secret from breaches of confidentiality even if the trade secret independently could have been obtained elsewhere or discovered by experimentation. For example, in *Sandlin v. Johnson,* 141 F.2d 660 (8th Cir. 1944), Sandlin developed a new and improved poultry picking device, which he treated as a trade secret. He revealed the new development to Johnson in confidence during licensing negotiations. The court held that if someone reveals a trade secret in confidence to another party, the secret likely will be protected from unauthorized use by that party. The court further stated that "the fact . . . that another has legitimately discovered the trade secret will not permit one to whom a confidential disclosure has been made to violate the confidence, where the matter has not been generally disclosed by any of the discoverers, so as to have become public knowledge and property." *Id.* at 661. Thus, the court prevented Johnson from revealing or using any of the confidential information he obtained from Sandlin.

3: Value to Trade or Business

The final requirement for trade secret protection is that the confidential information be used in the firm's business and gives it an opportunity to obtain an advantage over competitors who do not know or use it. Clearly, if the information does not assist a firm in some way, there is no reason to prevent others in the computer industry from gaining access to it.

B: Establishing Trade Secret Protection

As was noted previously, to acquire trade secret protection, a computer firm must treat its trade secrets as secret. The trade secret owner must, therefore, take both internal and external precautions to protect its secrets from use or discovery by others. Internal measures of maintaining secrecy involve various in-house procedures, such as limiting access to confidential information and keeping such information under lock and key when not in use. External measures of maintaining secrecy involve certain precautions that must be taken when a computer firm makes its trade secrets available to those outside its direct control.

1: Internal Measures

The most obvious way to assure that technological information remains a trade secret is physically to guard against its discovery. The computer firm, therefore, must implement and monitor compliance with stringent internal security procedures.

The following suggestions may be helpful to the computer firm seeking to maintain the confidentiality of its business secrets:

1. Limit access to computer programs and proprietary business data on a "need-to-know" basis.
2. Limit access to sensitive areas to approved personnel only. Keep such areas segregated and locked securely.
3. Institute proper sign-out procedures in tape libraries. Restrict access to such libraries to designated individuals.
4. Place terminals with access to confidential data in segregated and safe areas. Use passwords or keys to limit access to highly sensitive files. Make sure passwords and keys are changed periodically.
5. Monitor all copying of software, manuals, and other confidential documents.
6. Dispose of paper, tapes, notes, and other trash carefully.
7. Periodically instruct all personnel regarding security precautions. Post warning signs and security notes when appropriate.
8. Exclude all terminated employees from access to confidential data. If an employee leaves on bad terms, take further precautions such as changing terminal passwords and keys.
9. Label all confidential information as SECRET AND CONFIDENTIAL. Each page of proprietary computer printouts should also be labeled confidential.
10. Instruct employees not to leave confidential data unattended.
11. Monitor and review all proposed speeches and publications to ensure that employees do not divulge trade secrets and confidential data.
12. Periodically review the security program in effect at the firm.

Usually when an employee obtains knowledge of a trade secret from his employer, a duty not to disclose that secret is implied simply by virtue of the employment relationship. Thus, an actual written nondisclosure or noncompetition agreement may not be absolutely necessary. Such a written agreement, however, is strongly advised to protect against misappropriation of trade secrets.

The purpose of a formal nondisclosure agreement, whether it be with an employee or a nonemployee, is to obtain in writing a pledge not to disclose trade secret or confidential information obtained during one's dealings with the trade secret owner. Such an agreement should (1) specify the obligations of confidentiality, (2) identify the rights in or ownership of the trade secret, (3) make the individual aware that the owner considers the confidentiality of the trade secret essential, and (4) legally bind the individual not to use the trade secret or to disclose it to a third party. The written agreement not only specifies the terms of the relationship and duties thereunder but also may serve to intimidate others considering misappropriation. Such an agreement further serves to convince clients and other parties that the computer firm is sincerely committed to preserving the confidentiality of its trade secrets.

Nondisclosure agreements are important because they maintain the confidential status of the information while allowing the trade secret owner to disclose it to others. Therefore, anyone who has access to confidential information (partners, associates, clients, technical staff, and even lower-level employees, independent contractors, visitors, and friends) should sign some form of agreement.

2: External Measures

Because absolute secrecy is not required to assure trade secret protection, a trade secret may be made available to the public or to others in the industry with certain restrictions. External measures for protecting trade secrets are those precautions taken by the trade secret owner when it makes its trade secret available to outside parties.

For example, the owner of a software trade secret may choose to license, rather than sell, the program to others. A license restricts the licensee from any use of the program not expressly granted in the license and prohibits the licensee from allowing others to use the program without the express permission of the licensor/owner. A license agreement, therefore, may allow the computer firm to maintain its program as a trade secret while allowing others to use it.

If an owner does not license its trade secret but merely divulges it to a nonemployee, the owner should specifically inform the nonemployee that the information is regarded as a trade secret. One way to assure and prove that a nonemployee knows that information to which he has access is confidential is through the use of a written confidentiality and nondisclosure agreement. As was previously discussed, such an agreement specifically lists what information the company regards as confidential and places the nonemployee on notice as to his responsibilities regarding this information.

Other external measures involving the physical structure of computer software and hardware can be taken to assure trade secret protection. First, a computer firm can place on all software copies notices that limit or prohibit reproduction. Second, a firm can distribute software only in object code; this method, however, would not prevent the user from reverse engineering the source code. Third, software can be designed to require updating by authorized service personnel. Fourth, a firm can deliberately place data bugs that cause the software to be inoperative or to malfunction after a particular date unless the firm modifies the programs. Fifth, a computer firm, through process unit specialization, can design hardware to run only on a particular copy of software. Sixth, the firm can encrypt the software or can create a software or hardware "lock" on the diskette. Seventh, firmware can be covered with a special coating, such as epoxy, to prevent duplication.

3: Case Studies

There are no steadfast rules for determining what constitutes sufficient physical protection of computer trade secrets. In *Telex Corp. v. International Business Machines Corp., supra* at 330, the court observed that IBM had "significant security measures in place to protect its trade secrets and design information." These measures included magnetic locks on doors to allow access only to authorized persons; a control procedure for documents containing IBM trade secrets and for documents labeled "Registered IBM Confidential Documents;" signed nondisclosure statements from each employee; and an exit interview, during which IBM personnel reminded departing employees about the confidential nature of their work and their duties under the nondisclosure agreements. Other precautions such as guards, sensors, locks, and television cameras also were used. IBM's unusually stringent measures convinced the court that the company's proprietary information justified trade secret protection.

Such extreme measures, however, are not always necessary. For example, in *Structural Dynamics Research Corp. v. Engineering Mechanics Research Corp.,* 401 F. Supp. 1102, 1117 (E.D. Mich. 1975), the court noted that "although [Structural Dynamics] did not use the ultimate in policing measures, the professional calibre of its employees . . . made heavy-handed measures unnecessary." In *Com-Share, Inc. v. Computer Complex, Inc., supra* at 1234, the court found that inclusion of the words "Com-Share, Inc. Company Confidential" on all trade secret documents constituted "utmost caution" on the part of the employer to protect its secrets.

To summarize, a computer firm must make a genuine effort to maintain the confidentiality of its trade secrets. No established list of requirements, however, exists to ensure that a firm will receive trade secret protection for its proprietary information. Once the requirements of novelty, secrecy, and value to business are met, tight restrictions on access to and use of trade secret information increase the likelihood of acquiring and maintaining trade secret protection.

C: Legal Rights and Remedies

1: General Rights: What Can Be Protected under Trade Secret Law

"The protection [offered by trade secret law] is merely against breach of faith and reprehensible means of learning another's secret." Restatement of Torts Sect. 757, Comment b at 7 (1939). Thus, when the owner of a trade secret suspects that its confidential information has been misappropriated, it can obtain trade secret protection if it establishes that (1) a trade secret actually exists and (2) the trade secret misappropriation resulted from the breach of a confidential relationship or from some other illegitimate or "reprehensible" means.

While trade secret law will protect a computer firm from those who misappropriate confidential information, it will not protect against other firms that independently develop an existing trade secret. For example, suppose computer firm A develops a program that satisfies all of the requirements for trade secret protection (novelty, secrecy, and value to business). Suppose further that another firm, B, develops virtually the same program without any knowledge of A's product. Under trade secret law, A will have no recourse against B because B did nothing illegal or reprehensible to gain access to A's trade secret. As long as B developed the program independently from A, A will be unable to prevent B from using it.

Trade secret law also will protect a trade secret developed by two computer firms independently as long as both firms keep the information confidential. If, however, one "loses" the trade secret, the secret will be lost to both. In other words, if one computer firm does not maintain adequate security precautions or discloses the trade secret to a third party without first obtaining a signed nondisclosure agreement, both firms will lose the trade secret protection.

Unfortunately, once a trade secret becomes known, whether by legal or illegal means, trade secret protection generally will cease. This does not mean, however, that the trade secret owner is without recourse. A computer firm has several legal remedies available to it when someone "steals" its trade secret.

2: Legal Remedies

Once the trade secret owner proves that someone has misappropriated its secret, the offending party may be subject to both criminal and civil liability. Criminal sanctions for misappropriation of trade secrets are generally governed by state law. Civil remedies available to a computer firm include both injunctive relief and damages.

a: Injunctions: A court injunction requires the person to whom it is directed to do, or to refrain from doing, a certain act. Injunctions can be either preliminary (i.e., temporary) or permanent.

1. *Preliminary injunctions:* When a trade secret owner suspects that his trade secret has been misappropriated or that the threat of misappropriation is imminent and substantial, the owner should immediately petition the appropriate court for a preliminary injunction, which is a temporary measure designed to preserve the existing status of the parties until the court decides how to remedy the situation permanently. Such an injunction will prevent the person accused of misappropriation from further using or disclosing the trade secret until the court determines whether the information is a trade secret and has actually been misappropriated.

   Because a preliminary injunction limits an individual's freedom to engage in an activity that has not yet been declared unlawful, a computer firm must meet two stringent requirements before a court will issue such an injunction. First, the firm must show that unless the court immediately stops the person accused of misappropriation from using the firm's software or other proprietary information, it will suffer irreparable harm. Second, the firm must show that there is a substantial likelihood that it will prevail on the merits of the case and the court will hold the offending party liable for trade secret misappropriation.

2. *Permanent injunctions:* If the court makes a final determination that a trade secret has been misappropriated, then it will probably issue a permanent injunction. This will permanently prevent the offending party from further using the computer firm's trade secrets. Because an injunction is the only way to prohibit the continued illegal use of misappropriated trade secrets, a court most likely will award this remedy in cases involving proprietary rights in computer software and hardware. A permanent injunction, however, is not the only remedy available; damages are sometimes awarded as well.

b: Damages: Usually, in trade secret cases a court will award damages to compensate the computer firm for money lost because of the trade secret misappropriation. A court will not award damages that are based on speculative or assumed losses but will require the firm to calculate its damages accurately and precisely. Oftentimes, this requires the use of a computer expert skilled in economic analysis.

A court usually bases its damages on lost income resulting from (1) misuse or disclosure of a trade secret, (2) decreased sales, and (3) lost profits due to price reductions instituted to compete with the offending party. Attorneys' fees also may be awarded if the party who disclosed the trade secret has signed a nondisclosure agreement that allows such an award.

D: Problems with Trade Secret Protection

Trade secret law does not grant absolute protection to computer firms. While it provides some remedies, such as injunctions and damages, to firms whose trade secrets have been unlawfully misappropriated, the law does not protect firms who have lost their trade secrets "legally." For example, a simple act of carelessness—such as accidentally leaving trade secret information in a lobby, subway, or other public place—may result in the legal loss of the trade secret. A computer trade secret also may be lost legally if an outside party discovers the secret independently or through reverse engineering.

Another problem with acquiring trade secret protection is the cost of instituting adequate security measures. As previously discussed, such measures require constant monitoring and updating and, oftentime, restrain the free flow of ideas.

Another problem with trade secret protection is that such protection is governed by multiple and, oftentimes, conflicting state laws. The trade secret owner, therefore, must incur the time and expense of abiding by different versions of trade secret law if the secret is used in more than one state.

Finally, trade secret protection greatly restrains the marketability of a product. In most instances, wide dissemination of a product makes it virtually impossible to keep a secret from the public. Once the secret becomes public information, trade secret law will afford no protection. Therefore, if a computer firm considers marketability important, it should not rely exclusively on trade secret law to protect its secret from use by others. Rather, the firm may have to rely on copyright protection, which is discussed in Section 3.

Trade secret law thus provides only limited protection of proprietary rights in software and hardware. The computer firm must be careful to maintain a high level of secrecy and to demand loyalty from those with whom it shares its secrets. Trade secret law does not protect against independent discovery or accidental disclosure of a trade secret nor does it allow for wide distribution of confidential information. Nevertheless, if the computer firm is willing and able to incur the time and expense of maintaining the secrecy of its proprietary information, trade secret protection is an appropriate and effective means of safeguarding such information from unauthorized use by competitors.

PROTECTING YOUR PROPRIETARY RIGHTS
IN THE COMPUTER AND
HIGH TECHNOLOGY INDUSTRIES

SECTION 3
COPYRIGHT PROTECTION
FOR SOFTWARE

Section 3: Copyright Protection for Software

A: Scope and Purpose of Copyright Protection

Copyright protection is a second method of safeguarding proprietary rights in computer software. Unlike trade secret protection, which requires strict secrecy and prevents widespread dissemination of proprietary information, copyright protection gives a computer firm greater flexibility in marketing its software and allows the public greater access to the product.

1: What Can Be Copyrighted?

a: Definition of copyright: Title 17 of the U.S. Code, which specifically governs copyrights, establishes the following criteria for determining what can be copyrighted:

> Copyright protection subsists . . . in original works of authorship fixed in any tangible medium of expression . . . from which they can be perceived, reproduced, or otherwise communicated, either directly or with the aid of a machine or device.

17 U.S.C., Sect. 102(a). Title 17 further states:

> In no case does copyright protection for an original work of authorship extend to any idea, procedure, process, system, method of operation, concept, principle, or discovery, regardless of the form in which it is described, explained, illustrated, or embodied . . . .

17 U.S.C., Sect. 102(b).

To qualify for copyright protection, therefore, a work must be the *expression* of an idea. Copyright law does not protect the idea itself.

The expression must satisfy three additional criteria for copyright protection. First, the expression must be one of original authorship. The standard for original authorship is relatively low. It requires simply that the person claiming authorship must not have copied the work. For example, a simple algorithm or mathematical equation is not copyrightable, but a computer program that creates a new expression of a well-known routine or function is sufficient to satisfy the original authorship standard. Similarly, a database of names, statistics, or other publicly available information is an original work, since it constitutes an original compilation of data.

Second, to qualify for copyright protection the expression must be in a physical form, such as a computer program, a tape recording, or a handwritten work.

Third, the expression must be unavailable to the public in general.

b: Expressions versus ideas under the copyright laws: A number of recent federal court decisions have raised considerable questions as to what constitutes a protectible expression—as opposed to an unprotectible idea—under the copyright laws. In

SAS Institute, Inc. v. S&H Computer Systems, Inc., 605 Fed. Supp. 816 (M.D. Tenn. 1985), for example, a court concluded that the unauthorized translation of a copyrighted software program from one language to another constituted a copyright infringement. The court went on to state that

> The copying proven at trial does not affect only the specific lines of code [bearing a similarity to the copyrighted program]. Rather, to the extent that it represents copying of the *organizational and structural details* of SAS [the copyrighted program], such copying pervades the entire [infringing software] product.

Id. at 830 (emphasis added). The court clearly implied that the overall organization and structure of a program was a protectible expression under the copyright laws.

In a subsequent case, *Whelan Associates, Inc. v. Jaslow Dental Laboratories, Inc.,* 797 F.2d 1222 (3d Cir. 1986), the court addressed the question of "whether the structure (or sequence and organization) of a computer program is protectible by copyright, or whether the protection of copyright law extends only as far as literal computer code." *Id.* at 1224. In that case the idea underlying the software program was the efficient organization of a dental laboratory. Because this idea could be expressed through a variety of program structures, the program structure at issue in the case was declared to be "not a necessary incident" to that idea and, therefore, a copyrightable expression. The court concluded that copyright protection of a computer program extends beyond the program's literal source and object codes to its "structure, sequence and organization." *Id.* at 1248.

In *Broderbund Software, Inc. v. Unison World, Inc.,* 648 F. Supp. 1127 (N.D. Cal. 1986), the court went further than the court in *Whelan.* The *Broderbund* court held that a computer program's copyright protection extends not only to its overall structure but also to its audiovisual screen displays.

Two recent cases, however, have held that sequence and organizational features dictated by a program's functions may not be entitled to copyright protection. In one case, an appeals court evaluated a PC program for pricing and selling cotton that performed the same functions as and adopted features similar to a pre-existing mainframe program. The court held that when "market factors play a significant role in determining the sequence and organization" of the PC software, copyright protection will not extend to the sequence and organization of the mainframe software. *Plains Cotton Coop. v. Goodpasture Computer Service, Inc.,* 807 F.2d 1256 (5th Cir. 1987).

In a second case, Digital Communications sued Softklone for software copyright infringement. While the court prevented Softklone from distributing its program unless it changed one screen and certain documentation, the court held that copyright protection of a program does not extend to screen images and that a copyright in the arrangement and design of a screen does not preclude other software developers from using the same commands or symbols. *Digital Communications Associates, Inc. v. Softklone Distributing Corp.,* 659 F. Supp. 449 (N.D. Ga. 1987).

Software developers and marketers should note that both these cases could significantly undercut recent attempts to expand the scope of software copyright protection.

c: Term of copyright ownership: Generally, a copyright extends for a term equal to the life of the author plus 50 years. If a program is the result of joint authorship, the copyright extends for the life of the last surviving author plus 50 years. If a program is a work for hire, the copyright extends for either 75 years from the year of publication, or 100 years from the date of its creation, whichever is less. Given the limited useful life of software, the term of copyright ownership should be more than adequate to protect most programs.

d: Protection against foreign infringement: Many foreign countries and the U.S. have reciprocal copyright treaties. If the copyright owner in the U.S. has fulfilled the proper notice and registration requirements, these treaties generally will protect the owner against foreign copyright infringement.

e: Applicability of copyright law to computer software:

1. *History of copyright law as applied to software:* Although the original 1909 Copyright Act did not explicitly protect computer software, the Copyright Office first accepted computer programs for copyright registration in 1964 by categorizing them as "literary works." In 1976, Congress enacted a new copyright law to replace the 1909 Copyright Act. While the new law did not directly protect computer software, the legislative history indicated that programs were copyrightable literary works.

   In 1980, Congress adopted amendments to the 1976 Copyright Act that defined "computer program" as a "set of statements or instructions to be used directly or indirectly in a computer in order to bring about a certain result." 17 U.S.C., Sect. 101. The 1980 amendments, therefore, specifically recognized software as a copyrightable work of authorship.

2. *Copyrights in source code and object code:* Once Congress conferred copyright protection on computer software, controversy arose as to which part or parts of the program could be copyrighted. The courts seemed to agree that owners could copyright source code because it was intelligible to humans. Surprisingly, however, the courts initially held that object code could not be copyrighted because such code represented unintelligible machine language.

   The early Supreme Court case of *White-Smith Music Publishing Co. v. Apollo Co.,* 209 U.S. 1 (1908), exemplifies why, for some time, courts did not regard object code as copyrightable. In that case, Apollo manufactured perforated rolls of music for use in player pianos. White-Smith, which composed and copyrighted sheet music, claimed that Apollo "copied" two pieces of its sheet music by transposing them into perforated rolls of music for player pianos. The Court, however, found that the perforated rolls were not meant to be read as musical compositions by humans. Instead, the Court found that the rolls operated as a mechanical device and were actually part of a machine. Therefore, because humans could not read the perforated rolls and because the rolls were part of a machine, the Court held that they were not "copies within the meaning of the Copyright Act." *Id.* at 18.

   The courts followed the basic reasoning of *White-Smith* for some time. If a work was not intelligible to humans, it could not be copyrighted. The case of *Data Cash Systems, Inc. v. J. S. & A. Group, Inc.,* 480 F. Supp. 1063 (N.D. Ill. 1979), *aff'd on other grounds,* 628 F.2d 1038 (7th Cir. 1980), for example, shows how the courts applied *White-Smith* in determining the copyrightability of computer programs. In that case, Data Cash developed a program that made it possible for a computer to play chess at six different levels of difficulty. A year after Data Cash produced the game, J. S. & A. marketed a similar game, which contained a ROM (object code) identical to that used by Data Cash. Data Cash brought an action against J. S. & A. for copyright infringement and unfair competition. The court held that because "the ROM is not in a form which one can 'see and read' with the naked eye, it is not a 'copy' within the meaning of the 1909 Act. In its object phase, the ROM, the computer program is a mechanical tool or a machine part but it is not a 'copy' of the source program." *Id*. at 1069. Therefore, assuming that J. S. & A. copied Data Cash's object code, the "copying" was not proscribed by the copyright laws.

In *Apple Computer, Inc. v. Franklin Computer Corp.*, 545 F. Supp. 812 (E.D. Pa. 1982), the district court again followed the basic reasoning in *White-Smith* and *Data Cash*. Here, Apple sought a preliminary injunction against Franklin for infringing Apple's copyrighted operating system software. The court determined that the operating system software was not copyrightable because, unlike the application system software, it was not designed to communicate with humans but was instead used to operate a machine. For this reason, the court concluded that the operating system object code in ROM was not copyrightable. Accordingly, the court refused to grant Apple's motion for a preliminary injunction against Franklin.

On appeal, the Third Circuit Court of Appeals reversed the lower court and established the law as it stands today. *Apple Computer, Inc. v. Franklin Computer Corp.*, 714 F.2d 1240 (3rd Cir. 1983), *cert. dismissed*, 104 S.Ct. 690 (1984). The Circuit Court first addressed the lower court's distinction between operating software and application software. The Court found that there was no difference between operating system programs and application programs and concluded that both systems involve a set of instructions for the computer: An operating system compiler program instructs the computer to translate a language from source code into object code, while an application program instructs the computer to perform a certain task, such as preparing a balance sheet or financial statement.

The Court then proceeded to decide whether object code in ROM could be copyrighted. While acknowledging that object code was unintelligible to humans, the Court noted that the 1980 Copyright Act amendments specifically defined a computer program as "a set of statements or instructions to be used . . . in a computer to bring about a certain result." The court concluded that because the only way to "bring about a result" in a computer was through instructions written in object code, such code was clearly copyrightable. *Id*. at 1248.

The court also found object code copyrightable under the 1976 Copyright Act's definition of "literary work." Sect. 101 of the Act defines "literary work" as "works . . . expressed in words, numbers, or other verbal or numerical symbols or indicia, regardless of the nature of the material objects . . . in which they are embodied." 17 U.S.C., Sect. 101. The court concluded that because object code is an expression in numbers, it constitutes a copyrightable work under the statute. The court, therefore, enjoined Franklin from further infringing Apple's copyright in its operating system software.

2: Who Owns the Copyright?

The copyright in a work protected by the Copyright Act of 1976 "vests initially in the author or authors of the work." 17 U.S.C., Sect. 201(a). The author, however, does not always retain copyright ownership. Determining who owns the copyright to a program is a critical question that depends on the agreement between the author or programmer and the party who commissioned the program. There are several such agreements.

a: Royalty/license agreement: In a royalty license agreement the programmer often retains copyright ownership and is paid a fee based on the number of programs sold.

b: Work for hire agreement: The Copyright Act defines a work for hire as either

> a work prepared by an employee within the scope of his or her employment, or a work specifically ordered or commissioned for use as a contribution to a collective work . . . if the parties expressly agree in a written instrument signed by them that the work shall be considered a work made for hire.

17 U.S.C., Sect. 101. Under a work for hire agreement the employer or commissioning party owns the copyright to the work.

When an employee writes a program, the threshold question is whether the work created was "within the scope of his or her employment." If the work was within the scope of employment, it is considered a work for hire and the employer retains the copyright to the program. For a work to be within the scope of employment, the employer or commissioning party must have the right to direct or control the performance of the work. Additional factors relevant to whether a program is regarded as a work for hire is the extent to which (1) the work is related to the employer's business and (2) the employer's time and facilities are used to create the work.

"No one sells or mortgages all the products of his brain to his employer by the mere fact of employment." *Public Affairs Associates, Inc. v. Rickover,* 177 F. Supp. 601, 604 (D.D.C. 1959), *rev'd on other grounds,* 284 F.2d 262 (D.C. Cir. 1960), *vacated per curiam for insufficient record,* 369 U.S. 111 (1962). Thus, an employee who develops a new computer program will not be forced to give up his copyright ownership in the program if he used his own time, money, and materials to develop it—notwithstanding the fact that he agreed to provide his employer all programs written during his employment, both on and off the job.

A work for hire also encompasses "a work specifically ordered or commissioned for use as a contribution to a collective work." 17 U.S.C., Sect. 101. To qualify under this definition, the programmer and the commissioning party must agree in writing that the work shall be considered a work for hire. Furthermore, the work must be either (1) a contribution to a collective work, (2) a part of an audiovisual work, (3) a translation, (4) a supplementary work, (5) an instructional text, (6) a test, or (7) an atlas. 17 U.S.C., Sect. 101.

Some programs, particularly video arcade programs, may qualify as an audio visual work. *See Stern Electronics, Inc. v. Kaufman,* 669 F.2d 852 (2d Cir. 1982). Other programs or program documentation might be part of a collection and constitute contributions to a collective work. Finally, some manuals and documentation might qualify as instructional texts for use in "systematic instructional activities." 17 U.S.C., Sect. 101.

c: Assignment: A software developer may also "assign" his copyright in a program by selling or otherwise transferring his rights to another party. Absent operation of law, an assignment of copyright ownership must be made in writing and signed by the owner or his authorized agent. A copy of the written transfer agreement together with a check for $10.00 also must be recorded at the Copyright Office.

Merely transferring possession of the physical objects involved—such as the computer tapes, documents, or codes—is not sufficient to transfer copyright ownership. If conflicting assignments exist, the first one recorded and registered at the Copyright Office will prevail. Accordingly, each copyright assignment should be registered with the Copyright Office immediately.

d: Independent contractor: An independent contractor contracts to do work according to his own methods and is subject to his employer's control only as to the final result of his work. Copyright ownership in software developed by an independent contractor belongs to the contractor unless the contractor has executed a written agreement to the contrary. If the contractor has executed a written agreement specifying that the commissioning party owns the copyright in the contractor's work, then the work is regarded as a work for hire. Clearly, if a commissioning party is uncertain whether the programmer he has commissioned to develop software is an employee under his direct supervision and control or an independent contractor, the commissioning party should insist on a written agreement specifying that all work performed shall be considered a work for hire, and assigning copyright ownership (not merely program ownership) to the commissioning party.

e: Joint authorship: A "joint work" is a work prepared by two or more authors with the intention that their contributions be merged into inseparable or interdependent parts of a unitary whole. 17 U.S.C., Sect. 101. The "authors of a joint work are co-owners of copyright in the work." 17 U.S.C., Sect. 201(a).

Each co-owner of a joint work has the power to grant nonexclusive licenses to use the copyright of the work without the consent of the other co-owners. Any profits gained by a co-owner pursuant to such licenses must be shared equally with the other co-owners. The grant or assignment of the entire copyright requires the consent of all co-owners.

B: Required Steps for Copyright Protection

Under the Copyright Act of 1976, a work created on or after January 1, 1978 (the effective date of the 1976 Act) is automatically copyrighted. 17 U.S.C., Sect. 302(a). A work is created when it can be perceived, reproduced, or otherwise communicated for a period of more than transitory duration. 17 U.S.C., Sect. 101. Despite the principle of automatic copyright, however, a copyright owner should carefully follow the notice and registration requirements discussed next.

1: Copyright Notice Requirements

When a computer firm develops a new program, it may copyright the program merely by placing a copyright notice conspicuously on the work. Most copyright notices follow this format "© Copyright 1984 by John Doe. All Rights Reserved." The first part of the notice *must* include either (1) the internationally recognized symbol "©" or (2) the word "Copyright" or the abbreviation "Copr." As a general rule, however, the author should use both the copyright symbol and the term "Copyright."

Following the "©" or word "Copyright" or "Copr." is the year of publication of the work, which, under the 1976 Copyright Act is the date when the work was first made available to the public "by sale or other transfer of ownership . . .." 17 U.S.C., Sect. 101. The year of publication is crucial, because its omission renders the entire notice invalid.

The name of the copyright owner follows the date. If the work is for hire, or has been assigned, then the name should be that of whomever owns the copyright (e.g., the employer, commissioning party, or assignee).

The final part of the copyright notice—the phrase, "All Rights Reserved"—is not required in every country. It is advisable to use it, however, if the work will be marketed outside the U.S., particularly in South America.

The notice should also be clearly visible without the aid of a machine. Thus, the copyright notice on a computer program should appear not only on the terminal screen but also on the disk or cassette, printouts, manuals, and other documentation. Furthermore, the same copyright notices should appear on all published copies and throughout the source code listing.

2: Formal Registration with the Copyright Office

Once the author attaches a copyright notice to his program, the author may formally register it with the Copyright Office. A certificate of registration made within five years after the date of first publication of the program is evidence that the copyright is valid.

To register a program, the copyright owner must submit a Form TX, along with a check for $10.00 to the Copyright Office. (If the owner wishes to copyright the screens of a program, he should also file a Form PA, which can be obtained from the Copyright Office.) In addition to the Form TX and the $10.00, the copyright owner generally must file the first 25 pages and last 25 pages of the program in readable form (called a "deposit") as well as a copy of the copyright notice. It may be advisable to file more than these pages to ensure protection of the entire work.

The deposit can be either in source code or object code. If the applicant chooses to deposit object code, however, the Copyright Office will only grant a copyright under the "rule of doubt." This merely means that the office is unable to examine the object code to determine whether it can be copyrighted. As long as the copyright owner can verify that the object code is an independent work, however, the "rule of doubt" should not undermine the owner's copyright.

While formal registration with the Copyright Office is not required to obtain copyright ownership of a work, there are two distinct advantages to such registration. First, if the software copyright owner wishes to sue a party for infringement, the copyright must be registered with the Copyright Office. Second, registration allows the copyright owner to obtain statutory damages (discussed in Section 3.C.2.), as well as court costs and attorneys' fees. *See* 17 U.S.C., Sects. 504, 505.

3: Common Errors in Copyright Notice and Registration

Oftentimes, computer firms commit errors in drafting copyright notices and registering copyrights. The following are some common examples of such errors and their consequences.

a: Postdated and predated notices (17 U.S.C., Sect. 406(b)): If the copyright owner postdates the copyright notice by up to one year, the Copyright Office will accept the notice as valid. If the owner postdates the notice by more than one year, it is considered invalid. If the copyright owner predates the copyright notice, the notice is valid, but the term of the copyright ownership will begin on the notice date.

b: Date or name omitted (17 U.S.C., Sect. 406(c)): If the copyright owner omits the notice publication date or the owner's name, the Copyright Office considers the notice invalid.

c: Name incorrect or misspelled (17 U.S.C., Sects. 405, 407(a)): If the copyright owner uses an incorrect or misspelled name, the Copyright Office considers the notice valid. If the error misleads someone, however, and he innocently infringes on the copyright, he will not be liable for damages but may be prevented from further infringement.

d: © and/or the word "copyright" omitted: If the copyright owner omits both the "©" and the word "Copyright," the notice is invalid. If one of them is present, however, the U.S. and most other countries will hold the notice valid. The "©" is especially important in some foreign countries. If the owner omits it and markets the copyrighted work outside the U.S., the work may not be protected.

4: How to Remedy Notice and Registration Errors

When a copyright notice is defective, the copyright owner must make a reasonable effort to remedy the defect. He should replace the defective notices on all works that have not been publicly distributed and either recall the works that have been distributed or send substitute notice labels to those who have copies of the work.

Generally, as long as the copyright owner rectifies defects in the copyright notice within five years of the date of first publication, the owner can be protected against future infringements. The owner, however, is not protected against past infringements while the notice was defective. 17 U.S.C., Sect. 405.

C: Legal Rights and Remedies

Anyone who infringes a copyright may be subject to both criminal and civil liability. Criminal sanctions for copyright infringement are specifically governed by 17 U.S.C., Sect. 506 and 18 U.S.C., Sect. 2319. Civil remedies, such as those available under trade secret law, include both injunctive relief and damages.

1: Criminal Penalties

One who willfully infringes a software copyright may be subject to a fine of up to $25,000 and one year imprisonment. 18 U.S.C., Sect. 2319(b)(3). In imposing criminal sanctions, the court may also destroy all available infringing copies as well as the equipment and materials used to produce them. 17 U.S.C., Sect. 506.

2: Injunctions

The courts will generally grant both temporary and permanent injunctions to prevent copyright infringement. The applicable law and governing standards for such injunctions are the same as those under trade secret laws. 17 U.S.C., Sect. 502.

In addition, the 1976 Copyright Act allows Courts to impound copies "claimed to have been made or used in violation of the copyright owner's exclusive rights." 17 U.S.C., Sect. 503. The court can also order the destruction of all infringing programs, tapes, film, or other media as part of a final judgment or decree.

3: Damages

A victim of copyright infringement may also obtain damages from the infringer. If the software copyright owner properly registered his program with the Copyright Office within three months of actual publication, he may obtain statutory damages instead of his actual damages. Section 504(c) provides that statutory damages may not be less than $100 nor greater than $50,000 (if the infringement is willful) and that the court will make the final determination as to a just award. Statutory damages are usually used in cases where the infringement is obvious but the actual damages are difficult to prove. If the copyright owner properly registered his work with the Copyright Office, he will also be eligible to collect court costs and attorneys' fees as part of his statutory damages award. 17 U.S.C., Sect. 505. Unless the copyright was registered within three months of initial publication, statutory damages and attorneys' fees may only be awarded for infringement occurring after the date of registration. 17 U.S.C., Sect. 412.

D: Advantages and Disadvantages of Copyright Protection

One of the major advantages of employing copyright (rather than trade secret) protection of computer software ownership rights is that federal statute governs copyright law. This means that an owner who chooses copyright protection rather than trade secret protection will have to comply with only one law (federal law) rather than the varying state laws governing trade secrets.

Another advantage of copyright is that it provides a safeguard against third-party infringers. This discourages people from buying and selling "illegally" copied programs. One who knowingly purchases an illegally copied program is just as liable to the copyright owner as the person who actually copied the program.

Like trade secret law protection, however, copyright protection is not absolute. A copyright owner can take the legal precautions necessary (copyright notice and formal registration), and infringers will still be able to copy his work. In the case of the "hacker," for example, copyright law is ineffective since a computer owner would not find it economically feasible to track down novice pirates. The copyright owner can only hope that notice warnings on the software will scare the novice from infringing the copyright.

Copyright law also offers limited protection against the professional copyright infringer. Such an infringer usually will disguise the program he copies to make it almost impossible to detect an infringement. If a professional infringer is caught, however, the copyright owner should be able to obtain adequate judicial relief in the form of an injunction and/or damages.

The final problem with copyright protection is that copyright registration may require the owner to make the program code and other confidential information available to the public. Thus, if the program contains proprietary information, it may lose its trade secret status upon public registration with the Copyright Office. The Copyright Office, however, has promulgated regulations to protect trade secrets registered with the Copyright Office. The reader is advised to consult these regulations before registering trade secrets.

Much controversy exists as to whether trade secret protection and copyright protection can coexist. A computer firm, however, need not rely solely on one type of protection or the other. It can successfully combine the two, depending on the type of software to be protected, the competitive advantage afforded by the software, the cost of adequate protection, and the ease with which someone can independently develop the same program.

For example, copyright law may provide better protection than trade secret law if the program will be mass marketed or if it can easily be developed independently. The cost of maintaining internal and external secrecy of such a program far outweighs the relative importance of the secret. Copyright protection in this situation assures the firm's proprietary rights at a very low cost, while allowing mass marketing of the program.

Reliance on trade secret protection, however, might be appropriate when the proprietary information gives the computer firm a significant competitive advantage. Furthermore, if the program is available to a relatively limited market, the computer firm will likely not incur significant costs in maintaining secrecy.

A computer firm might also safeguard a program by combining trade secret and copyright protection. Under this approach, the firm would (1) place a copyright notice on the source code, but treat the code as a trade secret, and (2) register the object code with the Copyright Office pursuant to the "rule of doubt." This procedure allows the computer firm to register the program and acquire statutory copyright protection without revealing its source code to the public.

While neither trade secret law nor copyright law affords perfect protection against misappropriation or infringement, either may provide adequate protection depending upon the circumstances. A computer software firm is advised to review carefully each software program and evaluate its marketing potential and need for "strict" protection. A detailed evaluation of each program will allow the firm to apply the best possible protection or combination of protections at the lowest cost.

PROTECTING YOUR PROPRIETARY RIGHTS
IN THE COMPUTER AND HIGH TECHNOLOGY INDUSTRIES

SECTION 4
PATENT PROTECTION
FOR SOFTWARE AND HARDWARE

Section 4: Patent Protection for Software and Hardware

Patent protection is a third method available to safeguard a computer firm's proprietary rights in software and hardware. This section discusses the various requirements of patent protection, the application of patent law to computer products, and the problems arising therefrom.

A: Definition and Scope of Patent Protection

Like copyright law, patent law is governed by federal statute. Article I, Section 8 of the U.S. Constitution authorizes Congress "To promote the progress of science and useful arts, by securing for limited times to authors and inventors the exclusive rights to their respective writings and discoveries." Pursuant to this authority, Congress has enacted the Patent Act, which is incorporated in Title 35 of the U.S. Code. The Act provides that an inventor may obtain a patent for "any new and useful process, machine, manufacture, or composition of matter, or any new and useful improvement thereof . . . ." 35 U.S.C., Sect. 101. Patent protection does not extend to mental processes or newly discovered laws of nature.

Patent law essentially grants a patent owner a complete monopoly on his invention for 17 years. During this period, a patent owner can prevent unauthorized use, manufacture, and sale of his patented invention. A patent owner need not prove that an alleged patent infringer copied his invention; rather, he need only prove that the infringer used the invention in an unauthorized manner. Accordingly, unlike a trade secret or copyright owner, a patent owner can protect his invention from independent discovery.

Patent law clearly protects computer hardware if such hardware meets the requirements discussed next. Patent law, however, provides only limited protection for computer software. Originally, the Patent and Trademark Office denied patent protection to software on the ground that programs are unpatentable mathematical formulas within the "laws of nature." The Supreme Court changed this line of thinking in 1981 so that, in some circumstances, patent protection may be available to computer programs.

B: Patent Requirements

Before acquiring patent protection, a computer firm must demonstrate that its software product meets four requirements: (1) appropriate subject matter, (2) novelty, (3) utility, and (4) lack of obviousness.

1: Subject Matter

Under 35 U.S.C., Sect. 101, there are four classes of patentable inventions: processes, machines, manufactured items, and compositions of matter. Mere ideas do not qualify for patent protection.

Prior to 1981, the Supreme Court consistently held that computer programs did not fall into any of the four categories. Today, however, the Court recognizes that software may fall into either the process or the machine category. The following brief history of the case law concerning the patentability of software will make clear how the Patent and Trademark Office, the Court of Customs and Patent Appeals (now the Court of Appeals for the Federal Circuit), and the Supreme Court have viewed the patentability of software.

During the 1960s, the Patent and Trademark Office and the Court of Customs and Patent Appeals were constantly at odds over the applicability of patent protection to computer software. The Patent and Trademark Office consistently rejected patent applications for computer programs, while the Court of Customs and Patent Appeals generally found in favor of patentability. Whenever the Supreme Court stepped in, it traditionally reversed the Court of Customs and Patent Appeals and denied patentability, but it never held that computer software was *per se* unpatentable.

For example, in *Gottschalk v. Benson*, 409 U.S. 63 (1972), the Supreme Court held that an algorithm used to convert binary-coded decimal numerals into pure binary numerals was unpatentable. Basing its decision on the principle that ideas are not patentable, the Court found that the algorithm was "a procedure for solving a given type of mathematical problem," and that because the procedure could be performed mentally, without the aid of a computer, there was nothing new to patent. The algorithm in that case could only be used on a general purpose digital computer; it could not be applied to create a useful structure, or be put to any particular end use. Thus, the Court concluded:

> It is conceded that one may not patent an idea. But in practical effect that would be the result if the formula for converting . . . [binary-coded decimal] numerals to pure binary numbers were patented in this case. The mathematical formula involved here has no substantial practical application except in connection with a digital computer, which means that . . . the patent would wholly preempt the mathematical formula and in practical effect would be a patent on the algorithm itself.

Id. at 71-72. The Court specifically stated, however, that its decision did not preclude the patentability of programs in the future. *Id*. at 72.

Thereafter, the Court of Customs and Patent Appeals interpreted *Benson* narrowly and limited its application to patent claims for mathematical algorithms which did not cause physical changes. Thus, the Court of Customs and Patent Appeals left unsettled whether software, which did cause physical changes, could ever be patented.

The Court of Customs and Patent Appeals extended its interpretation of *Benson* in *In re Freeman*, 573 F.2d 1237 (CCPA 1978), and developed a two-part test for determining the patentability of computer software. The test required the court to make two determinations: (1) whether the patent claim included a mathematical algorithm and (2) if it did, whether granting a patent would completely preempt use of the algorithm. 573 F.2d at 1245. Applying this test, the Court of Customs and Patent Appeals reversed the Patent and Trademark Office and granted a patent to a program that used a nonmathematical algorithm to control a phototypesetter.

Subsequently, in *Parker v. Flook,* 437 U.S. 584 (1978), the Supreme Court considered whether to grant a patent to a program that improved an alarm system used in petroleum refining processes. The algorithm in that case was the only new part of the improved alarm system. Because the algorithm embodied a law of nature and because the other parts of the alarm system were well known, the Court held that the system was not patentable. The Court concluded that the entire process had to be new and useful for it to be patentable. The "process is unpatentable . . ., not because it contains a mathematical algorithm as one component, but because once that algorithm is assumed to be within the prior art, the application, considered as a whole, contains no patentable invention." *Id.* at 594. The Court succinctly stated that a "claim for an improved method of calculation, even when tied to a specific end use, is unpatentable subject matter . . . ." *Id.* at 595 n.18. Thus, after *Flook,* it appeared that in order to obtain a patent for a computer program, the entire process had to be both new and useful.

In 1981, the Supreme Court dramatically shifted its standards for evaluating the patentability of computer software. In *Diamond v. Diehr,* 450 U.S. 175, 177 (1981), the Court held that under 35 U.S.C., Sect. 101. "a process for curing synthetic rubber, which included in several of its steps the use of a mathematical formula and a programmed digital computer," constituted a new and useful process or machine. The Court stated that "a [patent] claim drawn to subject matter otherwise statutory does not become nonstatutory simply because it uses a mathematical formula, computer program or digital computer." *Id.* at 187.

In *Diehr,* the curing process employed a computer to measure continually the temperature of rubber in a press and, using a well-known formula, to calculate the time necessary for the rubber to be cured and molded. As the temperature changed, the program instructed the computer to recalculate the cure time and, when the recalculated time equaled the elapsed time, the computer signaled the press to open.

The Court in *Diehr* distinguished *Benson* and *Flook* on the basis that the earlier cases attempted to protect mathematical formulas that did not produce anything new and useful. In *Benson,* the formula did not produce anything new; it only provided a method for performing a function with a computer (changing binary-coded numerals to pure binary numerals) that could be performed without a computer. Similarly, in *Flook,* the formula merely provided an improvement for an old system. In *Diehr,* however, the formula helped to transform an article (synthetic rubber) into a totally different state (molded, precision synthetic rubber products).

The distinction is that the inventor in *Diehr* sought to patent his whole process, not just the formula. The patent would not prevent others from using the known formula; it would only prevent others from using it with the other steps in the curing process. Thus, the Court instituted a new test—similar to the Court of Customs and Patent Appeal's *Freeman* test—which required inspecting the claim as a whole:

> When a claim recites a mathematical formula (or scientific principle or phenome-
> non of nature), an inquiry must be made into whether the claim is seeking patent
> protection for that formula in the abstract. A mathematical formula as such is not
> accorded the protection of our patent laws . . ., and this principle cannot be
> circumvented by attempting to limit the use of the formula to a particular techno-
> logical environment . . . .. On the other hand, when a claim containing a mathemat-

ical formula [directly or indirectly] implements or applies that formula in a structure or process which, when considered as a whole, is performing a function which the patent laws were designed to protect (e.g., transforming or reducing an article to a different state or thing), then the claim satisfies the requirements of [35 U.S.C., Sect. 101].

Id. at 191-192.

Since *Diehr,* the Court of Customs and Patent Appeals has found some computer programs patentable. *In re Pardo,* 684 F.2d 912 (CCPA 1982), for example, a patent for a method of dealing with the internal operation of a computer was upheld. The court emphasized the Supreme Court's language in *Diehr* that a "claim drawn to subject matter otherwise statutory does not become nonstatutory simply because it uses a mathematical formula . . . " *Diehr,* supra, at 183.

Unfortunately, the test established in *Diehr* does not settle the issue of software patentability. The Court decided the case in a 5-4 vote. Thus, there is still opposition in the Supreme Court to granting patents to computer software. Only additional court decisions will clarify the exact state of the law on whether computer programs are proper subject matter for patents.

2: Novelty

Once an inventor proves that the invention meets the subject matter requirement for patentability, it must then be demonstrated to be sufficiently novel. Recall that a trade secret owner also must establish sufficient novelty to obtain trade secret protection. The standard for trade secret novelty is that the information not be common knowledge in the industry. The standard for patent novelty, however, is much higher and more difficult to meet.

Under patent law, a protectable computer program must be different from any invention previously discovered or known. 35 U.S.C., Sects. 102, 103. Specifically, the Patent and Trademark Office must determine that the program was not known or used in this country, patented, or described in a printed publication, in this or a foreign country, prior to its invention by the individual(s) credited as the inventor(s) in the patent application.

Unfortunately, it is difficult to determine exactly what kinds of computer programs meet the novelty requirement, because the Patent and Trademark Office has no precedents concerning previously discovered or known programs. As with the question of appropriate subject matter under patent law, only additional court decisions will clarify what types of software satisfy the patent novelty requirement.

3: Utility

"Utility" under patent law simply means that an invention is useful. Computer software has no difficulty meeting this requirement, because programs, which instruct computers to perform certain functions, are, by definition, useful.

The most difficult patent element to establish is lack of obviousness. Patent law provides that a patent may not be obtained "if the differences between the subject matter sought to be patented and the prior art are such that the subject matter as a whole would have been obvious at the time the invention was made to a person having ordinary skill in the art to which said subject matter pertains." 35 U.S.C., Sect. 103. A person having ordinary skill in the art of computer software is a skilled programmer who is familiar with various methods and tools used by others in the field. Thus, the standard applied to computer software is whether a skilled programmer considers the program to be truly innovative or merely the next logical step in the current state of programming. If the program is truly innovative, it is patentable; if it is merely a logical development, it is not patentable.

C: The Patent Application Procedure

A programmer obtains a patent for his software by first filing an application with the U.S. Patent and Trademark Office. The process takes an extraordinarily long period of time to complete—18 to 36 months—during which the program may be rendered obsolete. Title 35, Sects. 111-135, governs the application process and specifies the necessary requirements, which includes "specification" or full disclosure.

Under 35 U.S.C., Sect. 112, "the specification shall contain a written description of the invention, and of the manner and process of making and using it, in such full, clear, concise and exact terms as to enable any person skilled in the art to which it pertains . . . to make and use the same, and shall set forth the best mode contemplated by the inventor of carrying out his invention." Full disclosure is required so that when the patent expires others will be able to use the invention effectively.

The applicant must also disclose fully the prior art known by the applicant at the time of the application. He must disclose any and all facts—whether adverse or helpful to his claim—that may assist the Patent and Trademark Office in determining whether to grant the patent application. Deliberate failure to disclose such information can result in invalidation of the application.

In addition to specification and full disclosure of prior art, the patent application must also prove the basic elements discussed earlier: appropriate subject matter, novelty, utility, and lack of obviousness. The application must also include the name of the inventor(s) and a minimum filing fee of $150. The Patent and Trademark Office further requires that patents issued on applications made after January 1, 1980, pay additional fees of between $200 and $1200 periodically during the 17 year period of patent ownership.

During the patent application process, the Patent and Trademark Office maintains strict secrecy of the application. No information concerning the patent is given without the applicant's authorization. 35 U.S.C., Sect. 122. Thus, inventions may be maintained as trade secrets until the Office issues a patent.

If the Patent and Trademark Office rejects the application, the inventor may appeal the decision to the Court of Appeals for the Federal Circuit and eventually to the Supreme Court. If the Patent and Trademark Office accepts the application and grants a patent, the patent owner should immediately place a patent notice on the invention. Lack of notice precludes recovery of damages in case of infringement.

Finally, it is important that the potential patent owner file a patent application within one year of either public disclosure, public use, or any attempt at commercialization of his invention. If this is not done, the applicant will lose any chance of obtaining a patent. The potential owner must also be careful not to solicit investments in his invention or to publish any descriptions of his inventions unless he is prepared to file an application within one year. 35 U.S.C., Sect. 102. Both of these initiate the one year deadline. Experimental use that is not a test of marketability, however, does not initiate the one year filing deadline.

D: Legal Rights and Remedies

Patent law defines a patent infringer as anyone who "without authority makes, uses or sells any patented invention within the United States . . . or [who] actively induces infringement of a patent." 35 U.S.C., Sect. 271. Suits for patent infringement may be brought by either the legal title holder of the patent or by a licensee, if the license agreement so provides. When infringement occurs, the patent owner has several recourses similar to those available for trade secret and copyright infringement.

Like trade secret and copyright law, patent law allows patent owners to obtain injunctive relief against future infringement. Courts may award both temporary and permanent injunctions.

Courts also may award monetary damages to a patent owner to compensate for lost profits. At a minimum, the damages will be equal to "a reasonable royalty for the use made of the invention by the infringer." 35 U.S.C., Sect. 284. The court also has the power to award damages equal to three times the amount of actual damages. *Id.*

A court will not award damages when there is inadequate notice of a patent. Once notice is given, if the infringer continues to use the patented item, he will be liable for damages incurred from the point of notification. Courts also will not usually include attorneys' fees in an award for damages except in exceptional cases involving gross injustice, bad faith, or unconscionable conduct on the part of the infringer.

When a patent owner brings an action for patent infringement, the alleged infringer may present one of the following defenses: (1) no infringement occurred; (2) the "patent" lacks statutory subject matter, novelty, utility, or lack of obviousness and is, therefore, invalid; and (3) the patent is invalid because there was insufficient disclosure in the application. 35 U.S.C., Sect. 282.

One of the advantages of patent protection is that the law presumes that a patent is valid. Thus, an alleged infringer attempting to establish a defense on the basis of an invalid patent has the burden of proving that the patent is, in fact, invalid.

E: Advantages and Disadvantages of Patent Law Protection

1: Advantages

As was mentioned previously, patent law has the potential of providing the greatest amount of protection possible to an invention. A patent offers its owner the exclusive privilege to sell, manufacture, or use the invention for up to 17 years. Unlike trade secret and copyright law, it even protects against independent discovery or development. Once the Patent and Trademark Office issues a patent, it cannot be lost, unless, of course, it is subsequently found invalid.

A patent also does not require the strict maintenance of secrecy required by trade secret law. Therefore, elaborate and expensive security systems are not needed, and mass distribution is possible. Obviously, the exclusiveness of the rights offered by patent protection can also create great financial rewards.

2: Disadvantages

Unfortunately, when applied to computer software, the disadvantages of patent law protection far outweigh the advantages. As was shown by the *Diehr* decision, only programs that actually produce a new and useful product or process are patentable. Computer programs often will not satisfy this strict requirement. Rather, many programs will constitute unpatentable algorithms or mathematical formulas, similar to the program in *Benson*.

Another problem with patent protection is that it takes at least 18 to 36 months to obtain a patent. Much software is obsolete after that period of time. Because the application process is technical, high legal fees usually result. The process also requires full disclosure of the invention, and, if the patent application is denied, the inventor's secrets will be publicly available. Thus, while patent law offers the most comprehensive protection, it is usually unavailable or impractical as a means of protecting computer software.

PROTECTING YOUR PROPRIETARY RIGHTS
IN THE COMPUTER AND
HIGH TECHNOLOGY INDUSTRIES

SECTION 5
PROTECTING PROPRIETARY RIGHTS
THROUGH EMPLOYMENT CONTRACTS

Section 5: Protecting Proprietary Rights through Employment Contracts

Computer hardware and software firms often expend considerable time, resources, and money in developing and marketing various computer products, including custom software, firmware, and integrated circuits. The contents of such products, as well as the methods for their production and utilization, are typically viewed as confidential and as trade secret information by computer firms. In the normal course of computer product development and marketing, the employees of computer firms (and independent contractors) generate or must be provided with access to confidential and trade secret information regarding the products of their employers. Many computer and high technology firms, however, commit a crucial business error by failing to provide an employment contract that limits the employees' ability to divulge confidential and trade secret information and to compete with or otherwise damage the business of the employer.

Clearly, the absence of a carefully drafted employment contract can be devastating to a computer firm whose business survival depends on the protection of its proprietary rights. The following section discusses the basic elements of employment contracts in the computer industry from the perspective of the employer seeking to protect his business interests. Specifically, this section addresses the negotiation, drafting, execution, and enforcement of high technology employment contracts in light of recent case law, as well as the experience of employers in the computer industry. (For additional information regarding high technology employment contracts, the reader is referred to Appendix B.)

A: Negotiating the Employment Contract

Since the employment contract will ultimately govern relations between the employer and the employee, it is essential for a computer firm to establish careful procedures for negotiating the contract. Failure to comply with certain procedural and legal requirements before executing a contract may nullify its effect or preclude its enforcement. The following guidelines, therefore, should be followed by the computer firm engaged in contract negotiations with its prospective employees.

1: Watch What You Say During Contract Negotiations

During contract negotiations, company representatives should be extremely careful of what they say to the prospective employee. Even though a contract may be drafted to prevent an employee from enforcing oral commitments not embodied in the contract (see Section 5.B.7.), a court may in certain circumstances rely on oral statements made by the employer to determine the meaning and intent of the parties.

In one recent case, for example, *Weiner v. McGraw-Hill, Inc.*, 443 N.E.2d 41 (N.Y. Ct. App. 1982), a prospective employee was assured by a company representative that the firm's policy was to terminate employees only for "just cause" and that employment at the company had the advantage of job security. *Id.* at 442. The company's preprinted application forms also referenced the firm's personnel handbook, which represented that "the company will resort to dismissal for just and sufficient cause only." *Id*. After several years of employment, the employee was dismissed for "lack of application." *Id*. at 443. He subsequently brought suit against his employer for wrongful dismissal. Under these facts, the New York Court of Appeals held that the employee could sue his former employer based on the oral representations and assurances made to him prior to his employment, as confirmed by the statement of policy set forth in the firm's personnel manual. *Id*. at 445.

Clearly, an employer should not make any gratuitous oral promises during contract negotiations. Such promises, if relied upon by the prospective employee, may come back to haunt the employer at a later date.

2: Carefully Draft Personnel Policy Manuals

In addition to oral assurances made by the employer during contract negotiations, written statements in office handbooks or personnel manuals may be used to expand an employee's rights under a contract. In several recent court cases, for example, employees have been able to enforce personnel policy manuals as supplements to their employment contracts and thereby bind their employers beyond the specific terms of the individual contracts. *See, e.g., Weiner v. McGraw-Hill, Inc., supra* at 445-446; *Piper v. Board of Trustees of Community College District No. 514,* 426 N.E.2d 262, 267 (Ill. App. Ct. 1981); *Carter v. Kaskaskia Community Action Agency,* 322 N.E.2d 574, 576 (Ill. App. Ct. 1974).

While a personnel manual serves the useful function of informing employees of company policies, the computer firm must exercise extreme caution in drafting such a manual. The manual, for example, should include a statement that it is not intended to constitute any type of contract between the company and the employees. The statement should include words to the effect that the policies set forth in the manual, particularly those involving employee terminations, are meant only as guidelines, not as rigid standards. This disclaimer should not, however, be used as a substitute for careful drafting of the manual's contents; where the disclaimer contradicts other expectations raised by the contents of the manual, the ambiguity in the manual will be construed against the employer.

In addition, the manual should not include unnecessary detail about termination policies. The more specific the standards and procedures for termination, the more likely (1) an employee will claim substantive and procedural rights arising from the manual and (2) a particular termination will violate the standards set forth in the manual.

In short, a personnel or office manual may be used against an employer. The employer, therefore, should make every effort to limit the binding effect of the manual to avoid unforeseen liabilities to employees.

3: Give the Employee Ample Opportunity to Review the Contract

Often, computer firms present a proposed employment contract to a new employee on the first day of work, thereby giving the employee no meaningful opportunity to review the contract or negotiate specific terms. As a matter of policy, however, a computer firm should provide the prospective employee a copy of the employment contract *before* the start of employment. Following this procedure will guard against any allegation that the employee was placed at a disadvantage relative to the employer.

An employer who fails to provide a prospective employee with the opportunity to review the proposed contract may be unable to enforce the contract, particularly if a court concludes that the employee was not given a fair chance to negotiate the terms of his employment. In *PEMCO Corp. v. Rose,* 257 S.E.2d 885 (W. Va. 1979), for example, the defendant was offered and accepted employment with an engineering firm in West Virginia. Thereafter, the defendant canceled his housing lease in Washington, D.C., signed a contract to purchase a home in West Virginia, and moved all his personal belongings to his new place of residence. When the defendant arrived at his employer's offices for the first day of work, he was asked to sign an "agreement" restricting his right to compete with his employer should he leave the firm. Having already moved to West Virginia, the defendant had no choice but to sign the contract. In an action by the former employer to prevent the defendant from working for one of the employer's competitors, the court concluded:

> Under the circumstances in which the employee found himself, it is beyond cavil that his ability to negotiate with respect to the post-employment restraint was markedly diminished. At the very least, the employee was not as freely able to bargain concerning the provision as he was at the time he received the offer of employment. The covenant not to compete was not a freely bargained for term or condition of employment, but rather was a term or condition of employment extracted from or imposed on an employee under circumstances which deprived him of any fair ability to negotiate.

Id. at 890.

A computer firm should, therefore, provide the prospective employee a copy of the contract prior to employment. Failure to do so may seriously undermine the validity and enforceability of the employment contract.

4: Determine Whether the Prospective Employee Is Bound by a Prior Employment Contract

Given the frequency of job changes among professional employees at computer firms, an employer should know whether a prospective employee is bound by a contract with a former employer that restricts the scope of the employee's work. During contract negotiations, therefore, the employer should specifically ask the prospective employee whether the employee is still subject to a prior employment contract. If the employee is not bound, then the employer should obtain a written assurance to that effect. If, however, the employee is subject to a prior employment contract, the new employer should consult with counsel to determine (1) whether and to what extent the contract does, in fact, restrict the prospective employee's ability to work for the new employer, (2) whether the restrictions are enforceable, and (3) whether and in what manner the new employer should contact the old employer to discuss the scope and effect of the prior employment contract. Without a careful review of prior contractual restrictions on the prospective employee, the new employer and employee may find themselves subject to a suit for injunctive relief and/or damages by the former employer.

B: Drafting the Employment Contract

The terms and conditions of any employment contract generally depend upon the particular needs of the computer firm, as well as the prospective employee's scope of employment. The computer firm should draft the employment contract to protect its business interests and proprietary rights, while giving the employee a clear understanding of his contractual obligations. A computer firm should consider the following guidelines when drafting an employment contract.

1: Protect Trade Secrets and Confidential Information through Confidentiality and Nondisclosure Agreements

Perhaps the most important provision in any computer employment contract is a confidentiality and nondisclosure agreement. Under the terms of this agreement, the employee pledges to hold in confidence and not to disclose directly or indirectly trade secrets and confidential information obtained from the employer during the course of employment. Such trade secrets and confidential information may include (1) discoveries or inventions; (2) ideas or concepts; (3) software (object code and source code), regardless of the stage of development; (4) software documentation, including flow charts and diagrams; (5) designs, drawings, and models; (6) internal specifications and testing procedures; (7) data and databases; (8) marketing, development, and research plans; (9) novel techniques and procedures; (10) certain kinds of customer lists; (11) bidding policies and procedures; and (12) miscellaneous marketing information concerning finances, pricing policies, and price lists.

A confidentiality and nondisclosure agreement specifically restricts the employee from divulging to the public—particularly the employer's competitors—any information treated as secret or confidential by the employer. To ensure complete protection of its trade secrets, a computer firm should require its nontechnical support personnel, as well as its technical employees, to sign confidentiality and nondisclosure agreements. Nontechnical or lower-level employees often have access to considerable proprietary data. Without a specific agreement or evidence of a confidential relationship, an employer may be unable to prevent such employees from divulging trade secrets or confidential business information. *Shatterproof Glass Corp. v. Guardian Glass Co.*, 462 F. Supp. 854, 865, *aff'd on other grounds*, 462 F.2d 1115 (6th Cir.), *cer. denied*, 409 U.S. 1039 (1972).

Similarly, independent contractors and visitors may acquire or have access to a firm's trade secrets. To preserve the confidentiality of such information, the computer firm should also require these individuals to sign confidentiality and nondisclosure agreements.

Confidentiality and nondisclosure agreements, when carefully implemented, serve to place employees and other affected parties on notice that their jobs might involve trade secrets. Therefore, the employee is more likely to be secrecy conscious and to exercise prudence with respect to confidential matters entrusted to him. Confidentiality and nondisclosure agreements can also assist the computer firm in convincing its existing and potential clients that confidential information submitted to the firm will be protected from disclosure. Therefore, the computer firm is advised to require all prospective employees, independent contractors, and visitors with access to confidential information to sign such agreements.

2: Protect Trade Secrets and Confidential Information through Covenants Not to Compete

In addition to demanding that employees execute confidentiality and nondisclosure agreements, an employer should protect his confidential information and trade secrets by requiring professional employees to sign covenants not to compete. A covenant not to compete seeks to prevent an employee with access to sensitive proprietary information from competing with or working in the same line of business as his former employer within a given geographic area and for a given period of time. The practical effects of such a covenant are to prevent (1) the employee from directly or indirectly disclosing trade secrets to any new employer who might be in competition with the old employer, (2) other firms from "buying" confidential information by hiring employees of a competitor, and (3) the employee from appropriating confidential information to start his own business.

Because of their restrictions on worker mobility, covenants not to compete must be narrowly defined and carefully drafted. The enforceability of such covenants is discussed in Section 5.D.3.

3: Make Sure the Employment Contract Transfers to the Employer the Rights to All Works by the Employee

As discussed previously, under the Copyright Act of 1976, a computer program or other work prepared by an employee within the scope of his employment is a "work made for hire," 17 U.S.C. Sect. 101, and "the employer or other person for whom the work was prepared is considered the author" and owns all rights in the copyright. 17 U.S.C. Sect. 201(b). Accordingly, without an employment contract that provides otherwise, copyright in all the works produced by an employee in fulfilling his duties vests with the employer. Some questions, however, might arise as to whether an individual is an "employee"—under the direct control and supervision of the employer—or an independent contractor, *see, e.g., Epoch Producing Corp. v. Killian Shows, Inc.,* 522 F.2d 737, 744 (2d Cir. 1975), *cert. denied,* 424 U.S. 955 (1976), and whether work performed by an employee is within the scope of his employment. To avert any misunderstanding or confusion between the employer and the employee on these questions, the employment contract should include the following provisions, tailored to fit each employer's needs.

1. All work by the employee or independent contractor is deemed to be a "work made for hire" to which copyright vests with the employer.

2. To the extent any work performed by the employee or independent contractor is not a "work made for hire," copyright in the work is assigned and transferred to the employer.

3. Copyright in any work performed during work hours (including lunch), on the employer's premises, or using the employer's facilities or money vests with and is transferred to the employer.

4. The employee must disclose, assign, and transfer to the employer all patent and trademark rights to any ideas or inventions developed during the course of employment that involve the employer's business and products.

4: Consider Including Family Members in the Employment Contract

Too often, computer firms fail to place any contractual restrictions on the employee's family. To prevent the improper or unauthorized use of trade secrets and confidential information by the employee and his family members, computer firms should consider including a provision in employment contracts restricting the employee, directly or indirectly through a family member or agent, from serving as an officer, director, or employee of another company without prior approval of the employer, and from owning an interest in any competitor of the employer, if such interest is significant enough to interfere or conflict with the employee's responsibilities and obligations to the employer.

The courts have held that such policies are reasonable and not in violation of anti-discrimination laws. *See, e.g., Moore v. Honeywell Information Systems, Inc.,* 558 F. Supp. 1229, 1231 (D. H. 1983); *Klanseck v. Prudential Ins. Co. of America,* 509 F. Supp. 13, 17 (E.D. Mich. 1980); *Thomson v. Sanborn's Motor Express, Inc.,* 382 A.2d 53, 56 (N.J. Super. Ct. App. Div. 1977). In *Moore v. Honeywell Information Systems, Inc., supra,* for example, a federal district court upheld a policy restricting employees and their family members from working for or owning an interest in a computer firm's competitors. The court reasoned that where one family member, a spouse, is engaged in a competing business "it would be perfectly reasonable to conclude that the interests of both parties will eventually intertwine, since the success of the spouse's competing business will be of a real and direct benefit to both spouses." *Id.* at 1233.

The court went on to note that in the computer industry a company policy restricting family members is reasonable:

> Honeywell [the employer] is undoubtedly in possession of valuable trade secrets, such as software programs, marketing techniques, market studies, and other valuable information developed perhaps at great cost to the company. The employment policy here seems to be a reasonable means to prevent the improper and unauthorized use of such information by persons or businesses which may unjustly benefit themselves with such information.

Id.

To avert any conflict of interest, therefore, a computer firm is well advised to place restrictions on its employees' family members.

5: Make Sure the Contract Identifies a Jurisdiction or Forum Whose Law Will Govern

The law governing employment and contractual relations varies from state to state. Accordingly, a computer firm should specify in the employment contract the jurisdiction or forum whose law will control the interpretation and enforceability of the contract. The selection of a jurisdiction should be made in consultation with counsel, based on such factors as whether the employer and employee have sufficient contacts with the particular state, and whether the governing state law is favorable to the employer.

The contract should also require the employee to consent to jurisdiction in the appropriate state(s) most convenient to the employer. In this way, if legal action must be initiated against an employee to enforce the terms of an employment contract, the employer will not be required to litigate his case in a distant jurisdiction. Courts, however, will not enforce such provisions when they are so burdensome as to be unconscionable. *See Horning v. Sycom,* 556 F. Supp. 819 (E.D. Ky. 1983). *See also* T. Marzouk, "Unconscionability in Computer Contracts with Small Businesses," *2 Comp. L. Rptr. 214* (1983).

Finally, the employer might wish to require employees to submit certain contractual disputes to an arbitration board pursuant to standards and guidelines set forth in the employment contract. The use of arbitration to resolve contract disputes between an employer and an employee is usually less expensive and more speedy than court litigation and should be considered seriously by the employer.

6: Include a Severability Clause in the Employment Contract

A "severability clause" should be included in every employment contract. Such a clause states that every paragraph or condition in the contract is considered a separate entity and may be enforced separately, regardless of the validity of the remainder of the contract. If a contract lacks a severability clause, a decision by a court to strike one contract provision could void the entire contract. *See, e.g., Naseef v. Cord, Inc.,* 216 A.2d 413, 418 (N.J. Super. Ct. App. Div.), *aff'd on other grounds,* 225 A.2d3 343 (N.J. 1966). A severability clause, therefore, insures that if one paragraph in the contract is declared invalid, the other paragraphs will remain enforceable.

7: Include an Integration Clause in the Employment Contract

Another provision that should be in every employment contract is an "integration clause." Restatement, Second, Contracts, Sect. 209. This clause reflects the intention of the parties that the written contract is an integration of the entire agreement and constitutes the sole evidence of such an agreement. A typical integration clause reads:

> The employee agrees that this contract is the complete and exclusive statement of the agreement between the parties, which supersedes all proposals or prior agreements, oral or written, and all other communications between the parties relating to the subject matter of this agreement.

The purpose of an integration clause is to prevent both parties from relying upon statements made prior to, during, or after contract negotiations. In the absence of an integration clause, a court may be inclined to expand the contract terms by looking to the general subject matter of and the circumstances surrounding the contract, particularly if the contract is fragmentary, ambiguous, or uncertain. To guard against allegations by the employee that the employer made various promises and assurances not embodied in the contract, an integration clause should be included as a standard provision.

8: Remind the Employee of the Legally Binding Effect of the Employment Contract

Every employment contract should end with a statement that the employee acknowledges that he has read the agreement and agrees to abide by its terms. In addition, the contract should state that it is legally binding and that the employee has the right to consult with legal counsel concerning the contract terms. Such a provision will (1) stress to the employee the importance of the contract and the employer's intent to enforce it and (2) place the employee on notice that an attorney may be necessary to review the contract.

C: Executing the Employment Contract

Execution of the contract is largely a formal, uncomplicated procedure. The employer, however, should adhere to the following guidelines.

1: Have the Employee Sign Each Page and Initial Important Paragraphs of the Contract

As a matter of policy, the employee should sign every page and initial all important paragraphs, particularly paragraphs involving confidentiality and nondisclosure agreements and covenants not to compete. Following this procedure will guard against any allegation that the pages of the contract were replaced. In addition, the procedure will highlight significant clauses of the contract, thereby undercutting any claim by the employee that he did not read or was told to ignore certain important paragraphs.

2: Be Careful with Employment Contracts with Existing Employees

Many computer firms begin as a small group effort with "technically oriented" personnel who view attorneys as intruders in the firms' technical or business domain. This attitude has led to rude awakenings when, several years into operations, the firms realize that they have no formal confidentiality agreements and covenants not to compete from their employees. The prime objective then becomes the securing of such agreements at the least possible cost.

Before executing an employment contract with an *existing* employee, computer firms should consult with legal counsel to determine whether the governing law requires that additional consideration be provided to the employee. Consideration is, in effect, something of value given in exchange for a promise. For a prospective employee, the consideration is that he will be employed and will receive a given salary and certain benefits in exchange for signing the contract and for agreeing to be bound by its terms.

An existing employee who executes an employment contract, however, already has a job. Some jurisdictions have held that continued employment alone is not adequate consideration for an existing employee who is required to sign an employment contract containing restrictive covenants. *See, e.g., PEMCO Corp. v. Rose,* 257 S.E.2d 885, 890 (W.Va. 1979); *Maintenance Specialties, Inc. v. Gottus,* 314 A.2d 279, 281 (Pa. 974). *But see Puritan-Bennet Corp. v. Richter,* 657 P.2d 589,

592 (Kan. Ct. App. 1983), *aff'd as modified*, 679 P.2d 206 (Kan. 1984). *Matlock v. Data Processing Security, Inc.*, 607 S.W.2d 946, 948 (Tex. Civ. App. 1980), *aff'd as modified*, 618 S.W.2d 327 (Tex. 1981); *Davies & Davies Agency, Inc. v. Davies*, 298 N.W.2d 127, 130-131 (Minn. 1980). If an employment contract with an existing employee is governed by a jurisdiction that requires additional consideration, the employer should provide some benefit to the employee in exchange for signing the contract. The benefit could be a small cash bonus, a salary increase, or a job change. To ensure that no additional sums are spent, the computer firm could require existing employees to execute contracts prior to annual salary adjustments and treat the increase in salary as consideration for the contract.

D: Enforcing the Employment Contract

Most employees will abide by the restrictions in their employment contracts. In some instances, however, the computer firm will be required to enforce its contracts to ensure compliance by its employees. In this regard, a computer firm must be willing to take legal action when necessary and to implement certain in-house procedures to protect its interests.

1: Make Sure the Departing Employee Undergoes an Exit Interview

Whenever an employee terminates his employment, an exit interview should be held to remind the employee of his obligations under the contract. Specifically, the interviewer should stress the importance of maintaining the computer firm's confidential information and trade secrets and remind the employee of any covenants not to compete against the employer.

The employer also should require the departing employee to execute a termination agreement acknowledging obligations and restrictions set forth in the employment contract. Naturally, an employee's unwillingness to sign such an agreement will cast serious doubt as to whether the employee will preserve the employer's trade secrets and otherwise comply with the employment contract.

2: Establish "In-House" Policies Regarding the Use and Disclosure of Trade Secrets

As discussed in Section 2, trade secret protection for business information is available only if the employer makes efforts to maintain such information as secret. Accordingly, the computer firm must implement security procedures and monitor compliance with such procedures as set forth in Section 2.B.1.

3: Remember That Covenants Not to Compete Provide Only Limited Protection

The computer firm should realize that covenants not to compete do not provide unlimited protection against former employees. Indeed, the courts have placed various restrictions on the enforceability of such covenants. As was previously noted, some courts require the employer to give additional consideration to an existing employee who agrees not to compete against the employer. In addition, covenants that place unduly restrictive limitations as to subject matter, geographic area, or time period will not be enforced. *See, e.g., Trilog Associates Inc. v. Famularo*, 314 A.2d 287, 294 (Pa. 1974) (covenants, unrestricted in territorial application, are unreasonable restraints on trade and cannot be upheld); *Reading Aviation Service, Inc. v. Bertolet,* 311 A.2d 628, 629, 630 (Pa. 1973) (covenant void as unreasonable restraint of trade "since it was without limitation as to time or space"; "open-ended restrictions . . . impose an unsconscionable burden on [an employee's] ability to pursue his chosen occupation"). *But see Henry Hope X-Ray Products, Inc. v. Marron Carrel, Inc.,* 674 F.2d 1336, 1342 (9th Cir. 1982) (where employer marketed its products internationally, confidentiality agreement that contained no geographic or temporal limitations was reasonable since "disclosure or use of [the employer's] trade secrets anywhere could reasonably be expected to harm [its] business interests [and] . . . [t]he limitation to confidential information contains the implicit temporal limitation that information may be disclosed when it ceases to be confidential").

Courts revise such covenants so as to protect equitably the interests of both the employer and employee. *See, e.g., USA Chem, Inc. v. Goldstein,* 512 F.2d 163, 167 (2d Cir. 1975) (covenant barring employee from competing with former employer will be enforced only to the extent necessary to prevent former employee's use or disclosure of former employer's trade secrets); *Fidelity Union Life Insurance Co. v. Protective Life Insurance Co.,* 356 F. Supp. 1199, 1203 (N.D. Tex 1972), *aff'd mem.,* 477 F.2d 594 (5th Cir. 1973) ("if the covenant is adjudged unreasonable it does not follow that the entire covenant is void; rather, . . . contract may in effect be reformed to aid in enforcement thereof"). On the other hand, courts may strike the covenants in their entirety. *See, e.g., Trilog Associates, Inc. v. Famularo, supra,* at 294 ("such a failure to limit the territorial application of the covenant . . . renders the covenant invalid"). Accordingly, the employer is well advised not to be overly greedy in efforts to restrict an employee's job mobility.

Finally, in some jurisdictions, all covenants not to compete are deemed to be void as a matter of public policy. *See, e.g.,* Cal. Bus. Prof. Code, Sect. 16600. Therefore, the employer should consult legal counsel to determine the law governing such covenants with his employees.

4: Be Willing to Enforce Employment Contracts to Let the Employees Know You Mean Business

The computer firm should be willing and able to enforce its employment contracts for two reasons. First, active enforcement will alert other employees that their employer fully intends to hold them to their employment contracts. Second, selective enforcement or nonenforcement of restrictive covenants may undermine their effect. A court may conclude that the employer is not entitled to protection since other employees were allowed to violate their restrictive covenants. Therefore, the employer should initiate (and announce to its employees) a policy of regularly enforcing restrictive covenants in employment contracts.

Computer firms in recent years have grown more jealous about their secret processes and technologies because of the increasing cost of developing them. Furthermore, a start-up computer company often needs only a good idea, concept, or invention to obtain venture capital and begin competing with larger firms. With the rising number of start-up companies, the courts have witnessed an exponential increase in the number of trade secrets suits by employers against their former employees.

These suits hit start-up firms at their most vulnerable stage—when all available time and money must be devoted to the business. In addition, a lawsuit may scare off potential employees, customers, suppliers, and investors. Clearly, litigation between an employer and his former employees can be emotionally charged and financially draining to both sides. However, with the rise in the number of employees "jumping ship" from their former employers, litigation in this area will continue to increase given the high financial stakes in the computer and high technology industries.

E: Conclusion

Employment contracts are essential to computer firms, regardless of size. Carefully drafted employment contracts may protect the business interests and confidential data of the firm, while informing employees of their obligations to their employer. However, the computer firm should follow proper procedures in negotiating, drafting, executing, and enforcing its employment contracts. Only then may the firm receive the necessary protection available under law.

PROTECTING YOUR PROPRIETARY RIGHTS
IN THE COMPUTER AND
HIGH TECHNOLOGY INDUSTRIES

SECTION 6
MARKETING PROTECTION FOR
COMPUTER SOFTWARE AND HARDWARE

Section 6: Marketing Protection for Computer Software and Hardware

A computer firm seeking to market its products will encounter numerous problems in maintaining adequate protection for its software and hardware. Among the issues of greatest concern are the use of licensing agreements to market computer products, the protection afforded by trademarks and trade names, and the antitrust problems arising from the bundling or "tying" of computer goods and services.

A: Licensing

A license is a contract by which one person, the licensor, grants to another, the licensee, certain rights in specified property belonging to the licensor. This section discusses three kinds of software licensing agreements: (1) an agreement between a software designer and a software publisher, (2) an agreement between a provider of custom software and a purchaser of such software, and (3) an agreement between a publisher of mass-produced software and a consumer who purchases the software at a retail outlet.

1: Software Developer/Publisher Agreements

Licensing agreements between software developers and publishers are similar to and frequently modeled after standard author/publisher agreements that have traditionally been used for printed works.

a: Introduction: A software publishing license will generally have an introduction that identifies the parties to the licensing agreement, namely, the software developer and the publisher. The introduction will also identify the program that is the subject of the license.

b: Definitions: The definitions section will clarify the meanings that the parties to the agreement have agreed to assign to key terms, such as "net sales" or "derivative work." Misunderstandings with respect to these terms could seriously affect the royalties that the developer will ultimately receive or the extent of the publisher's rights in related programs that the licensor/programmer develops in the future.

c: Items provided by developer: A license will also contain a section that stipulates those items that the program developer is obligated to provide under the agreement's terms. It will undoubtedly include the program itself, but may also include such items as a manual or supporting documentation.

d: Delivery schedule: A section setting out the schedule for the delivery of the items specified may also be included. This section will be more important if the software has not been developed at the time the licensing agreement is executed.

e: Maintenance, modification, and training: The maintenance, modification, and training clause covers the responsibilities of the developer after he has delivered the program to the publisher. The maintenance clause concerns the programmer's duty to rectify any errors or bugs that exist in the delivered software. This duty is usually of limited duration and will generally be expressed in terms of the developer's "best efforts." In other words, the developer will not be penalized if, despite his best efforts, he is unable to locate the error within a reasonable time period.

Another issue is whether the programmer or the publisher will be responsible for the cost of recalls caused by programming errors. Who will bear the loss in this case is a matter that should be negotiated prior to signing the agreement.

The modifications clause is similar to the maintenance clause except that it relates to the programmer's obligations regarding improvements to the program rather than to the correction of errors in it. A modifications clause may provide that the program developer will supply any modifications that improve the program's performance at no charge to the publisher (but, presumably, with the expectation that the improvements will promote sales and, therefore, royalties). On the other hand, the clause may provide that the programmer will be paid for making such modifications. The clause also may allow the publisher to make any changes to the program that it feels will improve the program's marketability or, alternatively, to make such modifications and charge the cost to the developer's royalties, but only after giving the developer a right of first refusal to make the changes himself.

The training clause is self explanatory. It provides that the developer of a program will provide any necessary instruction in the use of the program to the publisher's employees for a set fee.

f: License provisions: The license section sets out the subject, scope, and duration of the licensing agreement.

1. *Subject clause:* The subject of the license is the program itself and any of the other items that may have been included in the "items to be supplied by developer" clause (manuals or supporting data, for example).

2. *Scope clause:* The purpose of the scope clause is to limit the publisher's right to market the program and to limit the scope of the license geographically. If, for example, the publisher did not have access to retail outlets in a certain region of the U.S., it would be unwise to extend the license to that area. A software developer is better off licensing the program to a publisher who would be able to market the program in that region. The scope of the license may also be limited to certain market segments. It may give one publisher the right to sell the program to the retail market and another publisher the right to sell to the educational market. Finally, the scope may be limited with respect to the publisher's right to sell the program for use with different computers. For example, one might want to give publisher A the license to sell the program for use on IBM computers and publisher B the license to sell the program for use on Apple computers.

3. *Duration:* The duration clause states the period of time that the publisher enjoys the rights granted by the license. At the expiration of this period, all rights in the program revert to the developer. The advantage to the developer of a short license duration is that it allows him to regain control over a successful program sooner and, thus, enables him to negotiate a better deal with the same publisher or one of its competitors.

The publisher will generally favor a long-term license because it gives him more time to recover the investment he made in the product. The usual way of satisfying both the developer's desire to participate in the profits of a wildly successful program and the publisher's desire to have a long enough license to justify the initial expense of marketing the program is to set the royalty rate on a sliding scale so that the programmer receives a higher royalty percentage as sales increase.

g: Acceptance: The acceptance clause gives the publisher a specified period of time (30 or 60 days, for example) in which to accept or reject the program that is the subject of the license. This allows the publisher time to determine whether the program lives up to its billing and can be marketed successfully.

h: Royalties: The royalties section determines how much the program developer will be paid for each sale of the program and the schedule on which payments will be made. The royalty can be based either on a percentage of the net profits or on a fixed dollar amount for each program sold. If the royalty is based on a percentage of net profits, that percentage can either be fixed for the entire license term or, as noted earlier, be set on a sliding scale with the percentage increasing as sales of the program reach specified thresholds.

The advantage of using a sliding scale has already been discussed—basically, it protects the interests of a programmer who develops a very successful program and that of the publisher who has expended considerable money advertising and marketing the program. The advantage of basing royalties on a fixed dollar amount per sale is that it assures the programmer of getting a reasonable return on each sale—irrespective of the price the publisher chooses to set for the program. Basing the royalty on a percentage of the net sales price introduces uncertainty into the royalty equation. On the one hand, it allows the publisher to set the price of the program at whatever level he believes will maximize profits, without the constraints of a fixed royalty amount. On the other hand, it entails uncertainty for the developer since his royalty could vary depending on the price the publisher sets. A publisher may have his own marketing reasons to set a low price on the program; he may wish to offer a "buy program A and get program B for half price" promotion, for example.

One way of protecting the developer's interests and maintaining pricing flexibility is to combine the "percentage of net sales" and "fixed amount" approaches so as to base royalties on a percentage of net sales but provide a minimum royalty on each sale. One might provide for a 10 percent royalty with a $15 minimum, for example, in which case the programmer would receive $20 per sale if the publisher's net profit on each program were $200 but would still receive the minimum $15 payment if the profits were only $50.

It is important to determine whether royalties will be computed based on the number of programs the publisher has shipped or on the payments that the publisher has received. If they are based on the latter formula, the programmer's royalties may be substantially diminished or delayed as a result of late payments or nonpayments.

A final note on royalties: Much of the ground that a programmer wins in negotiating a royalty percentage may be lost through inattention to the schedule on which the publisher is obliged to pay those royalties to the programmer. The situation to avoid, from the programmer's perspective, is one in which he is in the position of giving the publisher an interest-free loan between payments that are set too far apart. The objective should be to give the publisher enough, but only enough, time to allow him to receive timely payments from his customers and to carry out the required accounting procedures.

i: Accounting: The accounting section sets out the records that the publisher is required to keep regarding sales of the developer's program and the terms under which the developer is entitled to inspect those records.

j: Warranties: The warranty clause can contain various guarantees by the developer regarding the program he has delivered. The developer may warrant, for example, that he is, in fact, the owner of the program, that there are no pending lawsuits that could affect his right to license the program (a suit for copyright infringement, for example), or that the program will perform in the way the developer has promised.

k: Indemnification: The indemnification section sets out the obligations of the developer and publisher with respect to indemnifying each other against potential liabilities. Commonly, the developer will indemnify the publisher for his legal fees and damage awards in suits based on allegations that the program was stolen. The publisher, on the other hand, may be required to indemnify the programmer against suits based on allegations that there are errors or omissions in the program.

l: Copyrights: The copyright section specifies the name under which the copyright is to be registered and the party responsible for registering it and sets out the rights and obligations of the parties with respect to enforcing the copyright against infringers.

m: Termination: Termination of a licensing agreement generally occurs when the term specified in the duration section expires. It may also occur when there is a material breach of the agreement—the failure of the publisher to make royalty payments, for example—or when an express condition contained in the contract is not satisfied, as in the case of a failure to reach a specified level of sales. The termination provision sets out the rights and obligations of the respective parties in the event of a contract breach or termination.

n: Source-code escrow: Even if under the terms of the licensing agreement the developer retains the source code, the parties may nevertheless wish to identify conditions under which the publisher may gain access to the source code—the death of the programmer, for example—by designating someone to act as an escrow agent to keep a copy of the source code.

o: Miscellaneous provisions:

1. Marketing strategy: The developer may wish to have some control over the marketing plan that the publisher follows or the publisher may wish to make clear that he has the sole responsibility for making such decisions. The parties, on the other hand, may agree that the publisher has the final say in marketing matters, but that he is obligated to consult with the developer in determining marketing strategy.

2. Assignment and delegation: The parties may also wish to limit the ability of either party to assign rights and to delegate duties under the agreement. Generally, such limitations prohibit assignments and delegations by one party

without the other party's prior written consent, which shall not be unreasonably withheld.

3. Applicable law: An applicable law clause stipulates which state's law will apply should a dispute arise regarding the proper interpretation of the agreement. Choosing the applicable law provides a certain amount of predictability in the way the agreement will be construed. In addition, the choice of one state over another may benefit one party more depending on the trend of legal decisions by courts in that state.

2: Licensing Agreements for Custom Software

Licensing agreements with respect to custom software are similar to programmer/publisher agreements. The following discussion addresses the most common clauses in custom software licensing agreements.

a: Program products: The program products section either describes the products to be developed or incorporates by reference separate documents that describe those products. To protect both the licensor (the service provider) and the licensee (the service purchaser), the section should describe fully the functions that the software is supposed to perform.

b: Title: The title clause contains an acknowledgment on the part of the licensee that title lies with the licensor. It follows that the licensee's rights are restricted to those enumerated in the grant of license clause.

c: Grant of license: This clause defines the licensee's rights in the software that is the subject of the license. Basically, the licensee is permitted to use the software at a specified location and, perhaps, for a specified computer for the duration of the license.

d: Definitions: As was noted previously, a definitions section may be used to clarify the meaning of key contract terms. In reviewing and/or drafting definitions, each party should take care that his interests are being protected, since such definitions can seriously affect, for better or worse, a party's rights under the agreement.

e: Fees and payment: This section is largely self-explanatory. It states the fees to be charged for the programming services provided and the terms under which payment will be made for those services.

f: Nondisclosure: The nondisclosure clause constitutes a recognition by the licensee that the program, supporting data, manuals, and other material the licensor provides are proprietary in nature, that the licensee has an obligation not to disclose these data to third parties without the authorization of the licensor, and that the licensee will be liable for any damages caused by such disclosure.

g: Warranty of title: The warranty of title clause serves the same purpose as the analogous provision in the programmer/publisher agreement. It is a guarantee by the party providing the software (the licensor) that he is the owner of the software and that he will indemnify the licensee against any damages it incurs as a result of suits challenging the licensor's title in the software.

h: Breach and termination: Similar to the analogous clause in the programmer/publisher agreement, this clause sets out the rights of the party against whom a breach has been committed and the liabilities of the breaching party.

i: Warranties/limitation of liability: In this section, the licensor warrants that the software provided will carry out the functions described in the program products section. He may, however, limit his liability in various ways so as not to include, for example, consequential damages, lost profits, and the like. The licensor may also limit the period after purchase for which the warranty is effective.

j: Source code escrow: The source code escrow provision serves the same purpose as the analogous clause in the programmer/publisher agreement. It guarantees the licensee access to the valuable source code under given circumstances.

k: Miscellaneous:

1. *Applicable law:* As in the case of the programmer/publisher agreement, the parties to a custom software agreement may choose the law that will apply should a dispute arise.

2. *Severability:* A severability clause protects the validity of the agreement as a whole if one or more isolated provisions should turn out to be invalid or unenforceable. It essentially "severs" the offending clause, thus allowing the remainder of the agreement to remain in force.

3. *Integration:* An integration clause states that the written contract constitutes the entire agreement of the parties with respect to the subject matter of the agreement. Thus, prior negotiations or oral promises have no effect on the obligations of the parties to that agreement.

4. *Disputes:* A disputes clause contains a stipulation by the parties as to the method that will be used to resolve disputes. It will state, for example, whether the parties will bring claims in civil court or if they will submit disputes to formal arbitration.

3: Consumer/Publisher Licensing Agreements

It is unclear whether a customer who purchases prepackaged software at a retail outlet has entered into a license agreement with the software publisher. Software publishers have gone to considerable lengths in an attempt to create such a contractual relationship. The reason for these efforts should be obvious—publishers want to protect their very valuable proprietary rights in the software they market. We shall here consider two ways in which publishers have attempted to create such a contractual relationship with software purchasers.

a: The "tear-open" or "shrink-wrap" license: The tear-open or shrink-wrap license consists of a printed license agreement that appears on the outside of the software package, on the shipping carton, or in an accompanying user's manual that states that the purchaser (or licensee, as the case may be) of the program will be taken to have accepted the printed terms when he opens the package.

The concept of acceptance is taken from the Uniform Commercial Code which holds a buyer to have accepted a seller's goods when he (1) signifies to the seller that he will accept them, (2) fails to reject them after a reasonable opportunity, or (3) does any act inconsistent with the seller's ownership. U.C.C., Sect. 2-606.

The problem with arguing that a contract has been created, however, is that one first has to demonstrate that U.C.C. Article 2 is applicable. As the provision applies to the sale of goods (as opposed to services), this contention seems tenuous at best. In fact, one could argue that a sale, which necessarily involves the passing of title, does not encompass a license arrangement, in which title, by definition, remains with the software publisher/distributor.

Even if one accepts the general applicability of U.C.C. Article 2, it is highly doubtful that the concept of acceptance and the consequences that flow from it could ever adequately bind software customers in the way publishers would like. The consequences of acceptance under U.C.C. Sect. 2-607 relate solely to the buyer's obligation to pay for the goods and the effect of acceptance on the buyer's ability to sue the seller for breach of contract. These consequences are far removed from the obligations to which a licensee is bound.

b: License forms contained on the sales slip or within the software package: A second approach that mass software publishers have used to create a licensing agreement is to include a printed agreement on the sales slip or inside the software package and to induce the purchaser of the program to sign the agreement and return it in exchange for an extended warranty or a specified period of support and maintenance. The success of this approach is also problematic, however, albeit somewhat less so than the shrink-wrap license approach. One could easily question, for example, whether the consumer has provided consideration sufficient to create a binding contractual relationship or, if the license is in small print on the back of the sales slip, whether he is even aware that he has entered into such an agreement.

4: Summary

This section has examined the kinds of licensing agreements that one is likely to encounter as a developer, seller, or purchaser of software. The importance and enforceability of the programmer/publisher and custom software licensing agreements are well established. The validity of the tear-open and package or sales slip licenses is an open question that may require a statutory solution. (Louisiana, for example, enacted a statute in 1984 that establishes the enforceability of such licenses. That statute was subsequently stricken by a Louisiana Federal Court.) One fact is abundantly clear: The parties must draft their licensing agreements with great care to ensure proper protection of proprietary rights. For a discussion of the special problems related to computer contracts with small businesses, the reader is referred to Appendix C.

B: Trademarks and Service Marks

1: Definitions and Scope of Protection

a: Definitions: A trademark, as defined in the Federal Trademark Act of July 5, 1946, as Amended (Lanham Act) 15 U.S.C., Sect. 1051 *et seq.*, is "any word, name, symbol, or device or any combination thereof adopted and used by a manufacturer or merchant to identify his goods and distinguish them from those manufactured or sold by others." Lanham Act, Sect. 45, 15 U.S.C., Sect. 1127. A trademark constitutes a valuable property right for a computer firm and, as such, is entitled to protection under law.

As the name implies, a service mark can be distinguished from a trademark by virtue of its use as a means of identifying the services of one person from those of another. Lanham Act, Sect. 45, 15 U.S.C., Sect. 1127. Thus, where a trademark identifies and distinguishes tangible goods and products, a service mark identifies and distinguishes intangible services. *Application of Radio Corp. of America*, 205 F.2d 180 (C.C.P.A. 1953) (holding that record company slogan "The Music You Want When You Want It" identified records themselves rather than alleged "service" of providing free records to radio stations in exchange for on-air publicity).

While trademarks and service marks are conceptually distinct, they will be treated here together, since the legal protection they enjoy and the requirements for that protection are virtually identical. Unless otherwise indicated, the following discussion will apply equally to trademarks and service marks. Trade names, on the other hand, must be distinguished for legal purposes and will, therefore, be treated separately.

The Supreme Court has explained the importance of trademarks as follows:

> The protection of trade-marks is the law's recognition of the psychological function of symbols . . . .A trademark is a merchandising short-cut which induces a purchaser to select what he wants, or what he has been led to believe he wants. The owner of a mark exploits this human propensity by making every effort to impregnate the atmosphere of the market with the drawing power of a congenial symbol . . . . [T]he aim is . . . to convey through the mark, in the kinds of potential customers, the desirability of the commodity upon which it appears. Once this is attained, the trademark owner has something of value. If another poaches upon the commercial magnetism of the symbol he has created, the owner can obtain legal redress.

Mishawaka Rubber & Woolen Mfg. Co. v. S.S. Kresge Co., 316 U.S. 203, 205 (1942).

Simply stated, then, the purpose of a trademark is to distinguish one computer firm's product from another's. In addition, a trademark represents an important instrument of advertising and selling computer goods. The trademark also makes clear that all goods bearing the mark come from a single source and are of equal quality. McCarthy, *Trademarks and Unfair Competition*, Sect. 3:1.

Legal protection against trademark infringement is only available where there is a "likelihood of confusion" by consumers with respect to product identity. In using a confusingly similar mark, the infringer frustrates the purpose of trademarks, namely, directing consumers to the particular product they desire.

b: Protectable and unprotectable marks: Four different categories of trademarks exist: (1) generic marks, (2) descriptive marks, (3) suggestive marks, and (4) arbitrary or fanciful marks. *Abercrombie & Fitch Co. v. Hunting World, Inc.*, 537 F.2d 4, 9 (2d Cir. 1976). The requirements needed to justify protection of the mark and the extent of legal protection against infringing uses will vary according to the category in which the mark is placed.

1. *Generic marks:* A generic term is "one that refers . . . to the genus of which the particular product is a species." *Abercrombie & Fitch*, 537 F.2d at 9. Generic terms may *not* be used as trademarks. The prohibition on their use exists irrespective of whether the term has come to be identified with a particular source of the product. *See CES Publishing Corp. v. St. Regis*

Publications, Inc., 531 F.2d 11, 13 (2d Cir. 1975) ("Consumer Electronics" as title of trade magazine generic and not subject to trademark protection even if term had come to be identified with plaintiff's publication). Furthermore, a word that was once protectable may become generic if it comes into general use as a term describing genus rather than species. An example of this sort of gradual erosion of a mark's distinctiveness is the term "thermos" which has become generic and no longer subject to legal protection. *King-Seeley Thermos Co. v. Aladdin Industries, Inc.*, 321 F.2d 577 (2d Cir. 1963). *See also Bayer Co. v. United Drug Co.*, 272 Fed. 505 (2d Cir. 1921) ("Aspirin," having come to mean the article sold to general public, was generic and not subject to protection against use by competitors); *E.I. Dupont de Nemours & Co. v. Waxed Products Co., Inc.*, 85 F.2d 75 (2d Cir.), *cert. denied*, 299 U.S. 601 (1936). ("Cellophane" no longer associated exclusively with owner's product in minds of public and thus may be used by dealer in competing products to refer to other brands of transparent cellulose film.)

The rationale for forbidding the use of generic terms as trademarks is that it would be unfair to other computer product marketers to allow one firm to appropriate a generic term for its exclusive use and, in so doing, deprive others of the ability to describe the character or purpose of their products. For example, if one company were allowed to appropriate the term "software" and use it in such a way that it designated only software sold by that company, all other computer firms would have no way of describing their own software. Accordingly, generic terms are afforded no legal protection.

2. *Descriptive marks:* The second category of terms is descriptive terms. Unlike generic terms, descriptive terms may, under certain circumstances, be used as trademarks. While a generic term fully characterizes the product, a descriptive term describes some feature or quality of the product. Thus, while the term "software" is generic and may not receive trademark protection, the term "Quickwriter" is descriptive and would only be entitled to protection if it had come to be associated with a computer firm's product. When a descriptive term, through usage, acquires a special significance with respect to the product of a particular firm, it acquires secondary meaning. The existence of secondary meaning is a prerequisite before a descriptive term receives trademark protection.

Two examples of terms that courts have held to be descriptive are "Sure-Grip" for nonslip floor paint and "Tender Vittles" for semi-moist cat food. *See In Re Colonial Refining & Chemical Co.*, 196 U.S.P.Q. 46 (TTAB 1977); *Ralston Purina Co. v. Thomas J. Lipton, Inc.*, 341 F. Supp. 129 (S.D.N.Y 1972). In *Colonial Refining, supra,* the Trademark Trial and Appeal Board stated that the term "Sure-Grip:"

> requires no mature thought, imagination, or mental gymnastics to immediately comprehend the nature of applicant's product and its main and intended purpose or attribute; as such, it is merely descriptive thereof.

196 U.S.P.Q. at 47.

In *Ralston Purina, supra,* the court evaluated the term "Tender Vittles" and noted that "a product designation is descriptive . . . if . . . it conveys to potential consumers the characteristics, functions, qualities, ingredients, properties, or uses of the product." 341 F. Supp at 133. The term "Tender Vittles," the court held, means food which is "soft, juicy, and easily chewed. . . . [which is] precisely a description of Purina's semi-moist cat food." *Id.* The court went on to note that "[t]he unique characteristic of this product and the quality which sets it apart from other noncanned cat foods is that it is soft and juicy . . . [and] [t]his is just what is conveyed by the words "tender vittles." *Id.*

Given the court's determination that the term "tender vittles" was descriptive, the next issue was whether it had acquired the secondary meaning that would entitle it to protection from infringing uses. The court set forth the following requirements of secondary meaning:

> To establish secondary meaning, it must be shown that the *primary* significance of the term in the minds of the consuming public is not the product but the producer. This may be an anonymous producer, since consumers often buy goods without knowing the personal identity or actual name of the manufacturer. However it must be demonstrated that the purchasing public associates goods designated by the particular word or words in question with but a single, though anonymous source.

Ralston Purina, 341 F. Supp. at 133 (citations omitted).

Whether a term has acquired secondary meaning is a factual determination that is made based on such elements as length and exclusivity of use, sales levels, and extent of advertising and promotion. *Id.* Surveys of consumer brand awareness are also frequently introduced as evidence to show that a mark has acquired secondary meaning such that the "purchasing public associates it with the goods of a particular source." *Ralston Purina,* 341 F. Supp. at 134.

It should be emphasized as well that the evidentiary burden on a party attempting to establish secondary meaning is always a "rigorous" one, *Ralston Purina, id.* at 134, and that burden may be increased depending on the extent to which the mark is purely descriptive. That is, the evidentiary burden is especially great "where the proposed mark's original or primary meaning suggests the basic nature of the service to be rendered." *American Heritage Life Insurance Co. v. Heritage Life Insurance Co.,* 494 F.2d 3, 12 (5th Cir.1974).

3. *Suggestive terms:* Suggestive terms occupy a middle ground between descriptive marks, which have just been discussed, and fanciful and arbitrary marks, which will be treated in the next section. The distinction between suggestive and descriptive marks is a crucial one because descriptive marks require secondary meaning in order to be protected while suggestive marks do not. Thus, if a computer firm in an infringement suit successfully argues that its mark is suggestive, it need not prove that the mark has acquired secondary meaning.

Unfortunately, the distinction between suggestive and descriptive terms is not an easy one to draw. As one court put it, the descriptive/suggestive line is "scarcely 'pikestaff plain' . . . [and] is . . . often made on an intuitive basis rather than as the result of a logical analysis susceptible of articulation." *Union Carbide Corp. v. Ever-Ready, Inc.*, 531 F.2d 366, 379 (7th Cir.), *cert. denied*, 429 U.S. 830 (1976). The courts have applied two tests in evaluating suggestive trademarks: the "imagination" test and the importance to competitors test.

a. *The imagination test:* Under the imagination test a term is suggestive if it requires the consumer to exercise his imagination in order to draw a conclusion as to the nature of the goods or services to which it applies. In *Zatarains, Inc. v. Oak Grove Smokehouse, Inc.*, 698 F.2d 786 5th Cir. 1983, for example, the court considered the term "Fish-Fri" as a name for a prepackaged coating or batter mix applied to fish prior to cooking. The court refused to grant trademark protection on the ground that the connection between the term and the product was so close that even a consumer unfamiliar with the product would have an idea of its purpose or function. As the court wryly noted: "It simply does not require an exercise of the imagination to deduce that 'Fish-Fri' is used to fry fish." *Id.* at 793. *See also West & Co., Inc. v. Arica Institute, Inc.*, 557 F.2d 338 (2nd Cir. 1977) (term "psychocalisthenics" suggestive imagination test as applied to system of physical exercises designed to create specific mental, emotional, and physical results).

b. *The importance to competitors test:* The other major criterion that courts use in classifying a mark as suggestive is whether competitors would be likely to require the terms used in the trademark in describing their products. *Zatarains*, 698 F.2d at 793. If a trademark is likely to be used by competitors in the computer industry, therefore, it will not be classified as suggestive. *See, e.g., Vision Center v. Opticks, Inc.*, 596 F.2d 111, 116 (5th Cir. 1979), *cert. denied*, 444 U.S. 1016 (1980) (term "Vision Center," as applied to partnership selling optical goods, is descriptive not suggestive as "word 'vision' is virtually indispensable to the vocabulary of the goods industry"); *Stix Products, Inc. v. United Merchants & Manufacturers, Inc.*, 295 F. Supp. 479 (S.D.N.Y. 1968) (term "CON-TACT" as applied to self-adhesive decorative shelf covering product held suggestive as not so closely related to product as to be generally useful to others marketing similar goods).

4. *Fanciful and arbitrary marks:* Like suggestive marks, arbitrary and fanciful marks receive legal protection without proof of secondary meaning. Fanciful marks are essentially coined marks like "Kodak" and "Exxon," words that were introduced for the purpose of serving as trademarks. Arbitrary marks, while not coined, are terms that serve no descriptive function with respect to the product. Examples of marks that courts have recently classified as arbitrary are "Jellibeans" as applied to a roller skating rink, and "Ice Cream" as applied to chewing gum. *Jellibeans, Inc. v. Skating Club of Georgia, Inc.*, 212 U.S.P.Q. 170 (N.D. Ga. 1981), *aff'd* 716 F.2d 833 (11th Cir. 1983); *Borden, Inc. v. Topps Chewing Gum, Inc.*, (173 U.S.P.Q. 447 TTAB 1972).

Now that we have examined the kinds of marks that a computer firm can choose to name its product or service protect its proprietary rights therein, several conclusions can be drawn regarding the appropriateness of choosing one mark over another. First, an arbitrary or fanciful mark has one great advantage over a purely descriptive mark. Such a mark will be given broad protection without secondary meaning. The disadvantage of using a fanciful mark and, to an only slightly lesser extent, an arbitrary mark, is that such marks, by definition, provide a consumer with no information about the nature of the product or service to which they refer. That is, had "Kodak" and "Polaroid" not been drummed into the minds of consumers by advertising, they would not help a consumer at all in deciding whether the products to which they referred would be useful in the darkroom or in the kitchen. Accordingly, a computer firm choosing an arbitrary or fanciful trademark must be willing and able to expend substantial sums of money in advertising to acquaint the public with the firm's product.

Not surprisingly, the advantages and disadvantages of fanciful and arbitrary marks are reversed in the case of descriptive marks. That is, descriptive marks *do* provide a consumer with information about the computer product or service to which they refer. Thus, they are helpful immediately in directing consumers to the product. The disadvantage is that while a fanciful term like "Kodak" receives legal protection from the moment the product with which it is associated is introduced into the stream of interstate commerce, a descriptive term is only entitled to protection as a trademark after it has acquired secondary meaning. *See Aloe Creme Laboratories, Inc. v. Estee Lauder, Inc.,* 533F.2d 256, 258 (5th Cir. 1976) (descriptive term "After Tan" not accorded legal protection where existence of secondary meaning not proven); *In rem Consolidated Foods Corporation,* 200 U.S.P.Q. 477, 480-481 (TTAB 1978) (term "Pre-Inked" descriptive as applied to rubber stamp pads and unregisterable without proof of secondary meaning).

Suggestive marks have some of the advantages of both descriptive and fanciful marks. Like fanciful marks, suggestive marks do not require the user to prove that his mark has acquired secondary meaning in order to obtain protection for it. Like descriptive marks, however, suggestive marks may provide a consumer with some information about the computer product or services, though in theory less than descriptive marks.

Choosing a suggestive mark would seem to be the perfect compromise for the computer firm that wishes its trademark to serve some descriptive function without an accompanying need to prove secondary meaning in infringement suits. Unfortunately, suggestive marks have one serious drawback—they are virtually impossible to distinguish from marks that are merely descriptive. As one court noted, "it is difficult to perceive a clear-cut distinction in the case law between those terms which have been held to be descriptive and those suggestive." *West & Company, Inc. v. Arica Institute, Inc.,* 557 F.2d at 342 n.5. Some courts, in fact, have even more strongly expressed their frustration at being unable to distinguish the two concepts. *See, e.g. Union Carbide Corp. v. Ever-Ready, Inc.,* 392 F. Supp. 280, 286 (N.D. Ill. 1975) *rev'd* 531 F.2d 366 (7th Cir.), *cert. denied,* 429 U.S. 830 (1976) (suggestive/descriptive distinction "threatens to be one without a difference").

Despite the previously cited tests of suggestiveness, the determination of whether a mark is suggestive or descriptive is often based on intuition rather than on logical analysis. *Union Carbide, supra*, 531 F.2d at 379. Not surprisingly, consistency is not a hallmark of decisions based on intuition. *Cf. American Heritage Life Insurance Co. v. Heritage Life Insurance Co.*, 494 F.2d 3, 11 (5th Cir. 1974) (term "Heritage" descriptive as applied to services of life insurance company); *Glamorene Products Corp. v. Boyle Midway, Inc.*, 188 U.S.P.Q. 145, 164 (S.D.N.Y. 1975) (term "Spray 'N Vac" as applied to aerosol rug cleaner suggestive, not descriptive). The clear lesson to be learned is that a computer firm that picks what it believes to be a suggestive mark may be unpleasantly surprised when it learns later that the trademark is merely descriptive and, thus, unprotectable unless a showing of secondary meaning is presented.

3: Obtaining Legal Protection

Common law protection may be available for trademarks that have not been formally registered. Federal registration of trademarks, however, provides a trademark owner with certain procedural advantages, most significantly (1) a presumption that the mark is valid and (2) after five years, the possibility of acquiring uncontestable status for the mark. To gain the protection afforded by federal registration, the owner of a trademark must, in addition to selling its products in interstate commerce, file an application for registration with the Patent and Trademark Office.

The symbol "R" in a circle is used to indicate that a mark has been registered with the Patent Office and that it is entitled to legal protection. The symbol "TM" frequently appears alongside product names. The "TM" symbol should not be confused with the "R" symbol. When "TM" accompanies a product name, it means only that the user of the name claims a proprietary right in the name. While it may serve a notice function with respect to potential competing uses of the mark, "TM" does not indicate that the Patent and Trademark Office has accepted the mark for registration nor does it indicate that the mark meets any of the common-law requirements for protection. To illustrate, someone could use the term "soap" to refer to his brand of soap and affix to it the "TM" symbol. As was previously discussed, however, the term soap, when used in this way, is generic and, hence, unprotectable, irrespective of the user's use of the "TM" symbol.

Before attempting to file a trademark application, the computer firm should consider taking two steps. First, it should conduct a trademark search. The purpose of a trademark search is to determine whether the chosen mark is already being used on a related product by another individual. If so, another mark will have to be chosen. Second, the computer firm should consult a trademark attorney before proceeding with the application process. The aid of an attorney experienced in trademark matters can be of immeasurable help in avoiding omissions in the application process that could have serious negative consequences with respect to the protectability of the chosen mark. Moreover, an attorney can handle both the trademark search and the paperwork associated with the application process and can almost certainly do so in a more expeditious manner than the applicant himself. Finally, to protect its trademarks, a computer firm should alert its employees of such trademarks and encourage them to monitor their use in advertisements and other publications. Furthermore, employees should watch for other companies that use identical or similar trademarks. The Patent and Trademark Office issues a weekly publication, called the *Official Gazette*, which lists those marks that the Office has granted preliminary approval. A computer firm may challenge any new registration by filing a formal opposition within 30 days of publication.

4: Legal Rights in a Trademark

Under both federal statutory and common law, the computer firm that owns a valid trademark is entitled to protection from infringing uses of the mark. A use is infringing if (1) the firm was neither the first one to use the trademark (in the case of fanciful, arbitrary, and suggestive marks) nor the first to acquire secondary meaning in the mark (in the case of marks that are merely descriptive) and (2) the marks are used on similar products that are sold in the same geographic areas. The use of a similar or identical mark will constitute an infringement if is likely to confuse a reasonably prudent purchaser as to the source of the computer goods or services.

a: First use and acquisition of secondary meaning as prerequisite of legal protection: In trademark law (unlike patent law) the first person to use a mark rather than the first to register it is entitled to legal protection for the mark. *Haviland & Co., Inc. v. Johann Haviland China Corp.*, 269 F. Supp. 928, 935 (S.D. N.Y.), 154 U.S.P.Q. 287, 291 (1967); *Campbell Soup Co. v. Armour & Co.*, 175 F.2d 795, 797 (3rd Cir.) *cert. denied,* 338 U.S. 847 (1949).

To support federal registration the computer firm must use the mark by selling and transporting in interstate commerce the computer goods to which the mark is affixed. One interstate transaction may be sufficient to support registration. Courts, however, have distinguished between "token sales" (which are valid) and "sham transactions" (which are invalid). While an interstate sale may involve a very limited quantity of goods, it must be a *bona fide* commercial transaction. In one case, the court held that the interstate sale and subsequent shipment of one maternity "jumper" was sufficient to support registration. *Maternally Yours, Inc. v. Your Maternity Shop, Inc.*, 234 F.2d 538, 542 (2d Cir. 1956). In another case involving the Florida "Sunshine Tree" slogan for citrus juice, the vice-president of the corporation typed the words "Sunshine Tree" on self-adhesive labels and pasted them on six grapefruit juice cans he had previously received as personal samples. He then mailed the six cans to a business associate in another state. The court held that the transaction was a "sweetheart shipment," not an arms-length business transaction and was thus not sufficient to give the corporation any rights in the name. *State of Florida v. Real Juices, Inc.*, 330 F. Supp. 428 (M.D. Fla. 1971).

b: Likelihood of confusion: The first or "senior" user of a mark may prevent the registration and use of a similar mark if such mark is likely to confuse a reasonably prudent purchaser with respect to the product's source. The courts have character-ized the reasonably prudent buyer as "an ordinary purchaser using ordinary care and caution." *American Diabetes Association v. National Diabetes Association*, 533 F. Supp. 16 (E.D. Pa. 1981).

Likelihood of confusion may be proven through various means, including "visual, verbal, and intellectual similarity; the class of goods in question; the marketing channels; the intent of [the alleged infringer]; evidence of actual confusion; and the strength or weakness of the marks in question." *Carter-Wallace, Inc. v. Proctor & Gamble Co.*, 434 F.2d 794, 800 (9th Cir. 1970).

If, for example, the goods are expensive, a buyer of such goods will be presumed to exercise more care in selection than if he were buying very inexpensive goods. As one court noted, "[t]he greater the value of an article the more careful the typical consumer can be expected to be; the average purchaser of an automobile will no doubt devote more attention to examining different products and determining their manufacturer or source than will the average purchaser of a ball of twine." *McGregor-Doniger, Inc. v. Drizzle, Inc.*, 599 F.2d 1126, 1137 (2d Cir. 1979) (sophistication of buyers of expensive raincoats supported conclusion that no likelihood of confusion existed with respect to defendant's coat). *Accord Frisch's Restaurants, Inc. v. Elby's Big Boy of Steubenville, Inc.*, 670 F.2d 642, 648 (6th Cir. 1982), *cert. denied*, 459 U.S. 916 (1983) (casual degree of care exercised by purchasers of fast-food hamburgers supports conclusion of likelihood of confusion). Moreover, where the goods are to be sold only to professional or commercial buyers or other experts, an expert's higher level of expertise will be used as the measure of likelihood of confusion. *See, e.g., Vitek Systems, Inc. v. Abbott Laboratories, Inc.*, 675 F.2d 190, 193 (8th Cir. 1982) (knowledgeable purchasers of sophisticated laboratory equipment unlikely to be confused by similar mark on competing product).

1. *Related goods:* Infringement may result even if the alleged infringer's products or services are not in direct competition with the computer firm holding the trademark. In one case, for example, the court granted a supermarket's request for a preliminary injunction to restrain a real estate developer from using the Supermarket's mark in connection with their real estate business. *Safeway Stores, Inc. v. Safeway Properties, Inc.*, 307 F.2d 495 (2d Cir.), 134 U.S.P.Q. 467, 470 (1962). In other cases, identical trademarks on products as dissimilar as board games and wearing apparel, and snow skis and cigarettes have been held to be so closely related as to generate a likelihood of confusion. *See General Mills Fun Group v. Tuxedo Monopoly, Inc.*, 204 U.S.P.Q. 396 (TTAB 1979), *aff'd* 648 F.2d 1335 (C.C.P.A. 1981); *K2 Corp. v. Philip Morris, Inc.*, 192 U.S.P.Q. 174, (TTAB 1976) *aff'd* 555 F.2d 815 (C.C.P.A. 1977). In contrast, however, are other cases in which virtually identical trademarks on crackers and tortilla chips and on outboard motors and automobile engines were held to not be so closely related as to be confusingly similar. *See Vitarroz Corp. v. Borden, Inc.*, 644 F.2d 960 (2d Cir. 1981); *Kiekhaefer Corp. v. Willys-Overland Motors, Inc.*, 236 F.2d 423 (C.C.P.A. 1956).

As can be seen, it is not always obvious why courts conclude that two dissimilar products are so closely related as to preclude the use of identical trademarks to identify product sources. Among the factors that courts weigh in making this decision are (1) whether the marks are used in the same advertising medium, (2) whether the products are placed near each other on the same shelf in the same retail outlets, and (3) whether one of the parties has expended large sums of money on advertising to promote the product to which the mark is attached. *See, e.g., Pure Foods, Inc. v. Minute Maid Corp.*, 214 F.2d 792 (5th Cir.) *cert. denied*, 348 U.S. 888 (1954); Restatement of Torts, Sects. 729, 731.

2. *Geographically remote use:* Under early common law, if a "junior" user used a trademark in good faith to promote its product in an area into which the "senior" user had not entered and in which the mark was unknown, the junior user could enjoin the senior user's entry into the market. *See United Drug Co. v. Theodore Rectanus Co.*, 248 U.S. 90 (1918); *Hanover Star Milling Co. v. Metcalf,* 240 U.S. 403 (1916).

The Lanham Act, however, has modified this common law rule. Under the Lanham Act, registration eliminates the junior user's good faith argument by providing constructive notice of the senior user's ownership of the mark. Furthermore, once the senior user/registrant enters the junior user's market area, the junior user must stop using the mark. In fact, once the senior user can show a *present likelihood of entry* into the junior user's market, it is entitled to enjoin the junior user's use of the mark in that area. *Dawn Donut Co., Inc. v. Harts Food Stores, Inc.*, 267 F.2d 358, 365 (2d Cir. 1959).

5: Legal Remedies against Trademark Infringement

Three remedies are available against an infringing party. First, an aggrieved party may be entitled to money damages for the injury he has suffered as a result of the defendant's use of the infringing mark. The plaintiff's recovery would, in such a case, be measured by the defendant's profits that were attributable to the infringing use. Second, the aggrieved party may petition the Patent and Trademark Office to cancel the registration of the infringing mark (or oppose registration if it has not yet been obtained). Finally, the trademark owner may seek an injunction preventing the infringing use if, as is almost always the case in trademark infringement actions, money damages would be inadequate to compensate the owner for the harm caused by the infringer's actions. The great advantage of an injunction, of course, is that it gives the victim of infringement exactly what he wants, namely, an end, either temporarily or permanently, to the defendant's use of the infringing mark. None of the above remedies, however, is exclusive. Even if a plaintiff is granted a permanent injunction, for example, he may nevertheless seek money damages from the infringer.

C: Trade Names and Trade Dress

1: Trade Names

Trade names, that is commercial and corporate names, may be entitled to legal protection in the same way as trademarks. The tests for the protectability of a trade name and for infringement are also the same as those for trademarks and service marks. Under common law, therefore, a trade name will be protected if it is arbitrary, fanciful, suggestive, or descriptive (with proof of secondary meaning). As with trademarks and service marks, a showing of likelihood of confusion is required before a court will prevent the use of an allegedly infringing name.

The primary difference between trade names and trademarks is that trade names are not covered by the Lanham Act. This fact has two consequences. First, trade names are not registerable as are trademarks and service marks, and may not, therefore, enjoy the same presumption of validity as registered trademarks. Second, trade name owners do not enjoy the same rights with respect to geographically remote uses that trademark owners do. As has been noted, the owner of a registered trademark may prevent the use of a confusingly similar mark if it can prove a likelihood of entry into the remote user's market. Trade name owners, however, may not be able to prevent remote uses, unless such uses fall within the senior user's "natural zone of expansion under common law." *See Hanover Star Milling Co. v. Metcalf,* 240 U.S. 403 (1916) (good faith remote use by junior user may not be prevented unless use falls within senior user's natural zone of expansion). *See also United Drug Co. v. Theodore Rectanus Co.,* 248 U.S. 90 (1918).

While trade names, *per se,* are not protected under federal law, a corporate name will be protected if it is being used as a trademark. For example, "Data-Tech Software, Inc.," when used on company stationery, would not be protectable as a trademark; the term "Data-Tech" however might qualify for protection if it were affixed to a product in a manner that functioned as a trademark. The fact that only part of a trade name was used and incorporated in a corporate logo would make it more likely that it would be registerable as a trademark. If it were printed in full, however, and accompanied by a complete address, it would most likely be unprotectable as a trademark. If it were used on a product to which an independent trademark were also affixed, it would be presumed to be functioning as a trade name, rather than a trademark. *See Application of Antenna Specialists Co.,* 408 F.2d 1052 (C.C.P.A. 1969).

2: Trade Dress

The term "trade dress" refers to the total appearance of a product, including the product's packaging and labeling. Trade dress is protectable under the common law theory of unfair competition and under Section 43(a) ("False representation") of the federal Lanham Act, 15 U.S.C. 1125. As in the case of trademark infringement, the test of trade dress infringement is the likelihood of confusion of the reasonably prudent buyer. *See Chevron Chemical Co. v. Voluntary Purchasing Groups, Inc.,* 659 F.2d 695 (5th Cir. 1981), *cert. denied,* 457 U.S. 1126 (1982) (insecticide package with three-tiered, white, yellow, and red design protectable against confusingly similar competitor's product).

D: Antitrust Considerations: Tying Arrangements

The antitrust laws seek to maintain uninhibited competition among computer firms by outlawing private agreements and monopolies that restrain free trade. Both the Sherman Act, 15 U.S.C. Sects. 1, 2, and the Clayton Act, 15 U.S.C. Sect. 14, prohibit certain "tying arrangements" or product "bundling" which has become increasingly prevalent in the computer industry. The following discussion addresses how such tying arrangements can run afoul of the antitrust laws, as demonstrated by a recent decision involving Data General Corporation.

1: Definition of Tying Arrangements

A tying arrangement occurs when a selling party agrees to sell one computer product (the tying product) on the condition that the buying party agree to purchase another product from the seller (the tied product). Usually the buyer wants to purchase the tying product but does not necessarily wish to buy the tied product.

Tying arrangements constitute violations of the antitrust laws because such arrangements are inherently anticompetitive and injurious to the public. Tying arrangements create an unnatural demand for the tied product, which exists not because the tied product is the most popular, but because consumers have no choice except to purchase it. When consumers have no choice, an illegal restraint on trade is created.

Courts look for the presence of five elements to determine whether a particular tying arrangement is a *per se* violation of the antitrust laws.

1. There must be two separate products involved, where the purchase of one is conditioned on the purchase of the other.

2. The seller must possess sufficient economic power in the tying market to restrain appreciably competition in the tied market.

3. The tying arrangement must affect a not unsubstantial degree of commerce in the tied product market.

4. The party bringing suit must prove that it was actually damaged, and that the other party's antitrust violations actually caused the damage.

5. There must be no applicable business justification for the tying arrangement.

2: Case Example of an Unlawful Tying Arrangement

Digidyne Corp. v. Data General Corp., 734 F.2d 1336 (9th Cir. 1984), is an excellent case study of a computer firm involved in a tying arrangement. The case provides a detailed discussion of each of the elements of a tying arrangement and applies them specifically to computer firms. The case also explains what criteria a court is likely to use in establishing each element in the context of the computer industry.

a. Facts of the case: Data General Corporation manufactured a NOVA central processing unit (CPU) "designed to perform a particular 'instruction set' on groups of tasks," and a copyrighted NOVA operating system "called RDOS containing the basic commands for operation of the system." 734 F.2d at 1338. Digidyne Corporation also manufactured emulator CPUs, which were designed to perform the NOVA instruction set and thus to make use of Data General's RDOS operating system. Data General, however, only licensed its operating system to purchasers of its CPUs. Thus, buyers that did not want to purchase a Data General CPU could not purchase the RDOS operating system.

Digidyne brought an action against Data General and alleged that Data General's licensing policy created an illegal tying arrangement between the NOVA CPU and the RDOS operating system. Digidyne alleged that the tying arrangement severely restrained competition for CPUs since consumers who purchased an operating system from Data General were not free to purchase a compatible CPU from Digidyne or any manufacturer other than Data General.

Under these facts, the Circuit Court of Appeals for the Ninth Circuit held that Data General's policy constituted an illegal tying arrangement under the Sherman Act and the Clayton Act.

b: The court's rationale: Establishing the elements of a per se antitrust violation:
In *Data General*, the Court discussed in great length the elements of a tying arrangement that comprise a *per se* violation of the antitrust laws. The following summarizes the Court's analysis.

1. *Whether two separate products are involved:* Determining whether two computer items are separate products or components of a single product can be extremely difficult since all parts of a computer are necessary to operate the system. The threshold question, however, is not whether two products must be used together but whether they must be manufactured by the same company.

    In *Data General*, the Court applied two criteria. First, the Court determined whether the joint sale of the RDOS operating system software (the tying product) and the NOVA CPU (the tied product) resulted in cost savings apart from reductions in sales expenses and the like normally attendant to any tying arrangement. Second, the Court determined whether the products were normally sold or used as a single unit. If substantial cost savings resulted or if the products were normally sold or used together, the operating system software and the CPU could not be considered separate products.

    Data General claimed that selling the operating system and the CPU as a unit resulted in substantial cost savings because the company researched and developed the two products as a unit. It also claimed that it would be unable to recover its research and development costs if the operating system and the CPU were sold separately. The Court, however, rejected the claim that joint research and development called for joint sales. In fact, the Court found no reason why Data General could not sell its products separately at a price that reflected the research and development of each.

    The Court also concluded that Data General sold CPUs without requiring the purchase of operating systems. The Court held that these actions were evidence of the fact that the two products did not have to come from the same manufacturer. The court further found numerous other companies that manufactured only operating systems or only CPUs, thus establishing not only that the two products need not be manufactured by the same company but also that they were not normally sold as a unit.

    Under these circumstances, the Court concluded that the RDOS operating system and the NOVA CPU were separate products.

2. *Whether the seller possesses sufficient economic power in the tying market to restrain appreciably competition in the tied market:* The courts have identified three tests for determining whether a seller has the requisite economic power in the tying market to restrain competition in the tied market: (1)whether the seller occupies a dominant position in the tying market; (2) whether the seller's product is sufficiently unique to afford the seller some competitive advantage in the market for the tying product; and (3) whether a substantial number of customers may have accepted the tying arrangement solely because of the seller's economic power.

    When any of these tests have been met, the seller usually has sufficient economic power in the tying market to restrain competition in the tied market. The seller does not have to possess a monopoly or price-fixing power in the tying product—just enough market leverage so that consumers are induced to buy the tied product solely on the basis of the tying product. It need only appear that "a substantial volume of commerce is foreclosed." *Jefferson Parish Hosp. Dist. No. 2 v. Hyde,* 104 S.Ct. 1551, 1560 (1984). "Even in the absence of a showing of market dominance, the crucial economic power may be inferred from the tying product's desirability to consumers or from uniqueness in its attributes." *U.S. v. Loew's Inc.,* 371 U.S. 38, 45 (1962). "Whenever there are *some* buyers who find a seller's product uniquely attractive, and are, therefore, willing to pay a premium above the price of its nearest substitute, the seller has the opportunity to impose a tie to some other good." *U.S. Steel Corp. v. Fortner Enterprises, Inc.,* 429 U.S. 610, at 620, n.14 (1977) (emphasis added), quoting, "The Logic of Foreclosure: Tie-In Doctrine after Fortner v. U.S. Steel," 79 *Yale L.J.* 83, 93-94 (1969). What is required is a factual assessment of the tying product's uniqueness and desirability, not its market power.

The Court in *Data General* found "abundant evidence that [Data General's RDOS operating system] was distinctive and particularly desirable to a substantial number of buyers . . . ." 734 F.2d at 1341. The Court also concluded that the system could not readily be reproduced by other sellers without infringing Data General's copyright and using its trade secrets. "The requisite economic power is presumed when the tying product is patented or copyrighted." *U.S. v. Loew's Inc., supra,* at 45. Thus, because Data General's operating systems were particularly desirable and not easily copied, the Court concluded that the company had sufficient control over the tying product market to restrain competition in the tied market.

Data General, however, argued that it did not appreciably restrain the market for CPU's because the market was highly competitive, "characterized by a wide range of competitive hardware offerings, intense price competition, ease of entry, and rapid growth." *In re Data General Corp. Antitrust Litigation,* 529 F. Supp. 801, 818 (N.D. Cal. 1981). The Court stated, however, that a detailed analysis of the market conditions in the tied product was unnecessary. All that was required was that a greater than *de minimis* volume of commerce be foreclosed. *In re Data General Corp. Antitrust Litigation,* 490 F. Supp. 1089, 1117 (N.D. Cal. 1980). "[T]he mere presence of competing substitutes for the tying product . . . is insufficient to destroy the legal, and indeed the economic, distinctiveness of the copyrighted product." *U.S. v. Loew's Inc., supra,* 371 U.S. at 49.

The Court reasoned:

> The question is not whether other operating systems with which RDOS competed were as good as RDOS or better . . ., but rather whether RDOS, available only from [Data General], was sufficiently attractive to some customers to enable [Data General] to require those who wished to obtain it to also buy from Data General CPUs they might otherwise have purchased from others.

734 F.2d at 1345-46.

In conclusion, the Court held, "[i]f a seller's product is distinctive, not available from other sources, and sufficiently attractive to some buyers to enable the seller by tying arrangements to foreclose a part of the market for a tied product . . .," the seller has sufficient economic power to satisfy the second element of an illegal tying arrangement. *Id.* at 1345.

3. *Whether a not insubstantial amount of commerce in the tied product was affected:* In determining whether a not insubstantial amount of commerce in the tied product is affected, courts look to the total sales tied, not the total sales accounted for by the party who brought suit. Data General admitted that it sold 52,700 CPUs between 1970 and 1978, and that in 1977 its shipments were valued at $254 million. 490 F. Supp. at 1117. The court found that this was not an insubstantial amount ("more than *de minimis*") of commerce affected by the tying arrangement and that, therefore, Data General satisfied the third element of a *per se* antitrust violation. 734 F.2d at 1347; 490 F. Supp. at 1117.

4. *Whether the party bringing suit was actually damaged and whether the antitrust violations actually caused the damage:* Some degree of damage is all that is necessary to prove actual injury caused by antitrust violations. In Data General, the court found that Digidyne had, in fact, been injured because customers who used Data General's operating systems were prevented from using Digidyne's CPUs. The court, therefore, concluded that Data General's tying arrangement approximately caused Digidyne's injury.

5. *Whether business reasons justify the violation:* Tying arrangements are exempt from antitrust laws if business reasons justify such arrangements. Exemptions, however, are very narrowly construed and are rarely allowed.

Data General presented the Court with three business justifications for its tying arrangement. First, Data General argued that allowing its RDOS operating systems to be sold separately from its NOVA CPUs would harm the company's goodwill because of increased service problems. Data General stated that it was difficult for it to maintain its equipment when the owners combined the RDOS operating system with equipment made by different manufacturers. The Court did not find this argument persuasive since Data General could provide lesser warranties for operating software licensed on an unbundled basis than for software licensed for use with Data General's CPU. 490 F. Supp. at 1120-21.

Second, Data General argued that it needed to sell the products together to recover its research and development costs. As was discussed earlier, the Court rejected this argument because less restrictive means were available to recover research and development costs. Specifically, Data General could sell its RDOS operating system and NOVA CPU separately and price each product to reflect respective research and development costs.

Finally, Data General argued that the market demanded that the products be sold as a unit because of customer preference. The Court, however, found no evidence to support this argument and concluded:

> Data General can achieve the legitimate end of responding to the market's demands by employing means less restrictive than a tie-in. The record establishes beyond dispute that Data General could license its software

under both bundled and unbundled-lesser warranty options. Customers who desire single vendor accountability could choose the bundled option; those who prefer hybrid systems, and the record establishes that there are such customers, could select the unbundled option. Data General need not pit the dictates of the market place against the mandate of the antitrust laws. The two interests can be simultaneously promoted by way of marketing practices less restrictive than tie-ins.

490 F. Supp. at 1123.

The Court thus found that Data General's actions satisfied the fifth and final element of a tying arrangement.

PROTECTING YOUR PROPRIETARY RIGHTS
IN THE COMPUTER AND
HIGH TECHNOLOGY INDUSTRIES

SECTION 7
IMPORT PROTECTION FOR
SOFTWARE AND HARDWARE

Section 7: Import Protection for Software and Hardware

A: Remedies Afforded by the International Trade Commission

The American high technology electronics and software industry has available to it an increasing number of legal weapons to combat unfair methods of competition from foreign imports. Least known and most misunderstood, but highly effective and increasingly employed by sophisticated American businesses, are the relief measures provided by the U.S. International Trade Commission (ITC) under Section 337 of the Tariff Act of 1933. For a more detailed discussion of high technology litigation before the ITC, the reader is referred to Appendix D.

1: Scope of Section 337

Section 337 of the Tariff Act of 1930, as amended, states:

> Unfair methods of competition and unfair acts in the importation of articles into the United States, or in their sale by the owner, importer, consignee, or agent of either, the effect or tendency of which is to destroy or substantially injure an industry, efficiently and economically operated, in the United States, or to prevent the establishment of such an industry, or to restrain or monopolize trade and commerce in the United States, are declared unlawful, and when found by the Commission to exist shall be dealt with, in addition to any other provisions of law, as provided in this section.

19 U.S.C., Sect. 1337(a).

Long considered only a method to remedy international patent infringements, Section 337 as administered by the ITC is, because of its speed and effectiveness, becoming a favored device to halt the importation of infringing high technology products that have flooded the U.S. market in recent years. Section 337 litigation, however, is often unfamiliar to both foreign and domestic respondents, and can offer significant strategic advantages to the experienced practitioner. The attractiveness of the ITC as a forum for domestic complainants is further augmented by the fact that the rapidity of Section 337 proceedings can be used as a tactical weapon against a respondent whose counsel is not fully aware of, or experienced in, the unique aspects of Section 337 practice.

2: ITC Procedures under Section 337

a: Complaint: A domestic company that believes it has suffered or may suffer substantial injury from an unfair act in connection with imported computer software or hardware may file a complaint with the ITC. Also, the Commission may initiate an investigation *sua sponte.* 19 U.S.C., Sect. 1337(b)(1), 19 C.F.R., Sect. 210.10(b). The fact that other similar or related legal actions have been filed in other forums prior to, concurrent with, or subsequent to the ITC action will not, under most circumstances, prevent the investigation from proceeding.

b: Informal inquiry: Upon receipt of the complaint, the ITC may conduct an informal inquiry to collect data, judge the scope of the problem, and consolidate proceedings before it. Under the Trade Act of 1974, 19 U.S.C., Sect. 2482 and 19 C.F.R., Sect. 210.11(b), such an investigation will conclude with the decision to commence a formal investigation or to drop the matter entirely. *See, e.g., ITC Informal Inquiry, Eastern Airbus Lease* (June-Dec. 1977) (informal inquiry into financing terms under which European A300 Airbus was leased to Eastern Airlines led to a decision not to institute a formal investigation). During the pendency of this informal inquiry, the Commission will not order any formal discovery or issue exclusion orders.

c: Formal investigation: Once the Commission receives a complaint, irrespective of whether an informal inquiry has been conducted, the Commission has 30 days within which to decide whether to institute a formal investigative proceeding. 19 C.F.R., Sect. 210.12. If the Commission decides to proceed with a formal investigation, a notice of the proceeding is published in the *Register, id.*, and the Commission has 12 months (18 months for "more complicated" cases) in which to complete the investigation. 19 C.F.R., Sect. 210.15. Thereafter, all named respondents are served with a notice of the investigation and the complaint, and a presiding Administrative Law Judge is appointed. 19 C.F.R., Sect. 210.13.

Each respondent then has 20 days within which to file a response. 19 C.F.R., Sect. 210.21(a). Failure to comply with this time limit may result in a default judgment against the respondent, with statutory remedies applied accordingly. 19 C.F.R., Sect. 210.21(d).

Prior to the hearing, both parties may amend their pleadings, supplement their prior submissions, and file appropriate motions. 19 C.F.R., Sects. 210.22, 210.23, 210.24. The party opponent must answer all motions within 10 days or else be deemed to have consented to them. 19 C.F.R., Sect. 210.24(c). (At least one ITC Administrative Law Judge routinely shortens the response time to five days.)

The parties to the proceeding may use the discovery process to "flesh-out" their positions. The parties may take depositions, serve interrogatories, and seek stipulations of admissions for all nonprivileged relevant information. 19 C.F.R., Sect. 210.30. The Administrative Law Judge will determine the limitations on discovery and is empowered to issue protective orders limiting disclosure of certain confidential, proprietary, or trade secret information. 19 C.F.R., Sect. 210.30(c)-(d), 210.44. The Commission investigative staff is also authorized to propound discovery requests and otherwise participate as a full party in the litigation. 19 U.S.C., Sect. 1333, 19 C.F.R., Sect. 210.41(b).

Failure to comply with discovery requests may result in adverse *ex parte* rulings against the noncomplying party. 19 C.F.R., Sect. 210.36(b). *See, e.g., Certain Multicellular Plastic Film,* Inv. No. 337-TA-54 (June 1979) (manufacturer/exporter did not comply with discovery and was subjected to exclusion order for its products, based on inferences drawn against it). Such rulings will apply to foreign respondent parties who have not subjected themselves to the personal jurisdiction of the ITC forum, because the ITC has full authority to impose appropriate relief on the basis of *in rem* jurisdiction over the imported articles.

In a complex federal court trial, the parties might take years to discover all relevant documents and data. In an ITC proceeding, however, because of the extremely short time period involved, most evidence-gathering must be completed within five to six months after the commencement of the proceeding.

d: Hearing: The statute provides for a public evidentiary hearing, which generally takes two weeks, with full rights of notice, cross-examination, presentation of evidence, objection, motion, and argument. 19 U.S.C., Sect. 1337(c), 19 C.F.R., Sect. 210.41. At the end of the hearing, the parties file post hearing briefs, and the Administrative Law Judge must issue an initial determination, based on findings of fact and conclusions of law. The initial determination must be filed within nine months—14 months for cases designated "more complicated" by the Commission—from the date of commencement of the investigation. 19 C.F.R., Sect. 210.53. The parties, including the ITC investigative staff, may then request the Commission's reversal of all or part of the initial determination. 19 C.F.R., Sect. 210.54.

e: Commission review: The Administrative Law Judge's initial determination is then reviewed by the full Commission, composed entirely of Presidential appointees. The Commission decides whether to adopt, modify, or reject the judge's initial determination, and what remedy, if any, to apply. 19 C.F.R., Sect. 210.56(c). The Commission reviews the initial determination for legal and evidentiary soundness and then makes its decision in light of "public policy" considerations. In reaching its conclusion, the Commission must consult other administrative agencies—at a minimum, the Department of Health and Human Services, the Department of Justice, and the Federal Trade Commission—and may hear arguments from private parties, including parties to the action. 19 U.S.C. Sect. 1337(b)(2), 19 C.F.R., Sect. 210.14(c)(2), 210.56(a).

If the Commission finds a violation, or reason to believe that there is a violation, it will, within 12 months of the commencement of the proceedings, publish its order in the *Federal Register* and send a copy to the President for review in light of executive office policy considerations. 19 U.S.C., Sect. 1337(g). Unless the President disapproves of the Commission's decision for policy reasons within 60 days, the decision and order become final. 19 C.F.R., Sect. 210.57. During the course of Presidential review, the infringing hardware and software may be imported under bond. U.S.C., Sect. 1339(g)(3).

If the Commission finds a violation of Section 337, it must—absent public policy considerations—direct that the foreign articles be excluded from entry into the U.S. 19 U.S.C., Sect. 1337(d). In appropriate circumstances, the Commission may issue interim Temporary Exclusion Orders whereby entry is permitted under bond while the investigation proceeds. 19 U.S.C., Sect. 1337(e). In lieu of or in addition to a temporary or permanent exclusion order, the Commission may issue an appropriate cease and desist order. 19 U.S.C., Sect. 1337(f)(2).

Any party that violates a Commission order is subject to a federal court-imposed civil penalty of $10,000 per day or an amount equal to the domestic value of the articles imported or sold on each day in violation of the order, whichever is greater. 19 U.S.C., Sect. 1337(f)(2). Adversely affected parties may petition the Commission for reconsideration within 14 days (19 C.F.R., Sect. 210.58), or seek review in the U.S. Court of Appeals for the Federal Circuit. 19 U.S.C., Sect. 1337(c), 19 C.F.R., Sect. 210.61.

Section 337 affords a computer firm several useful advantages against unfair importers:

1. Section 337 actions are faster and more effective than court proceedings.
2. Section 337 actions provide the complainant a tactical advantage against the infringing party because of the rapidity of the proceeding.
3. Section 337 actions are *in rem* proceedings.

a: Speed and effectiveness: While proceedings in federal court often drag on for several years, the Tariff Act of 1933 requires that ITC investigations be completed within 12 months. (The Act allows 18 months for "more complicated" investigations.) 19 U.S.C., Sect. 1337(b)(1) and 19 C.F.R., Sect. 210.15. ITC proceedings, as discussed above, follow a strict time table for filing responses, issuing orders, and answering motions. The speed and effectiveness of such proceedings clearly redound to the benefit of a computer firm seeking immediate protection of its software and hardware from infringing imports.

b: Tactical advantages against the opposing party: In the fast-paced procedure of a Section 337 investigation, the best prepared party has a clear advantage over those caught by surprise. Because the complainant has knowledge of the proceedings well in advance of the commencement of the investigation, which is when the public first becomes aware of the proceedings, the complainant can prepare its entire case before the action has even been instituted. Therefore, the complainant can control the sequence of events during the proceedings by having its discovery requests and motions substantially researched and ready for filing before the respondents even learn of the complaint. Thus the complainant has a distinct advantage in the course of the proceedings if respondents fail to secure adequate representation.

There are a variety of allegations of unfair acts a complainant may make under Section 337: (1) patent infringement; (2) copyright violations; (3) misappropriation of trade secrets, trademarks, or trade dress (passing off or palming off); (4) false designation of origin; (5) false packing, advertising, or labeling; and (6) a range of antitrust violations. The complainant must also allege that the act complained of has the tendency to injure or destroy an efficiently operating domestic industry, to prevent the establishment of such an industry, or to violate the antitrust laws. If the complainant meets his burden of proof, the ITC will exclude the unfair imports from the U.S.

c: "In Rem" proceeding: Before a court or agency is able to review a particular case, it must first determine whether it has jurisdiction to hear the matter. One means of asserting jurisdiction is through personal or *in personam* jurisdiction. *In personam* jurisdiction means that the court or agency has jurisdiction over the person or company involved in the case. Another method of asserting jurisdiction is through *in rem* jurisdiction, whereby the court or agency has authority over the product giving rise to the controversy.

The ITC has full authority to impose appropriate relief on the basis of *in rem* jurisdiction over the imported articles. Therefore, Commission rulings apply to foreign parties that have not subjected themselves to the personal jurisdiction of the ITC. In other words, the mere presence of the imported computer software or hardware in the U.S. gives the ITC complete jurisdiction over the matter, whether or not the person responsible for the illegal importation is present.

4: Case Study: Apple Computer

The case of the infringing Apple-compatible computers from the Far East is a recent example of the use of Section 337 as a remedy against unfair imports. In January 1983, Apple Computer, Inc. filed a Section 337 complaint with the ITC alleging patent, copyright, and trade dress infringement of its microcomputers—the Apple II, II+, IIe, and III. *In re Certain Personal Computers and Components Thereof*, Inv. No. 337-TA-140 (March 1984). Complainant Apple named 20 respondents, mostly Taiwanese manufacturers and exporters, who had been producing infringing microcomputers and shipping them to the U.S. under brand names such as "Gold II," "Orange," "Orange +," and "AP II." The products were exact copies of the patented Apple hardware circuitry, housed in lookalike cases; some were fitted with read-only-memory (ROM) chips, which contained pirated copies of the Apple operating system and BASIC Interpreter. Those units that did not contain infringing ROMs—including "ROM-less" or "ROM deficient" circuit boards—were designed to be fitted with ROM chips after their arrival in the U.S.

The ITC undertook an investigation and, on March 9, 1984, found for the complainant on all counts. All of the respondents were judged guilty of infringing Apple's patents. In addition, the ITC concluded that (1) the "knockoffs," which contained ROM, directly infringed Apple's copyrights and (2) the microcomputers and circuit boards, which did not contain infringing ROMs, contributorily infringed the same copyrights. (Apple had dropped its trade dress allegations during the course of the investigation.) The Commission ordered a total exclusion of all infringing microcomputers from entry into the U.S.

5: Current Developments

The remedies available to the prevailing complainant involve the exclusion of infringing products from entry into the U.S. In recent years, owing to the alarming increase in counterfeit goods entering the U.S., as well as the concern over American economic productivity in general, Congress has considered stronger remedies. Among the additional remedies that have been suggested during recent Congressional hearings are (1) creating a conclusive presumption of injury; (2) allowing Section 337 actions even when the products have not yet entered the marketplace and no industry has been damaged; (3) extending the life of an infringed patent for a new 17 year term as to any foreign firm adjudicated an infringer by the ITC; (4) requiring importers to certify that their products do not infringe American intellectual property rights before such products are allowed into the U.S. stream of commerce; and (5) imposing stiffer monetary and product exclusion penalties on infringing foreign firms, including forfeiture and/or destruction of illicit merchandise, instead of mere exclusion from entry. *Unfair Foreign Trade Practices: Hearings before the Subcomm. on Oversight and Investigations of the House Comm. on Energy and Commerce*, 98th Cong., 1st Sess., Parts I and II (1983). Another enforcement agency, the Federal Bureau of Investigation, has similarly taken a more active role in preventing the infringement of intellectual property rights. Recently, the Bureau has authorized video game manufacturers to affix to their products warning labels which have the initials "FBI" and the Bureau logo in bold print, in addition to the following:

WARNING

Federal law provides severe civil and criminal penalties for the unauthorized reproduction, distribution, or exhibition of copyrighted audio-visual works and video games.

The Federal Bureau of Investigation investigates allegations of criminal copyright infringement.

Id. Part II at 127, 115.

B: Enforcement of Proprietary Rights by the U.S. Customs

The Copyright Act, 17 U.S.C., Sects. 602, 603, and the Lanham Act, 15 U.S.C., Sect. 1124, prevent the importation of goods into the U.S. that infringe copyrights, patents, trademarks, and trade names. The U.S. Customs Service, which is an agency of the U.S. Treasury Department, enforces these provisions. Customs officers screen computer goods imported into the U.S. for possible proprietary rights infringements before the goods are actually allowed in the American market. Under 19 C.F.R., Sects. 133.1-133.53, the Customs Service has established certain procedures by which copyright, patent, trademark, and trade name owners can record their goods for protection, and customs officers can identify and exclude infringing goods.

1: Procedures of the U.S. Customs Service

A computer firm can obtain statutory protection against importation of infringing goods by the following two-step procedure. First, the firm must register the proprietary work with the appropriate office (e.g., Copyright Office or Patent and Trademark Office).

Second, the firm must record the copyright, patent, trademark, or trade name with the Customs Service. The firm need only provide the Customs Service with (1) a written request for recordation including information about the good(s) to be recorded and (2) a certified copy of the copyright, patent, trademark, or trade name registration, together with a fee of $190. Once the owner registers and records his proprietary work, the Customs Service will exclude the infringing goods.

Under 19 C.F.R., Sect. 133.42, the Customs Service may prohibit the importation of "actual copies or substantial copies of recorded copyrighted work produced and imported in contravention of the rights of the copyright owner." When a Customs officer believes that imported goods might be in violation of the statute, he immediately informs the importer and withholds delivery of such goods until a final determination is made. The importer then has 30 days to deny that his work is an illegal copy of a recorded work or to allege that withholding his product will result in substantial harm. The Customs Service assumes that the goods are copies and automatically seizes the goods if the importer ignores the officer's actions. If the importer denies the customs officer's allegations, however, the officer will release the goods, unless, within 30 days, the owner of the recorded goods files a demand for the exclusion of the imported goods in question. The owner of the recorded goods must also post a bond in an amount determined by the Customs Service to prevent damage to the importer in the event that the final determination is made against the owner. During this 30-day period, the Customs Service provides the proprietary owner with a sample of the imported product. The owner may then evaluate whether or not the imported product is an infringement.

The Commissioner of Customs decides whether the imported goods are illegal copies after the parties have presented their evidence. All decisions of the Commissioner and all actions of the Customs Service are subject to judicial review by the federal district courts.

If the goods in question are subject to copyright, the Customs Service will release the goods and the bond to the importer should the Commissioner determine that the imported goods do not infringe the recorded goods. If the Commissioner decides that the imported goods infringe recorded goods, however, the Customs Service will seize and destroy the imported goods and will return the bond to the proprietary owner.

If the goods in question infringe on a registered trademark or trade name, their disposition depends on whether their use constitutes counterfeiting or infringement. Counterfeiting occurs when the imported goods bear a trademark or trade name identical to that of the genuine goods, which will deceive the buyer into believing that he is purchasing the genuine goods. Customs may seize and destroy goods that bear counterfeited trademarks or trade names. Infringement occurs when the imported goods bear a trademark or trade name similar to that of the genuine goods, which may confuse the buyer. Customs will allow the importation of these goods once the importer removes the infringing mark.

2: Customs Problems Special to Computer Software and Hardware

Unauthorized infringement of proprietary rights in computer software or hardware is extremely difficult to discover, since computer products can be easily altered to avoid detection. In recent years, however, the Customs Service has increased its technical capability to identify infringing high technology goods. The Customs Service now has seven major laboratory facilities to test for infringing electronics products, such as computer chips, and a nationwide automated data processing system that contains extensive information on infringing importers and their goods. *Unfair Foreign Trade Practices: Hearings before the Subcomm. on Oversight and Investigations,* 98th Cong., 1st Sess., Part II (1983). The Customs Service also sponsors continuous seminar programs to keep enforcement personnel aware of the different computer products entering the U.S. *Id.* at 170.

Computer firms, however, are advised not to rely solely on recordation and registration with the Customs Service to protect their proprietary rights. Firms can offer additional help to customs officers and thus better protect their interests. First, computer firms should provide the Customs Service with a sample of their products, and should immediately notify it when they become aware of specific instances of infringements. Second, computer firms can provide the Customs Service with special machines or decoding devices that will help it identify unauthorized infringements. Finally, with respect to contributory copyright violations by ROM-less computers, computer firms may obtain exclusion orders from the ITC and require the Customs Service to halt the importation of such products. *See In re Certain Research Computer and Components Thereof,* Inv. No. 337-7A-140 (Mar. 1984).

In short, the Customs Service is well aware of the special infringement problems faced by computer software and hardware developers. Although Customs officers are trained and equipped to identify infringing computer software programs, they cannot keep abreast of the latest technological advances or the most sophisticated methods of infringement. Thus, computer firms must assist the Customs Service whenever possible to assure the best protection against unfair competition from infringing imports.

C: Remedies in Federal Court

When an American computer firm suspects that a foreign company is importing goods that infringe the firm's copyrights, patents, trademarks, or trade names, the firm may bring an *in personam* action in federal court seeking both injunctive relief and damages against the importer. Initially the firm may seek emergency relief by means of a temporary restraining order. Although limited in duration (usually only 10 days), a temporary restraining order takes effect immediately to prevent the goods in question from being imported until the court makes a final determination as to whether or not they actually infringe proprietary rights. Temporary restraining orders are difficult to obtain, however, because they are often issued *ex parte*. Thus, the party seeking the order must make a strong showing of immediate, irreparable harm and a likelihood of success on the merits. The party must also show that the hardship he would suffer without the order far outweighs the hardship the importer would suffer under the injunction. In addition the firm seeking the injunction must post a bond in the event that the court eventually decides against it.

Thereafter, the computer firm may obtain a preliminary injunction, which is effective pending a decision of a trial on the merits. A party may also request the court to seize and impound the infringing goods. To do so the party must satisfy all the requirements for a temporary restraining order and post a bond.

The court will then hold a trial and decide the merits of the case (i.e., whether or not the importations infringe a recorded copyright, patent, trademark, or trade name). If the court decides that an infringement has occurred, it will issue a permanent injunction to prevent the importation of the goods and will award damages, if applicable, to the owner of the infringed goods. If the Court finds no infringement, the imported goods will be released to the importer and accepted for importation.

PROTECTING YOUR PROPRIETARY RIGHTS
IN THE COMPUTER AND HIGH TECHNOLOGY INDUSTRIES

SECTION 8
EXPORT PROTECTION OF
SOFTWARE OWNERSHIP RIGHTS:
COPYRIGHTS

MARZOUK

Section 8: Export Protection of Software Ownership Rights: Copyrights

Generally, copyright infringement outside the U.S. is not actionable under the U.S. Copyright Act. There are two major multilateral treaties, however, that provide protection to U.S. computer firms whose software is available outside the U.S.: the Universal Copyright Convention (UCC) and the Berne Convention.

A: The Universal Copyright Convention

Countries that belong to the UCC provide the same copyright protection to foreign copyright owners that they afford to their own nationals. Under this principle of "national treatment," therefore, U.S. software firms are protected regardless of where their software is published.

The UCC became effective on September 16, 1955, and only protects works created after that date. Not all present member countries joined the UCC on that date, however, and software published after the UCC's effective date, but before a particular country became a member, will not be protected in that country. A list of UCC member nations and the corresponding effective dates follow:

Country	Effective Date
Algeria	August 28, 1973
Andorra	September 16, 1955
Argentina	February 13, 1958
Australia	May 1, 1969
Austria	July 2, 1957
Bahamas	December 27, 1976
Bangladesh	August 5, 1975
Belgium	August 31, 1960
Brazil	January 13, 1960
Bulgaria	June 7, 1975
Cameroon	May 1, 1973
Canada	August 10, 1962
Chile	September 16, 1955
Colombia	June 18, 1976
Costa Rica	September 16, 1955
Cuba	June 18, 1957
Czechoslovakia	January 6, 1960
Democratic Kampuchea	September 16, 1955
Denmark	February 9, 1962
Ecuador	June 5, 1957
El Salvador	March 29, 1979
Fiji	October 10, 1970
Finland	April 16, 1963

France	January 14, 1956
German Democratic Republic	October 5, 1973
Germany, Federal Republic of	September 16, 1955
Ghana	August 22, 1962
Greece	August 24, 1963
Guatemala	October 28, 1964
Guinea	November 13, 1981
Haiti	September 16, 1955
Holy See	October 5, 1955
Hungary	January 23, 1971
Iceland	December 18, 1956
India	January 21, 1958
Ireland	January 20, 1959
Israel	September 16, 1955
Italy	January 24, 1957
Japan	April 28, 1956
Kenya	September 7, 1966
Laos	September 16, 1955
Lebanon	October 17, 1959
Liberia	July 27, 1956
Liechtenstein	January 22, 1959
Luxembourg	October 15, 1955
Malawi	October 26, 1965
Malta	November 19, 1968
Mauritius	March 12, 1968
Mexico	May 12, 1957
Monaco	September 16, 1955
Morocco	May 8, 1972
Netherlands	June 22, 1967
New Zealand	September 11, 1964
Nicaragua	August 16, 1961
Nigeria	February 14, 1962
Norway	January 23, 1963
Pakistan	September 16, 1955
Panama	October 17, 1962
Paraguay	March 11, 1962
Peru	October 16, 1963
Philippines	November 19, 1955
Poland	March 9, 1977
Portugal	December 25, 1956
Senegal	July 9, 1974
Soviet Union	May 27, 1973
Spain	September 16, 1955
Sweden	July 1, 1961
Switzerland	March 30, 1956
Tunisia	June 19, 1969
United Kingdom	September 27, 1957
United States of America	September 16, 1955

Venezuela	September 30, 1966
Yugoslavia	May 11, 1966
Zambia	June 1, 1965

B: Berne Convention

Like the UCC, the Berne Convention provides copyright protection to foreign works. While the U.S. is not a member of the Berne Convention, domestic companies are often able to take advantage of the protection offered by the treaty. The Berne Convention states that if the copyright owner of a non-Berne member country first publishes its work in a Berne member country, then the owner receives copyright protection in all Berne member countries.

The Berne Convention also provides protection when the first publication occurs simultaneously in Berne member and non-Berne member countries. What constitutes a "simultaneous publication" differs from country to country, however. Generally, a work must be more than nominally available to the public for the convention to consider it "published." "Simultaneous" published works can mean works published on the same day or within 30 days of each other, depending on the country.

Copyright owners who seek international copyright protection through the Berne Convention must be aware of the different procedures and standards of each country. When dealing with international copyright protection, copyright owners should always refer to the copyright laws of each nation. A list of Berne Convention member nations and the corresponding effective dates follow:

Country	**Effective Date**
Argentina	June 10, 1967
Australia	April 14, 1928
Austria	October 1, 1920
Bahamas	July 10, 1973
Belgium	December 5, 1887
Benin	January 3, 1961
Brazil	February 9, 1922
Bulgaria	December 5, 1921
Cameroon	September 21, 1964
Canada	April 10, 1928
Central African Republic	September 3, 1977
Chad	November 25, 1971
Chile	June 5, 1970
Congo	May 8, 1962
Costa Rica	June 10, 1978
Cyprus	February 24, 1964
Czechoslovakia	February 22, 1921
Denmark	July 1, 1903
Egypt	June 7, 1977
Fiji	December 1, 1971
Finland	April 1, 1928
France	December 5, 1887
Gabon	March 26, 1962

German Democratic Republic	December 5, 1887
Germany, Federal Republic of	December 5, 1887
Greece	November 9, 1920
Guinea	November 20, 1980
Holy See	September 12, 1935
Hungary	February 14, 1922
Iceland	September 7, 1947
India	April 1, 1928
Ireland	October 5, 1927
Israel	March 24, 1950
Italy	December 5, 1887
Ivory Coast	January 1, 1962
Japan	July 15, 1899
Lebanon	September 30, 1947
Libya	September 28, 1976
Liechtenstein	July 30, 1931
Luxembourg	June 20, 1888
Madagascar	January 1, 1966
Mali	March 19, 1962
Malta	September 21, 1964
Mauritania	February 6, 1973
Mexico	June 11, 1967
Monaco	May 30, 1889
Morocco	June 30, 1917
Netherlands	November 1, 1912
New Zealand	April 24, 1928
Niger	May 2, 1962
Norway	April 13, 1896
Pakistan	July 5, 1948
Philippines	August 1, 1951
Poland	January 28, 1920
Portugal	March 29, 1911
Romania	January 1, 1927
Senegal	August 25, 1962
South Africa	October 3, 1928
Spain	December 5, 1887
Sri Lanka	July 20, 1959
Surinam	February 23, 1977
Sweden	August 1, 1904
Switzerland	December 5, 1887
Thailand	July 17, 1931
Togo	April 30, 1975
Tunisia	December 5, 1887
Turkey	January 1, 1952
United Kingdom	December 5, 1887
Upper Volta	August 19, 1963
Uruguay	July 10, 1967
Venezuela	December 30, 1982

Yugoslavia	June 17, 1930
Zaire	October 8, 1963
Zimbabwe	April 18, 1980

C: Other Treaties

Countries, many of which are neither UCC nor Berne Convention members, may also enter into private treaties that provide copyright protection. For example, while Canada is a member of both conventions, it also offers copyright protection by means of a special certification from the Minister charged with administration of the Copyright Act. This certificate provides "national treatment" to the countries it names. The U.S. accepted such a certificate from Canada on January 1, 1924.

In addition to private treaties, other treaties may protect the proprietary rights of American computer firms. The Buenos Aires Convention, for instance, protects American firms that fulfill the copyright formalities of the U.S. and use the phrase "All Rights Reserved" on all published software.

D: General Comparison between American and Foreign Copyright Laws

It is difficult, if not impossible, to generalize as to the nature and scope of foreign computer laws. The following, however, are very broad comparisons between U.S. and foreign copyright laws. Copyright owners should always consult the laws of each country before publishing software internationally.

1: Subject Matter

Appropriate subject matter for foreign copyrights is generally no different than that in the U.S.

2: Co-Authorship

Under U.S. copyright laws, joint ownership occurs when two or more authors make contributions that are either inseparable or interdependent. Under most foreign copyright laws, joint authorship requires that the contributions be inseparable. For example, most foreign countries would not consider music and lyrics a joint authorship. Foreign copyright laws also usually require the consent of all the joint authors before validating a license agreement. U.S. law requires only the consent of one of the authors.

3: Notice

Most foreign countries do not require a copyright notice or any other formalities to obtain copyright protection.

4: Duration

Software created in the U.S. cannot be protected in a foreign country beyond the period prescribed by that country's copyright laws.

PROTECTING YOUR PROPRIETARY RIGHTS
IN THE COMPUTER AND
HIGH TECHNOLOGY INDUSTRIES

SECTION 9
PROTECTING PROPRIETARY RIGHTS
WHEN CONTRACTING WITH
THE FEDERAL GOVERNMENT

Section 9: Protecting Proprietary Rights When Contracting with the Federal Government

In recent years, the U.S. federal government has demanded increasing control over computer software, technical data, and patent rights developed by independent contractors at government expense. The government generally seeks to retain royalty free access to proprietary software, data, and patented inventions to ensure the operation and maintenance of equipment and supplies and to enhance competition in the federal market. Whenever possible, the government will acquire this information without compensation.

The federal government, however, realizes that contractors also have a significant interest in these rights, particularly if the contractors expend private funds for research and development of proprietary data later used by the government. The contractor could suffer serious economic harm if the government made privately funded research and development available to the general public. Recognizing that private contractors will lose their incentive to develop innovative computer products and technical data if their products are exploited, the federal government attempts to strike a balance between the public interest and the interests of private contractors. In so doing, the government must decide what type and level of information it requires to satisfy its minimum needs. The government also must determine whether the contractor's software, technical data, and patent rights should be protected and whether the government should have limited or unlimited rights in them.

Part 27 of the Federal Acquisition Regulation (FAR) governs proprietary rights in contracts with the federal government. The regulations as issued, however, only cover the acquisition of rights in patents. There are no final regulations for rights in software, data, and copyrights; each agency has its own distinct rules. Thus, it is important that contractors consult the appropriate agency regulations when negotiating contracts involving software, technical data, and copyrights.

The Department of Defense (DoD), in its Defense Acquisition Circular (DAC) 84-1 (March 1, 1984), is one agency that has promulgated extensive regulations governing proprietary rights in software, data, and copyrights. DAC 84-1 amends the Department of Defense FAR Supplement to add a new Sect. 27.4 on "Technical Data, Other Data, Computer Software, and Copyrights." While DAC 84-1 is by no means the final word for agencies other than the DoD, the circular addresses the relevant issues and will serve as an example of applicable agency regulations for purposes of this discussion.

A: Patent Rights

The Patent and Trademark Amendments of 1980 marked a shift in the government's policy of favoring federal acquisition of patent rights to one of preferring contractor retention of such rights. The amendments only provided that small businesses and nonprofit organizations would enjoy enhanced patent rights. On February 18, 1983, however, President Reagan extended the policies of the 1980 amendments to all research and development contracts—not just those involving small businesses or nonprofit organizations. In dealing with other than small businesses, though, agencies are not bound by all of the 1980 amendments and may elect not to comply with these provisions, pursuant to FAR 27.302(b) (1984).

The 1980 amendments specifically provide that contractors may claim title to inventions developed under federal contracts unless the government is accorded title under the contract. The amendments authorize the Office of Federal Procurement Policy to issue uniform regulations and prescribe contract clauses to effectuate this policy. These regulations are set forth in FAR Part 27.3 (1984). A contractor may claim title to patent rights for any invention developed under a government contract unless:

1. The contract provides that rights in an invention will accrue to the government.
2. The contractor fails to disclose the subject invention to the government within the time set forth in the contract.
3. The contractor fails to elect to retain title to the invention within the time period prescribed by the contractor.
4. The contractor fails to file a timely patent application, or fails to prosecute the patent application and to defend challenges to his title.

Patent rights accrue to the federal government in any country where the contractor elects not to retain title, fails to file a patent application, or no longer wishes to retain title. FAR 27.302(d) (1984).

Whenever the contractor claims patent rights, the federal government reserves for itself a nonexclusive, nontransferable, paid-up license to use all inventions developed under the contract and to authorize use of the inventions on behalf of the U.S. If provided for in the contract, the government can also license inventions to foreign governments and international agencies pursuant to treaties. 35 U.S.C. Sect. 202(c)(4), FAR 27.302(c) (1984). In exercising its rights, however, the government must keep confidential all information about inventions for a reasonable period during which a patent application may be filed by the contractor and for the period during which the patent application is pending. 35 U.S.C., Sect. 205, FAR 27.302(i) (1984).

Even when the federal government allows contractors to retain title to inventions developed under federal contract, it continues to prefer that American industry manufacture the inventions. Therefore, a contractor may generally not grant an exclusive license to its invention unless the licensee agrees that any products "embodying the subject invention or produced through the use of the subject invention will be manufactured substantially in the United States." FAR 27.304(g) (1984). In addition, the government may use "march-in rights" to require the patent owner to license his invention to third parties when the contractor fails:

1. to develop a practical application for the invention;
2. to meet the requirement for public use specified in applicable regulations;
3. to meet various health and safety considerations; or
4. to comply with the statutory preference for U.S. industry.

35 U.S.C., Sect. 203, FAR 27.302(f) (1984).

By use of an appropriate contract clause, the federal government will acquire all patent rights to an invention if the agency is required by statute or pursuant to treaty to retain title, the invention is developed at a government-run research facility, or government acquisition of rights is in the interests of national security. FAR 27.302(b) (1984). When the government retains title, the contractor will receive a revocable, nonexclusive, royalty-free license to use that invention throughout the world. The license may be transferred with the contracting officer's permission. FAR 27.302(h) (1984). Even when the contract calls for the government to retain title to all inventions, the contractor may petition for greater rights to a specified invention pursuant to FAR 27.304.-1(a) (1984).

When the federal government takes exclusive title to inventions developed under federal contracts, the "Patent Rights—Acquisition by the Government Clause" is used. FAR 27.303(c). This clause, which appears at FAR 57.227-13 (1984), establishes circumstances under which contractors may retain certain rights, and sets forth various disclosure, identification, and reporting requirements. When the federal government does not demand title, one of two other patent rights clauses will be used: (1) "Patent Rights—Retention by the Contractor Clause (Short Form)," which applies to small businesses or nonprofit organizations and (2) "Patent Rights—Retention by the Contractor Clause (Long Form)," which applies to all other businesses and organizations. FAR 27-303 (1984). The clauses, which appear at FAR 52.227-11, 52.227-12 (1984), establish the circumstances under which contractors may claim title in inventions developed under federal contract; establish conditions under which the government may obtain title if the contractor fails to meet his obligations; and set forth disclosure, identification, and reporting requirements. The long form, which applies to other than small businesses and nonprofit organizations, contains more extensive and more frequent reporting requirements than the short form.

Contractors should also be aware of clauses seeking royalty information and royalty reports. Before awarding contracts, contracting officers often insert provisions into contracts and solicitations requiring information relating to any proposed or actual charges for royalties that the contractor will incur.

B: Rights in Computer Software and Technical Data: Department of Defense Regulations

The Department of Defense (DoD) recognizes that there are "innovative contractors who can best be encouraged to develop at private expense items of military usefulness where their rights in such items are scrupulously protected." DOD FAR Supp. 27.403-1(c)(1) (1984). The government's policy is to acquire only computer software and data rights essential to its needs. DOD FAR Supp. 27.403-2(a)(1), 27.404-1(c) (1984).

The Department of Defense distinguishes "limited rights" in software and data—which restrict the federal government's use—from "unlimited rights" in software and data—which allows the government to use, duplicate, or disclose the software and data as it chooses and to license others to do so for the government's benefit. DOD FAR Supp. 27.401 (1984). The DoD accepts limited rights in unpublished data "pertaining to items, components, or processes developed at private expense." DOD FAR Supp. 27.403-2(c) (1984). It seeks unlimited rights in contract software and data which is work specified in a government contract or is generally available or disclosed to the public. DOD FAR Supp. 27.403-2(b), 27.404-1(a) (1984). With respect to software, the DoD will accept "Restricted Rights" when such software is developed at private expense. DOD FAR Supp. 27.404-1(c) (1984).

1: Unlimited Rights to Software and Technical Data

The DoD will obtain unlimited rights in software or technical data when:

1. Development of the software or data was required by, or was the direct result of research and development required by, the contract.
2. The software or data constitutes changes or modifications to existing government software or data.
3. The data take the form of manuals and instructions for installation, operation, maintenance, and training regarding the equipment required by the contract. (Such data may include program documentation.)
4. The software or data is of the type normally disclosed by a contractor without restrictions, or is already in the public domain. (Even though published, copyrighted data and software are not in the public domain.)

FAR Supp.27.403.2(b), 27.404-1(a) (1984).

In addition, the federal government may demand unlimited rights to data normally furnished with limited rights when the data are necessary to ensure that subsequent contract procurements are competitive. In that case, specific acquisition of unlimited rights will be set forth and priced as a contract item.

The federal government may acquire unlimited rights to software or data under a "Rights to Data—Special Works" contract clause for the production of reports, surveys, histories, training materials, and audio-visual works that the government intends to publish.

2: Limited Rights to Technical Data

Unpublished technical data, including software documentation, will be accepted with limited rights when it is not required to be furnished with unlimited rights, and was produced at private expense. Limited rights data cannot be disclosed outside the government, licensed to private parties, or used in government manufacturing without the express permission of the contractor. The government may, however, release the information to a private party or foreign government for the purpose of emergency overhaul or repair. In either case, the party or foreign government is subject to the same limitations on use, release, and disclosure as the U.S. release of limited rights information to a foreign government may also be authorized because such release is in the best interests of the U.S. DOD FAR Supp. 27.401 (1984).

3: Restricted Rights to Software

When the federal government buys or leases computer software, it must, at a minimum, be allowed to run the software at its intended installation, make back-up copies, and modify the software as necessary. DOD FAR Supp. 27.401 (1984). A contractor, however, is free to negotiate specific restrictions on the government's use of the software, so long as the restrictions are not inconsistent with these minimum rights. To be binding on the government, all restrictions must be set forth in the contract, or in a licensing agreement incorporated therein. DOD FAR Supp. 27.404 (1984).

When the contract provides for "restricted rights" to software, the contractor must mark all copies of the software and documentation with the following restrictive legend:

RESTRICTED RIGHTS LEGEND

Use, duplication or disclosure is subject to Restrictions stated in Contract No. _____ with [Name of Contractor].

The legend must be in human-readable form that can be easily seen. The documentation must contain a detailed statement of the restrictions that apply. If the legend is omitted, the government will receive the software with unlimited rights, unless the contractor proves his omission was inadvertent. DOD FAR Supp. 27.404-2(c), (d) (1984).

Documentation for software acquired with restricted rights is received with limited rights. The government agrees, however, not to use the documentation to recreate software. DOD FAR Supp. 27.404-1(e). Databases are software for these purposes, but where the government provides the data, or where such data exist in the public domain, the government acquires the database with unlimited rights. DOD FAR Supp. 27.404-1(a)(3) (1984).

Restrictions may cease to apply if the software becomes "mixed." Mixed software exists when the DoD uses restricted rights software and develops it further with government funds. The government owns unlimited rights in the end product when it changes the original software so that it is no longer discernible. The government has no duty to protect the end product if the original, privately developed, software is not disclosed in the governmentally developed end product. The government, however, is still bound by the restrictions when it makes only minor changes to the contractor's original software.

Software is severable—as opposed to mixed—when it is possible to make a clear distinction between portions developed at private expense and those developed at government expense. When software is severable, restricted rights apply only to the part or parts developed at private expense. The federal government takes unlimited rights in those parts developed primarily with federal funds.

Without written approval from the contracting officer, the contractor may not provide to the federal government software or data, or portions thereof, in which copyright/ownership vests in a third party, unless the contractor can also secure for the government a nonexclusive, paid-up, worldwide license to use the included works.

Finally, although the federal government has statutory authorization to infringe copyrights, it must provide reasonable compensation to the copyright owner. 28 U.S.C. Sect.1498(b).

4: Copyrights

Contractors also may secure computer software and technical data rights by placing copyright notices to guard against infringement. The DoD awards the contractor copyright ownership in work produced under federal contract unless the work is a "special work;" then copyright ownership is retained by the government. FAR 27.402(c) (1984).

When the federal government pays for the development of copyrighted material, but allows the contractor to own the copyright, the government acquires at least an irrevocable, transferable, nonexclusive, royalty-free license to the work. Similarly, when data or software provided under a contract incorporates material previously developed and copyrighted, the contractor grants to the government a transferable, irrevocable, paid-up worldwide license to use and copy the work.

5: Contract Clauses Affecting Software and Data Rights

Contract clauses that affect the contractor's proprietary rights include Contract Data Requirements Lists, Rights in Technical Data and Computer Software Clauses, and Software and Data Identification Clauses.

a: Contract data requirements lists: When the DoD executes a contract it must attach a Contract Data Requirements List. The list must describe any and all software and data that the federal government requires, including contract specification data. FAR 27.404-2 (b)(1). Contractors do not have to deliver any data or software omitted from the Contract Data Requirements List, unless it is identified in an approved contract modification. The absence of a required contract provision negates the federal government's otherwise enforceable right to data.

Federal contracts may include a Deferred Delivery Clause when the federal government wishes to defer delivery of software or data specified in the Contract Data Requirements List. Similarly, a Deferred Ordering Clause may be included when the federal government is unable to identify specific software or data needed at the time of the contract. Because the contractor must include the cost of deferred software and data orders in his bid, deferred ordering can be problematic for the private contractor who may be forced to provide more software or data to the government than was accounted for in the contract price.

b: Rights in technical data and computer software clauses: The Rights in Data and Computer Software Clause is included in every contract under which computer software and technical data may be originated, developed, or delivered. The clause establishes the circumstances under which the government secures limited and unlimited rights in technical data and restricted and unlimited rights in software. FAR 27.404-2(b)(2). By means of an addition to this clause, the government may relinquish its right to publish unlimited rights data for sale in favor of the contractor. The contractor must then publish the work within a stated period and make it reasonably available to the public. The government will not publish the same work until the expiration of the copyright period, when such work enters the public domain. DOD FAR Supp. 27.407 (1984).

c: Software and data identification clauses: Along with a Rights in Data Clause, a contract will often include a Software and Data Identification Clause. Software and data that the contractor had intended to furnish with limited or restricted rights may be transferred to the government with unlimited rights if the contractor fails to comply with identification requirements set forth in the contract.

All data, software, and software documentation provided under the contract must be marked with the contract number, and the name of the prime contractor. If data and software are subject to restricted or limited rights, a restrictive legend must be included. In the case of technical data, the contractor must use "restrictive markings" to designate specific information for which confidentiality is claimed.

A restrictive legend protects against federal government disclosure. The federal government, however, is under no duty to protect the data if the contractor omits a legend. The government will allow restrictive legends to be added to a work after the date of submission at the contractor's expense if the contractor can prove that the omission was inadvertent.

A restrictive legend does not in itself limit the government's rights. The government may challenge the use of a legend, cancel, or ignore restrictive markings if they are not authorized, and "require the contractor to furnish clear and convincing evidence of the propriety of any restrictive markings used by the contractor on data furnished to the government under contract." FAR 27.403-3(d)(1) (1984). The government, however, must notify the contractor in writing before canceling restrictive markings or a restrictive legend.

6: Protection from Disclosure under the Freedom of Information Act

Congress enacted the Freedom of Information Act, 5 U.S.C. Sect. 552, to assure greater public access to government documents. The Act, however, exempts from disclosure all proprietary documents and information. Contractors, therefore, should stamp proprietary data legends on confidential information submitted to the government to prevent it from releasing the information without the contractor's knowledge and/or express agreement. A typical proprietary legend would be:

> This material contains trade secrets and other commercial or financial information that is privileged and confidential pursuant to 18 U.S.C. Sect. 1905 and 5 U.S.C., Sect. 552(b)(3) and (b)(4). This information may not be disclosed in whole or in part without the advance written permission of the submittor. Release of this information is punishable under federal law by one year imprisonment and a $1,000 fine.

C: Conclusion

The federal government recognizes that contractors have a significant interest in software, patent, and technical data rights. The government will, however, seek to retain control over these rights whenever possible. Thus, contractors must aggressively protect their proprietary rights by following the guidelines established by the Federal Acquisition Regulation and inserting appropriate protective clauses in their contracts to ensure protection. Contractors also must carefully distinguish between limited and unlimited rights, and must be explicit in the restrictions placed on computer software, data, and patented inventions used by or sold to the federal government.

MARZOUK

PROTECTING YOUR PROPRIETARY RIGHTS
IN THE COMPUTER AND
HIGH TECHNOLOGY INDUSTRIES

SECTION 10
RECENT CASES INVOLVING
FEDERAL PROCUREMENT OF COMPUTER
EQUIPMENT AND SERVICES

Section 10: Recent Cases Involving Federal Procurement of Computer Equipment and Services

A computer firm that contracts with the federal government to provide automatic data processing equipment and services must be apprised of not only its proprietary rights in patents, copyrights, software, and technical data, but also of the regulations and guidelines under which the government awards computer contracts. During the past two years, the General Accounting Office/Comptroller General—the agency responsible for deciding government contract disputes—has rendered several significant decisions concerning the federal procurement of computer equipment and services. The following summarizes the major decisions as they relate to four basic principles of government computer procurement law: (1) maximum competition, (2) minimum needs, (3) benchmarking, and (4) contract cancelation.

A: Maximum Competition

In procuring automatic data processing equipment and services, the government must encourage maximum competition to meet its minimum computer needs. Indeed, "[f]ull and open competition" is a "a basic objective of the government," under the Federal Procurement Regulations. 4 C.F.R., Sect. 1-4.1103-1. The following cases discuss the extent to which the Comptroller General will require the contracting agency to tailor its specifications so that the maximum number of computer firms may compete on a common basis. For a detailed discussion of federal procurement of corporate equipment and services, the reader is referred to Appendices E, F, and G.

1: Genasys Corporation, B-213830, 84-1 CPD Para. 102

Genasys alleged that several of its former employees who were responsible for preparing its proposal subsequently went to work for a competitor and used Genasys' price information in helping the competitor establish its price in the same procurement. Genasys alleged that the competitor's use of such pricing information violated the Request for Proposal's (RFPs) certificate of independent price determination. The Comptroller General dismissed the protest. The purpose of the certificate of independent price determination is to ensure that bidders do not collude to set prices or restrict competition by inducing others not to bid. There is no violation of the certificate absent collusion between bidders or an indication that a firm was prevented from bidding. A dispute between private parties will not be adjudicated by the Comptroller General.

2: Science and Management Resources, Inc.; James W. Collins and Associates, Inc., B-212628, B-212628.2, 84-1 CPD Para. 88

The Department of Commerce issued an RFP under a 100 percent small business set-aside. Four offerors, including both protesters, were found to be within the competitive range, and oral discussions were held with those firms. During the negotiations, the procuring agency became aware that the two protesters lacked the requisite experience to perform a full line of technical word processing services. Thus, a decision was made not to award the contract to either firm, and the Department of Commerce canceled the RFP and resolicited it on an unrestricted basis. The Comptroller General upheld the agency's decision. Cancelation of a small business set-aside RFP and resolicitation under an unrestricted RFP is proper where all small business proposals are found to be technically unacceptable and the agency's decision is found to be reasonable.

3: Amdahl Corporation, B-213150, 84-1 CPD, Para. 47

A procuring agency in the District of Columbia required all vendors to provide customer references and a demonstration of the specific operating system for two proposed central processing units, even though the agency would not need the actual installation of the operating system until approximately two years after award of the contract. Amdahl protested that it would have the operating system capacity before the agency required it, and that it could not provide the required references or demonstrations by the proposal deadline. Since only one vendor—IBM—could comply with these requirements, Amdahl contended that the agency was engaging in a de facto sole-source procurement. The protest was sustained because the solicitation did not reflect the agency's actual requirements and unnecessarily precluded vendors from competing on a common basis.

4: Masstor Systems Corp., B-211240, 84-1 CPD Para. 23

Masstor Systems, a supplier of IBM-compatible, mass storage equipment, contended that the RFP requirement of a single prime contractor for all hardware equipment, including mass-storage devices, violated the government contracting principle of maximum practicable competition. The Comptroller General held that a contracting agency's decision to procure by means of a "total package" approach rather than by separate procurements for divisible portions lies within the agency's discretion and will not be upset without a clear showing of unreasonableness on the part of the agency.

5: Command, Control and Communications Corporation, (4 C), B-210100, 83-2 CPD Para. 448

In 1979, the U.S. Army issued a competitive RFP for a mobile computer system. The award was made to Management and Technical Services Company (MATSCO). In 1982, the Army decided to upgrade the existing computer system by issuing a separate sole-source contract to MATSCO rather than by modifying MATSCO's existing competitively procured contract. The protester, 4-C, contended that the sole-source award of this contract was improper because: (1) the Army did not justify the "urgency" on which the sole source was apparently based and (2) the contract was not for a complex technologically advanced system but rather for a commercially available system. The Army contended that the sole source was justified because of the urgent time-frame requirements of the project and the need for a single contractor to supply the mobile microcomputer systems. The Comptroller General sustained the protest. A sole source acquisition is authorized when the legitimate needs of the government so require, (e.g., when time is of the essence and only one known source can meet the agency need within the required time frame; when the needs of the agency can be met only by items that are unique; when it is necessary to assure compatibility between the procured and existing equipment; or when award to a contractor other than the proposed sole source contractor poses unacceptable technical risks). The Comptroller General, however, will not approve a sole source procurement which exceeds the agency's immediate needs. In this case, the Army failed to justify the sole source award of the contract beyond the minimum quantity needed to satisfy its immediate need.

6: M/A-COM Alanthus Data, Inc., B-210415, 3-2 CPD Para. 429

The U.S. Geological Survey procured six Renex controllers at a cost higher than that for similar equipment offered by a protestor. The Comptroller General held that a government agency need not purchase the least expensive equipment if other factors outweigh the price difference. Here, the Geological Survey had previously purchased equipment from the protestor and had been dissatisfied by its performance. An agency's decision to buy higher-priced equipment must be properly justified in such a decision by the procuring agency. It will not be overturned unless it is shown to be unreasonable.

7: Federal Computer Corporation, B-211595, 83-2 CPD Para. 373

Federal Computer protested an RFP issued by the U.S. Army to upgrade 24 Vion 733-1 single-density disc drives, on the grounds that the RFP required offerors to obtain certification from an existing disc drive manufacturer and maintainer. Federal Computer claimed that this requirement was unduly restrictive of competition. The Army contended that the purpose of this requirement was to ensure compatibility between the existing and the newly acquired hardware. The Comptroller General denied the protest. Generally, the requirements for prequalification by manufacturers and independent testing laboratories are held to be unduly restrictive of competition. In this case, however, the Comptroller General found support for the necessity of the certification clause, since the government personnel did not have the requisite knowledge of the technical requirements needed to upgrade the existing hardware. Because of this lack of knowledge, the Army was required to rely on the proprietary knowledge of the incumbent vendor.

8: Acumenics Research and Technology, Inc., B-211575, 83-2 CPD Para. 94

The Department of the Interior's National Parks Service issued a three-phase RFP for the development, implementation, and operation of a financial accounting and cost-tracking system. Acumenics performed the work on Phases One and Two of the RFP, and produced all system documents identified in the definition and design stages listed in Phase Three. Acumenics, however, protested a special conflict of interest provision in Phase Three which prohibited any contractor from competing in the procurement if it had been instrumental in developing data systems specifications which would become part of the mandatory specifications. Acumenics contended that the National Parks Service's determination of ineligibility was improper. The Comptroller General denied the protest and held that the responsibility for determining whether a firm has a conflict of interest and the extent to which the firm should be excluded from competition rests with the procuring agency, and will be overturned only when it is shown to be unreasonable.

9: Sidereal Corp., B-210969, 83-2 CPD Para. 92

The Federal Aviation Administration (FAA) decided to purchase data processing equipment which it had been leasing, and advertised the intended purchase in the *Commerce Business Daily* (CBD), stating that affirmative responses from other capable firms would be considered on a competitive basis. Sidereal Corporation responded to the CBD advertisement. For unknown reasons, the FAA contracting officer was not informed of Sidereal's response and, subsequently, the FAA sole-source board approved the purchase of the sole-source equipment. The Comptroller General sustained the protest because the FAA failed to consider Sidereal, thereby precluding maximum practicable competition for the procurement.

10: Amdahl Corporation; ViON Corporation, B-212018, B-212018.2, 83-2 CPD Para. 51

The U.S. Army issued an RFP for an IBM Model 3083-J08 or equal computer. Among the mandatory requirements were that the item be "commercially available, state-of-the-art technology, and in current production." The contract was awarded to IBM. Protestors alleged that the equipment provided by IBM did not comply with the mandatory requirements. In sustaining the protest, the Comptroller General stated that the terms at issue in the protest had "sufficient latitude in their common, ordinary meanings to embrace all of the interpretations which the parties have proposed." The Army was ordered to clarify the meaning of those terms in the RFP and to initiate a new round of best and final offers. If a more advantageous offer were received, the Army was to take appropriate action to terminate the contract. This case illustrates the principle that specifications must be sufficiently definite and free from ambiguity so as to permit competition on a common basis. An ambiguity exists if specifications are subject to more than one reasonable interpretation.

11: Informatics General Corporation, B-210709, 83-2 CPD Para. 47

Informatics contended that its proposal for teleprocessing services was technically competitive under the RFP as issued by the Department of Transportation and that it should not have been excluded from the competitive range solely because its price was higher than that of the other competitors. The Comptroller General disagreed. An agency may properly exclude a vendor's proposal from the competitive range without discussion, solely because its cost proposal is much higher than that of the other offerors. The procuring agency has broad discretion to exclude technically acceptable but otherwise noncompetitive offers. On reconsideration, the Comptroller General affirmed its decision. *See* Informatics General Corporation 3-2 CPD Sect. 580.

12: Sperry Univac Division of Sperry Corporation, B-209379, 83-1 CPD Para. 571

This case addresses the issue of software conversion costs in the procurement of automatic data processing equipment and services. Although the protest was dismissed because of untimeliness, the issue is of major concern. Protestor, Sperry, was competing in a two-phase procurement process for the replacement of IBM data processing systems at two U.S. Navy sites. According to Sperry, the Navy biased the procurement in favor of IBM equipment by assessing a $5 million penalty for software conversion costs as a part of its evaluation of the system life costs of non-IBM systems. Sperry contended that the assessment of software conversion costs was improper because it tended to restrict competition, and the amount assessed was not justified. According to Sperry, the result of this Navy assessment was the creation of a two-tier price structure in which IBM or contractors offering IBM products would be evaluated by one standard, and all others by another. This, they contended, had a chilling effect on competition.

13: Burroughs Corporation, B-210201, 83-1 CPD Para. 446

Burroughs contended that the evaluation of its proposal was inconsistent with the evaluation criteria set forth in the RFP. Although the exact weight to be accorded each factor was not specifically set forth, the RFP indicated which factors would be weighted more heavily. In denying the protest, the Comptroller General indicated that the RFP need not outline the specific percentages accorded to each factor. A description of the weighting of the evaluation criteria is sufficient. This case, however, demonstrates that RFP's that do not specify particular weights for each evaluation factor may invite protest.

14: NCR Corporation; General Systems Corporation, B-208143, and B-208143.2, 83-1 CPD Para. 403

The Federal Maritime Commission awarded a contract for automatic data processing equipment and related software under the public exigency exception to the requirement for formal advertising (FPR Sect. 1-3.202 1964 ed., amend. 192). The contract award contained option period provisions. Protesters contended that the contract should not have included any option periods. The Comptroller General agreed. Under the "public exigency" exception to formal advertising, contract awards should not be for a period longer than is necessary to cover urgent needs. The Comptroller General recommended, therefore, that the additional option periods of the awarded contract not be exercised by the procuring agency.

15: Northern Telecom, Inc., B-209412, 83-1 CPD Para. 382

The Veterans Administration (VA) awarded a contract for a telephone system at a VA hospital under a two-step Invitation for Bids (IFB). Three vendors had passed the technical aspects of the first step of the procurement; in the second step, the pricing phase, the VA awarded the contract to Universal Communications Systems, Inc. (UCS). UCS's bid in the second step listed all pricing information as proprietary and not for public disclosure. Northern Telecom, Inc. (NTI) alleged that USC's restriction on the release of pricing data rendered the bid nonresponsive, and that the contracting officer should have rejected the bid. The GAO agreed. A bid which restricts the disclosure of price renders it nonresponsive. Bidders must permit disclosure of sufficient information to permit competing bidders to know the product offered and the quantity, price, and delivery terms. The procuring agency must ensure that bidders receive appropriate instructions regarding the handling and disclosure of proprietary information, consistent with applicable procurement regulations.

16: Alanthus Data Communications Corp., B-206946, 83-1 CPD Para. 147

The Department of Labor rejected the protestor's proposal for word processing equipment on the grounds that the vendor failed to meet the mandatory specifications of the RFP. The protestor was eliminated without first being provided an opportunity to participate in discussions and to modify its proposal accordingly. The protestor asserted that (1) its product met the mandatory requirements as defined in the RFP, (2) the RFP's requirements were vague, and (3) the specific requirements were not defined. The Comptroller General agreed with the protester. A fundamental principle of government procurement law is that solicitations must be drafted in clear and unambiguous terms, since there can be no effective competition on a common basis unless all offerors know the contract requirements. Here, the Department of Labor failed to state its requirements with sufficient particularity to ensure a common understanding of its needs.

17: Cray Research, Inc., B-207586, 82-2 CPD Para. 376

The Department of the Navy awarded to Control Data Corporation (CDC) a contract for the installation of a large-scale scientific computer system. Upon installation testing, the CDC computer (Cyber 203) was found to be inadequate in that it lacked sufficient memory and could not meet the processing time requirements of the benchmark. CDC offered to replace the computer with a much faster and more powerful one (Cyber 205) at no additional cost to the government. The Navy accepted this offer without making any changes to the performance specifications in the contract. Protestor, Cray Research, complained that the substitution of the Cyber 205 for the Cyber 203 exceeded the contract scope and should have been the subject of a new procurement. The issue here was whether a changed contract was materially different from the completed contract so that the contract, as modified, should have been the subject of a new procurement (unless a sole source acquisition was justified). This issue is often referred to as the "cardinal changes" doctrine. *See AIR-A-PLANE Corporation v. U.S.*, 408 F.2d 1030 (Ct. Cl. 1969). The Comptroller General denied the protest. A modification does not exceed the contract scope as long as the modified contract is substantially the same as the contract that was completed. An agency's acceptance of a firm's post-award offer to change the way it will perform to meet its obligation is not outside the contract scope, even if that change reflects a more advanced or sophisticated approach, where there is no change in the nature of the obligation of either party to the contract. Agencies will be granted remedial powers to obtain computer systems that will meet their contract requirements. Remedies may include major enhancements of the system as long as the contract performance requirements are not altered. This case is troublesome in that it allows a vendor whose delivered system has failed the acceptance tests to escape termination by installing a more advanced system.

18: SMS Data Products Group, B-205360, 82-1 CPD Para. 390

The Department of Justice (DOJ) awarded a contract to IBM for the lease of an IBM Model 4341L01 computer. DOJ's evaluation criteria included consideration of membership in two IBM user groups, SHARE and GUIDE, which require use of an IBM computer. Protestor argued that DOJ's assessment of the value of membership in the SHARE and GUIDE user's groups was arbitrary and that the criteria unduly restricted competition. The Comptroller General sustained the protest. Without a clear showing that the direct, identifiable, and quantifiable benefits of membership in a user organization outweigh the attendant costs, such membership may not be considered as an evaluation factor beyond some minimal value, that might be used only to discriminate between otherwise essentially equal proposals. Such was not the case here.

19: Compuserve Data Systems, Inc., B-202811,82-1 CPD Para. 137

The National Aeronautics and Space Administration (NASA) issued a Request for Information for teleprocessing services to be provided under the GSA Teleprocessing Service Program. On review, NASA found that only one company had met all mandatory requirements, and a contract was thus awarded. Protestor alleged that it was disqualified owing to technical noncompliance with a certain software procedure. The Comptroller General held that protestor had met all mandatory requirements. As a policy matter, the GAO, without a clear showing that contracting officers acted arbitrarily or unreasonably, will generally not evaluate proposals or substitute its judgment for that of the contracting officers by making independent determinations as to which offeror should receive an award or how many points each proposal should receive for each item. In this case, however, the Comptroller General found that NASA's evaluation was unreasonable. Since the specifications were vague, the protestor had met the functional requirements. This case illustrates the government contracting principle that functional requirements will be read into otherwise vague specifications.

20: Amdahl Corporation, B-203882.2, 82-1 CPD Para. 421

NASA issued an invitation for bids, restricted to a certain IBM make and model (IBM Model 3033 or 3033N) for use with a specific IBM operating system (TSS/370) oriented to a time sharing network already in place at the NASA site. NASA justified the make and model restriction on the ground that a non-IBM computer would not provide the necessary support for the time-sharing system. The Comptroller General denied Amdahl's protest that the solicitation was unduly restrictive. Make and model restrictions on the acquisition of a computer are reasonable and not unduly restrictive where they are based on a requirement for software support which the agency reasonably determines is available only on the specified make and model. This case illustrates the government contracting principle that maximum practicable competition will end when software requirements or factors mandate otherwise. (Note: The Comptroller General subsequently affirmed its decision in this case. *See Amdahl Corporation,* 82-2 CPD Para. 336.)

B: Minimum Needs

Besides encouraging competition in the procurement of automatic data processing equipment and services, the federal government must meet its minimum computer needs. Several recent decisions of the Comptroller General address the minimum needs standard for computer products.

1: Burroughs Corporation, B-211511, 84-1 CPD Para. 24

Burroughs, a computer hardware and software vendor, was eliminated in the first step of a two-step procurement because its proposed software programming language differed from that required by the specifications of the contracting agency. The Comptroller General denied Burroughs' protest and held that (1) a procuring agency is not required to hold discussions with a vendor prior to rejecting a technically unacceptable proposal that cannot reasonably be made acceptable and that (2) an agency's decision will not be questioned unless there is evidence of fraud, prejudice, abuse of authority, arbitrariness, or capricious action.

2: Arwell Corporation, B-210792, 83-2 CPD Para. 684

In response to a synopsis published in the *Commerce Business Daily* for the procurement of data processing equipment, protestor requested from the procuring agency (the U.S. Army) a Request for Quotation (RFQ). The U.S. Army refused to supply the RFQ because it determined that the protestor was unable to supply new equipment as required. The Comptroller General held that a procuring agency need not supply an RFQ if it determines that the proposed vendor is unable to meet its minimum requirement. A contracting agency is in the best position to ascertain its needs, based on its familiarity with the particular requirements and environments in which the products will be used. Thus, an agency's determination of its minimum needs will not be overturned unless such determination is unreasonable.

3: Four-Phase Systems, Inc.—Request for Reconsideration, B-201642.2, 83-1 CPD Para. 430

Four-Phase Systems protested the award for computer systems by the FAA on the grounds that the RFP was ambiguous and that the requirements were in excess of the FAA's minimum needs. That protest was denied. Subsequently, the General Accounting Office (GAO) issued a report analyzing the FAA's handling of the procurement that had been the subject of the previous protest decision. In that report, the GAO found that the FAA indeed procured a computing power far in excess of its needs. Based on these findings, the Comptroller General recommended that the FAA cancel the contract. This decision is important in two respects. First, the case indicates than an agency must write its RFP specifications according to its minimum agency needs. Second, the Comptroller General will make every effort to ensure that an agency's minimum requirements are in fact met. *See also Four-Phase Systems, Inc.* (Second Request for Reconsideration), B-20142.3; B-201642.4, 83-2 CPD Para. 473, in which GAO affirmed its decision.

4: Spectrum Leasing Corporation, B-205367, 82-1 CPD Para. 199

The U.S. Marine Corps published in the *Commerce Business Daily* (CBD) its intent to procure an IBM computer under its contract with IBM unless it received, within 15 calendar days of publication, a written response from another vendor indicating an ability to satisfy the procuring agency's needs more advantageously. Protestors submitted a timely written response which was technically competitive, but deficient in that it could not meet the same delivery and maintenance requirements as IBM. The Comptroller General held that a procuring agency may properly not consider a vendor's written response if it fails to address its capability or willingness to satisfy certain critical requirements. GSA regulations permit an agency to place certain orders against scheduled contracts when certain conditions are satisfied. One condition is that the agency consider all written responses to a CBD synopsis, and determine that the use of the scheduled contract is the lowest cost alternative. Here, the Marine Corp's announcement in the CBD adequately communicated the urgency of the procurement and the mandatory nature of the delivery requirement. Protestor's incomplete response—when time was so critical and negotiation was not possible—did not constitute an acceptable affirmative response by the protestor.

C: Benchmarks

The primary method of system validation of major federal procurements of automatic data processing hardware is "benchmarking." Oftentimes referred to as "live test demonstration," benchmarking is nothing more than "user-witnessed running of a [mixed] group...of programs representative of the user's predicted workload on a vendor proposed computer system in order to validate system performance." Federal Information Processing Standards Publication (FIPS PUB) 42-1, *Guidelines for Benchmarking ADP Systems in the Competitive Procurement Environment*, May 15, 1977. The Department of Commerce, which established uniform technical standards for data processing equipment, has published guidelines for benchmarking that discuss the various steps in the benchmarking process, including (1) workload definition and analysis; (2) construction, validation, and documentation of benchmarks; (3) procedural documentation and preparation for vendors; (4) vendor construction of required demonstrations; and (5) conduct of benchmark tests. *Id*. Under the guidelines, the primary factors affecting the validity of benchmarks are the estimation of workload and the selection of programs and data processing requirements that are representative of the user's actual minimum needs. *Id*.

1: NCR Corporation, B-209671, 83-2 CPD Para. 335

NCR protested its elimination from the competitive range under an RFP issued by the Internal Revenue Service (IRS). The RFP required an Operational Capability Demonstration (OCD) to confirm the ability of a vendor system to meet certain mandatory requirements. On the basis of NCR's demonstration, the IRS concluded that NCR's offer did not meet the mandatory requirements. NCR contended that its elimination from the competitive range was improper. The Comptroller General denied the protest. An offeror's failure to demonstrate the ability to satisfy mandatory minimum requirements of a solicitation is sufficient basis to exclude that offeror from further participation in the competition. Benchmarks are to be considered as an extension of the technical evaluation of proposals, the principal purpose of which is to provide a demonstration of the capability of offered hardware and software to perform the required functions. Strict pass/fail benchmarks that lead to the automatic exclusion of otherwise potentially acceptable offerors are disfavored. Such tests provide "strong evidence" of system capabilities which must be considered in determining technical acceptability. The determination of whether a proposal is within the competitive range, particularly with regard to technical considerations, is primarily a matter of administrative discretion, and will not be disturbed without a clear indication that the determination lacks a reasonable basis. Where the failure occurs in the course of a benchmark, the agency has a duty to point out the failure and permit the offeror to rerun that portion of the benchmark to see if it can be completed successfully. Here the IRS offered NCR the opportunity to rerun the OCD but NCR refused. Thus, IRS acted reasonably in excluding NCR from the competitive range.

2: Onyx, Inc., B-211489, 83-2 CPD Para. 137

Onyx protested the use of a benchmark developed by the Department of the Navy because it contained software written for machines designed to process EBCDIC rather than ASCII-coded software. Onyx claimed that the EBCDIC coding could only be run on machines manufactured by IBM, and was improper for two reasons. First, it violated the Federal Information Processing Standards Publication 1-1, which adopts ASCII as the government standard. Second, Onyx claimed that the EBCDIC coding was written in such a way as to prevent machine conversion. The Navy agreed with Onyx's assertions, but the GAO found the protest untimely and therefore dismissed it.

3: Westinghouse Information Services, B-204225, 82-1 CPD Para. 253

Protestor contended that the benchmark requirement under the RFP for teleprocessing services for the GSA was unnecessarily large and complex and, as a result, unduly restricted competition. Westinghouse alleged that if the benchmark had been less complex, more vendors could have competed for the contract award. The Comptroller General denied the protest. In deciding a protest involving a benchmark, the standard of review employed by the Comptroller General's Office is the same as for any other evaluation procedure (i.e., the establishment of qualification and testing procedures is a matter within the technical expertise of the cognizant procuring agency). Such procedures will not be questioned unless they are without a reasonable basis. Thus, if a benchmark is rationally based, its use as an evaluation tool is within the discretion of the procuring agency.

D: Contract Cancelation

Under some circumstances, the federal government may cancel a computer contract. The following decisions discuss two instances of contract cancelations.

1: Dictaphone Corporation, B-208836, 83-2 CPD Para. 151

The U.S. Army procured dictating equipment from the Dictaphone Corporation under a nonmandatory, Automatic Data and Telecommunications Service schedule contract. The Army canceled the contract to permit an award for comparable equipment to Lanier Business Products, Inc. under Lanier's mandatory Federal Supply Service scheduled contract. While the Comptroller General denied Dictaphone Corporation's protest, this case illustrates that the Comptroller General generally will not consider protests of an agency's cancelation of a contract. One limited exception to this rule, however, is when the decision to cancel is based on an alleged impropriety in the original contract award. Review under such circumstances is appropriate for the limited purpose of ascertaining whether award defects perceived by the agency, in fact, justify cancelation.

2: Pacific Scientific Company, Gardner-Neotec Division, B-208193, 83-1 CPD Para. 61

The U.S. Department of Agriculture (USDA) received only two responses on an invitation for bids issued for the procurement of a microcomputer system. While reviewing the proposals, USDA discovered a major deficiency in its own specifications. USDA had failed to indicate the need for a minimum 16-bit capacity in the required system. The protestor, the manufacturer of an 8-bit microprocessor, protested the cancelation of the solicitation and alleged that its product could meet the functional requirements of the specification. The issue presented was whether and when a procuring agency may cancel its solicitation. The Comptroller General has long recognized that a contracting officer may have discretion to determine whether a solicitation should be canceled and the contract reprocured. Such review is limited to the question of reasonableness in the exercise of discretion. Generally, the use of inadequate specifications provides a sufficient basis for invitation cancelation. Specifications are inadequate when they do not state the government's actual needs. Here, the government acted reasonably in canceling the solicitation. Accordingly, the Comptroller General denied the protest.

PROTECTING YOUR PROPRIETARY RIGHTS
IN THE COMPUTER AND HIGH TECHNOLOGY INDUSTRIES

SECTION 11
CRIMINAL SANCTIONS FOR
COMPUTER THEFT

Section 11: Criminal Sanctions for Computer Theft

A: Introduction

Computer use in both business and personal affairs has increased dramatically in the last decade. As computers have become more simple to operate and more available to the public, however, they have become more vulnerable to criminal activity. With the expansion of computer technology, the opportunity for computer crime has increased. Indeed, the more sophisticated computers are, the more difficult it is to detect and prevent computer crime, particularly crimes that affect a firm's proprietary software and data rights.

Unfortunately, major obstacles exist to developing an effective method of combating computer crime. First, computers encompass a broad range of activities. Experts, therefore, disagree on the definition of computer crime, as well as the best ways to prevent it.

Second, no federal legislation has yet effectively addressed the question of computer crime, and only a few states have enacted computer crime statutes. The lack of specific laws means that prosecutors must pigeon-hole computer crimes into other traditional crimes—such as burglary, larceny, or embezzlement—for which specific statutes exist. Too often, however, the computer crime will not fit other statutes exactly, and the charges are dismissed. In *U.S. v. Seidlitz,* 589 F.2d 152 (4th Cir. 1978), *cert. denied,* 441 U.S. 992 (1979), for example, a defendant used a terminal in Virginia to access and obtain data from a computer system in Maryland. The court acquitted him of unlawful interstate transportation of stolen property on the ground that electronic impulses were not tangible property under state law. (The court did find him guilty of interstate wire fraud.)

Finally, victims are generally unwilling to report computer crime because they (1) have little hope of catching the culprit, (2) are unwilling to publicize security breaches, or (3) are simply unaware of computer crimes.

The following section discusses the different types of computer crime and the problems of combating each. The section concludes with a brief discussion of one state statute (The Virginia Computer Crimes Act) that specifically deals with computer crime. This statute will serve to exemplify laws that should be enacted by state legislatures in the near future.

B: Types of Computer Crime

Computers act as both the target of and the tool for criminal activity. As the target, computers and computer-related data and information are the actual victims of crime. These crimes include the theft of software (object code, source code, etc.), printouts, instruction manuals, and hardware.

As the tool, computers act as the facilitators of crime. In other words, criminals use computer capabilities to commit crimes. This is the most difficult and complicated type of computer crime because of its different forms and its difficulty to detect.

There are three categories of crime that criminals can use computers to commit:

1. the unauthorized use of computer services
2. the theft of computer information
3. the alteration of computer files or data

Within each category, there are several different types of crimes.

1: Unauthorized Use

Unauthorized use of computer services occurs when an operator uses a computer to perform unauthorized tasks for his personal advantage. Gaining undetected access to a computer for unauthorized use can be relatively simple. An operator—through the use of the proper passwords and codes—can assume the identity of a person authorized to use the computer. The degree of unauthorized use, therefore, largely depends on the level of security at a particular firm.

2: Theft of Information for Personal Use

Numerous types of business and personal information are stored in a computer database. In the wrong hands, such information can cause a company substantial injury.

Theft of computer-stored information can occur when confidential data, programs, or printouts are not maintained in a secure place or are carelessly discarded. Accordingly, a computer firm is well-advised to protect its computer-stored information from disclosure to unauthorized individuals and maintain proper safety procedures at all times.

3: Alteration or Omission of Data

Alteration or omission of data occurs in different ways. For example, an operator may wish to erase certain negative data from employment records and replace it with positive data. A more serious case of tampering occurs when an operator adds or erases pertinent business records which are essential to the operation of a particular company. In the case of hospital records, this type of tampering can be life threatening.

C: Difficulties in Preventing Computer Crime

Computer crime is difficult to prevent for several reasons.

First, computer crimes often go undetected because the crime itself usually takes a very short amount of time to commit. Furthermore, the quantity of information affected is often so insignificant that no one notices any wrongdoing.

Second, detection of computer crime depends upon the type of internal security measures at a particular firm. As discussed in Section 2, security measures can be very expensive. Accordingly, many small companies that cannot afford adequate security systems risk becoming easy victims of computer crime.

Third, once the crime has been uncovered, identifying the culprit is often extremely difficult. Tampering with a computer requires not only access, but also technical knowledge. While this may narrow the field of possible guilty parties, in most firms that use computers, any number of people have access to and the requisite knowledge of computers.

Finally, law enforcement officers, such as the Federal Bureau of Investigation and state and local authorities, as well as judges and juries, often lack the technical knowledge to detect computer crimes. Explaining the crime generally can be so complex that the real issue—the wrong committed—becomes lost in the technicalities of the subject matter.

As with other crimes, once the computer crime is suspected, law enforcement officers must obtain a search warrant before they can seize any evidence from the alleged site of the crime. Again, lack of technical knowledge among officials responsible for issuing appropriate warrants becomes problematic. Search warrants must describe in detail the area to be searched and the object/evidence to be seized. Law enforcement officials untrained in the computer field encounter substantial difficulty in determining in what form the evidence will be found.

The major problem in prosecuting computer crimes is the lack of laws that relate specifically to such crimes. A few states, however, have passed computer crime legislation. These statutes are highly effective and provide a workable method for prosecuting criminals.

D: The Virginia Computer Crimes Act

The State of Virginia is one jurisdiction that has enacted a comprehensive computer crime law, the Virginia Computer Crimes Act. The law alleviates many of the problems in prosecuting and detecting computer crime previously discussed. A brief discussion of the law's various purposes and goals follows.

1: Establishing A Model Computer Crime Statute for Other States

The Virginia legislature sought to enact a statute that would be used as a model by other states. The legislature defined in detail over a dozen terms used in the computer field, including "computer," "computer data," "computer network," "computer services," "computer software," "owner," and "property." These definitions provide a guideline for law enforcement officers and others in the computer industry. The definitions are sufficiently narrow to identify particular criminal behavior, yet are broad enough to encompass technology that may be developed at a later date.

2: Creating a New Category of Crime: Computer Crime

The statute recognizes the prosecution problems presented by a lack of a specific computer crime statute. Accordingly, the law defines five new crimes concerned specifically with computers: computer fraud, computer invasion of privacy, theft of computer services, personal trespass by computer, and embezzlement through the use of a computer. These new crimes have their own list of requisite elements, which make it easier for officials to prosecute computer criminals successfully. No longer will officials be required to fit computer crimes into a more traditional category of crime.

3: Allowing Civil Relief for Damages

The statute also allows the computer crime victim to recover actual damages in a civil action. Specifically, the statute states:

> Any person whose property or person shall be injured by reason of a violation of any provision of this article may sue, therefore and recover for any damages sustained, and the costs of suit. Without limiting the generality of the term, damages shall include loss of profits.

Sect. 18.2-152.12A.

4: Providing Specific Procedural Devices When Dealing with Computer Crimes

Given the difficulty of detecting computer-related crimes, the Virginia law lengthened the statute of limitations for bringing action to "(1) five years after commission of the last act in the course of [criminal] conduct...or (2) one year after the existence of the illegal act and the identity of the offender are discovered...." Sect. 18.2-152.9. The statute of limitations for civil relief is of similar length.

The Virginia statute is an attempt to bring computer crime more easily within the realm of the law. It recognizes problems endemic to computers and offers effective, practical solutions. Clearly, the statute will serve as a model for other states (and perhaps even for the federal government), as they enact legislation in the future.

PROTECTING YOUR PROPRIETARY RIGHTS

IN THE COMPUTER AND HIGH TECHNOLOGY INDUSTRIES

**SECTION 12
CONCLUSION**

Section 12: Conclusion

Protecting proprietary rights in the computer and high technology industries is not a simple one- or two-step process. Computer firms must always be on guard for insiders and outsiders seeking to misappropriate their proprietary rights in software and hardware. Clearly, computer firms must institute and maintain appropriate safeguards at all times to ensure maximum legal protection in the development and marketing of their computer products.

The foregoing discussion has sought to provide the reader with a basic understanding of how to protect proprietary rights in software and hardware. Rather than ignore the legal "hoops" required to obtain adequate protection, computer and high technology firms are well advised to seek legal counsel before their computer property rights are lost or stolen. Only then will such firms be able to compete in the marketplace with full knowledge that their proprietary interests are properly protected.

PROTECTING YOUR PROPRIETARY RIGHTS

IN THE COMPUTER AND HIGH TECHNOLOGY INDUSTRIES

APPENDIX A

Computer Law Reporter

Suite 200, 1519 Connecticut Ave., N.W., Washington, D.C. 20036

TRADE SECRET TRENDS AFFECTING COMPUTER AND HIGH TECHNOLOGY FIRMS

by

Tobey B. Marzouk*

Abstract

The following discussion focuses on trade secret developments in three areas: (1) noncompetition clauses; (2) government contracting; and (3) trade secret protection procedures. The cases selected for treatment in the discussion were selected because of their applicability to concerns that are frequently encountered in the computer industry.

While trade secret cases often involve similar issues and considerations, several recent decisions raise concerns that are of particular significance to computer and high technology firms. The following discussion summarizes three cases that demonstrate how firms can adequately protect their confidential and proprietary information.

1. *Hekimian Laboratories, Inc. v. Domain Systems, Inc.*, 664 F.Supp. 493 (S.D.Fla. 1987)

Hekimian Laboratories, Inc. ("HLI") requested that the court grant a preliminary injunction to enjoin Domain Systems, Inc. ("Domain"), an engineering firm, from employing John A. Boyer, Sr. The principle issue in the case was whether a one-year noncompetition clause (with no geographical limitations) in Boyer's employment contract with HLI was enforceable. An unusual feature of the clause was that during that one-year period, Boyer was to receive one-half of his base salary.

HLI and Domain both produced and marketed remote access testing equipment for the telecommunications industry. As this was a very specialized field, HLI and Domain directly competed throughout the United States and in foreign markets, for a rather small number of customers who were primarily telecommunications companies. Furthermore, HLI and Domain shared some of the same customers, who divided their business between the two companies.

Boyer was originally employed by HLI in 1983. His employment contract with HLI included a restrictive covenant providing, in part, that: (1) Boyer would not work for any competitor of HLI for a period of one year after leaving the employment of HLI; (2) during this period, Boyer would not solicit current or prospective customers of HLI, nor recruit current HLI employees; (3) Boyer would not disclose any confidential or trade secret information pertaining to HLI; and (4) Boyer would not disclose any confidential customer information for a period of two years after leaving HLI's employment.

The employment contract, including the restrictive covenant, was reexecuted every year by both parties. The latest contract term was to expire on July 12, 1987, but Boyer formally resigned from HLI and informed HLI of his intention to work for Domain.

During the course of his employment with HLI, Boyer served as Director of Systems Engineering. In that capacity, he was privy to much sensitive and confidential information. Boyer was directly involved in the design and implementation of HLI's remote access equipment, and was the "father" of HLI's "React" System, a highly sophisticated remote access testing system, on which HLI spent more than $1.4 million in research and design. Boyer supervised and coordinated the development of the software for the "React" System, and the integration of this software with HLI's existing hardware.

Boyer was also exposed to and intimately familiar with the development and implementation of HLI's long-range planning and product development strategy. While employed by HLI, Boyer received weekly the company's highly confidential product development schedule, which contained long-range goals for HLI's product development and marketing strategies.

Boyer also had direct communication with HLI customers and was knowledgeable about their individual needs and expectations. HLI allowed its potential customers to use its remote access testing equipment on a "trial" basis before actual purchase.

Boyer was directly involved in one such trial for Bell South Services in North Carolina, and "became privy to confidential communications in which Bell South Systems advised HLI of ways to tailor its present system to meet their specific needs." At the same time, Domain was conducting a similar trial for Bell South Systems.

Finally, Boyer made a trip to Taiwan to speak with the Taiwanese government concerning the formulation of a procurement bid for a contract worth over $5 million. No bids had been formally submitted to the Taiwanese government when the present lawsuit was filed, and the contract had yet to be awarded. The court noted that "Boyer had direct and personal knowledge of what HLI planned to bid on the contract, what equipment HLI would use to perform the contract, and the specific interests and concerns of the Taiwanese government." Domain and HLI were currently in direct competition for the contract.

In granting a preliminary injunction, the court focused primarily on the restrictive covenant in Boyer's employment contract. The court applied Maryland law and observed:

> The general rule in Maryland is that if a restrictive covenant in an employment contract is supported by adequate consideration and is ancillary to the employment contract, an employee's agreement not to compete with his employer upon leaving the employment will be upheld "if the restraint is confined within the limits which are no wider as to area and duration than are reasonably necessary for the protection of business of the employer and do not impose undue hardship on the employee or disregard the interests of the public." ...[A] comparative examination of the cases in this State [of Maryland] ... demonstrate that Maryland follows the general rule that restrictive covenants may be applied and enforced only to those employees who provide unique services, or to prevent the future misuse of trade secrets, routes or lists of clients, or solicitation of customers.

Specifically, the court looked to four factors: (1) whether the employee was a skilled employee whose services were unique; (2) whether the noncompetition covenant was necessary to protect trade secrets and confidential data or prevent unfair solicitation of customers; (3) whether the employee unfairly exploited contacts with the former employer's customers; and (4) whether enforcing the covenant would impose an unfair hardship on the employee or adversely affect the public interest. The court held that each of these factors did not preclude consideration of the covenant and that, under Maryland law, the covenant was enforceable.

The court concluded that the restrictive covenant was supported by adequate consideration, particularly in light of HLI's agreement to pay Boyer half salary during the one-year noncompetition period. The court also held that the agreement's temporal limitation was reasonable and that the lack of geographical limitations did not mitigate against the enforceability of the covenant. A one-year time period was acceptable, given the fact that "Maryland courts have upheld agreements containing restrictive covenants of greater duration." Furthermore, the absence of a geographical limitation was reasonably necessary since "Domain and HLI are competing head to head all over the country, and are currently in direct competition for the Taiwan contract."

As to the covenant's effects on Boyer, the court found that the restrictive covenant did not impose an undue hardship on Boyer. The provision allowing Boyer to receive half salary during the noncompetition period "is unique to any of the restrictive covenants that have been uncovered by the Court's research, and the Court finds this provision quite a significant factor for the purposes of balancing the interests of Boyer and HLI."

Finally, the court concluded that the covenant did not disregard the public interest, particularly since HLI was not a "monopolist."

The court enjoined Boyer from: (1) working for Domain and Commtest in any capacity, (2) soliciting HLI's customers and potential customers, and (3) divulging or disclosing any HLI trade secrets or confidential and sensitive information. HLI was ordered to pay Boyer the payments to which he was entitled under the employment contract, including any back payments owed since the time that he formally left the employment of HLI.

The case is particularly interesting in that it illustrates one technique of protecting trade secrets. To ensure that noncompetition covenants are enforceable, a high technology firm should consider including a contract clause providing partial salary payments during the noncompetition period. Such payments not only demonstrate that the firm is serious about protecting its trade secrets, but also allow the firm to argue that the covered employees are not financially burdened by the restrictive covenant.

~~~

2. *CACI Field Services, Inc. v. United States*, 12 Cl. Ct. 440 (1987)

CACI Field Services addresses the question of when a party can obtain access to proprietary information during a federal procurement action. In that case, the General Services Administration ("GSA") issued a Request for Proposal ("RFP") for the operation of a scientific equipment commodity center. CACI, as well as other competitors, submitted proposals. On three separate occasions, the GSA requested that CACI provide additional information and CACI complied.

Thereafter, GSA notified CACI that its proposal had been rejected because CACI lacked the experience and understanding necessary to run the scientific equipment commodity center. GSA also rejected the other proposals and decided to cancel the RFP and not contract out the commodity center operation.

CACI immediately filed a complaint in the Claims Court alleging that: (1) GSA had failed to conduct meaningful discussions with CACI because CACI was not allowed to revise its proposal and correct alleged deficiencies; (2) GSA did not request best and final offers; and (3) GSA rejected CACI's offer based on factors not stated as evaluation criteria in the RFP.

During discovery, CACI requested all technical proposals (and GSA's evaluations thereof) submitted by all other bidders. GSA filed a motion for a protective order and argued that the information requested was confidential and proprietary, as well as irrelevant to the proceeding.

The Court, in granting the protective order, noted that all of CACI's allegations related to GSA's relationship with and treatment of CACI, not other offerors. Accordingly, CACI failed to show that full discovery of other bidders' technical proposals was relevant.

The court recognized that it "might otherwise be inclined to permit ... discovery on a theory that it might lead to other admissible evidence." Other considerations "in the bid protest context," however, militated against granting the discovery requests.

The court noted procedural Rule 26(c)(7) allows a court to protect a party so that "a trade secret or other confidential research, development, or commercial information not be disclosed or be disclosed only in a designated way." The Federal Acquisition Regulations, which governed the procurement at issue, provided an additional basis for protecting the information that CACI sought. Under Section 15.413-1, no information contained in proposals "or concerning the number or identity of offerors shall be made available to the public or to anyone in the Government not having a legitimate interest." The Court concluded that "the plain impact of these and related regulations and statutes shows that courts must exercise significant caution prior to ordering disclosures of information from other bidders."

CACI argued that other bidders could not be prejudiced by disclosure since CACI had withdrawn the solicitation and announced that it would not resolicit. The court, however, concluded that the Government still had an interest in not disclosing the bidders' proposals. Because the Government might contract out the operation of other centers, it "wants to maintain the cooperation of future bidders in providing useful information concerning the potential contracts and protect persons who submit financial or commercial data to government agencies from any competitive disadvantage."

For these reasons, the court granted the Government's request for a protective order and prevented CACI from obtaining the requested information. The Court, however, did allow some discovery to determine whether the Government held meaningful discussions with CACI. Specifically, CACI was allowed to obtain: (1) clarifications sent to the other bidders, sanitized so as to protect the bidders' names; (2) general instructions to evaluators concerning how to rate proposals; and (3) information regarding the frequency and general content of conversations with other bidders.

From a trade secrets perspective, this case is noteworthy for two reasons. First, in data processing procurement litigation, the courts will generally hold the discovering party to a more stringent standard of relevance and confidentiality than would otherwise exist in civil litigation. Second, notwithstanding this standard, federal procurement bidders will not be shielded entirely from discovery and the court may order the production of relevant information as long as confidentiality can be maintained and the procurement process protected.

~~~

3. *Formax, Inc. v. Hostert*, ___ F.Supp. ___, (N.D.Ill. 1987)

In the final case, Formax, Inc. ("Formax") filed a complaint alleging that The Dale Service Group ("DSG"), conducted a fraudulent scheme to profit through the misappropriation of Formax trade secrets, blueprints and patents, and the incorporation of this confidential information into the design, manufacture and sale of Formax machine repair parts. DSG was an unincorporated association, formed by a former Formax employee, which serviced food processing equipment and made replacement parts for Formax machines.

Formax asserted that DSG violated the RICO statute by conducting a fraudulent scheme to profit from the misappropriation of Formax trade secrets and the infringement of two Formax patents. Formax further asserted that DSG violated the Consumer Fraud and Deceptive Business Practices Act through the misappropriation of Formax blueprints containing trade secret information and Formax parts from a Formax supplier, and that the removal of the prints constituted a breach of the employee's fiduciary duty to Formax, "intentionally injur[ing]" Formax's business, property and reputation.

In its counterclaim, DSG asserted that, since 1979, Formax had intentionally interfered with DSG business opportunities and that Formax violated Section 2 of the Sherman Act by "trying to manipulate the market for Formax machine repair parts." DSG also alleged that the information contained in the Formax blueprints was not a trade secret and that one of the Formax patents was invalid.

DSG initially sought to dismiss Formax's claim that defendants violated the RICO statute. The court agreed, stating:

> Formax has not sufficiently pled mail fraud/wire fraud as predicate acts for its RICO claim. Formax's allegations are vague and conclusory; they do not state either the content of communications or the particular defendant involved ... Formax has not alleged that defendants made any fraudulent misrepresentation or omission to the public as to the Formax prints. Neither has Formax shown how defendants' collection efforts furthered defendants' alleged fraudulent scheme. In short, defendants' alleged conduct did not involve fraudulent misrepresentation or omission reasonably calculated to deceive persons of ordinary prudence or comprehension.

Formax also unsuccessfully argued that DSG violated the Uniform Deceptive Trade Practices Act by: (1) misappropriating 786 Formax parts prints; (2) passing off the DSG "perforator-cuber" and "patty snacking" machines as rebuilt Formax machines; and (3) causing a likelihood of confusion as to "the source, sponsorship, approval or certification of goods and services." The court held that Formax presented insufficient evidence for a "reasonable jury" to conclude that DSG passed off Formax prints as their own; in fact, there was no evidence that DSG made any "representation to the consumers concerning the prints." Formax did, however, present evidence to support the "likelihood of confusion" claim, and the court found that "[w]hile the evidence is not strong, it is enough to allow Formax's unfair competition claim (as to the DSG machines) to survive summary judgment."

With regard to Formax's allegation that its former employee breached his fiduciary duties by providing trade secret information to DSG, the court was very clear as to the criteria for evaluating a trade secret misappropriation claim:

While an employer with an enforceable restrictive covenant can protect non-trade secret information, absent such an agreement, an employer can prevent former employees from using only trade secret information. Unless, therefore, the information in Formax's blueprints qualifies as trade secret, [the former Formax employee] did not breach his fiduciary duty to Formax.

In determining whether particular information qualifies as trade secret information, courts can consider: (1) the extent to which the information is known outside the business; (2) the extent to which it is known by employees and others involved in the business; (3) the secrecy of the information; (4) the value of the information to the employer and his competitors; (5) the amount of effort/money expended in developing the information; [and] (6) the ease with which the information could be properly acquired or duplicated. Most important, the trade secret information must be confidential ... an employer must have taken reasonable measures to maintain confidentiality and ... the information must in fact be relatively confidential; the trade secret cannot be generally known."

Formax claimed that procedures were "created and enforced" to maintain the confidentiality of the trade secret information contained in the Formax blueprints. The Court held that four agreements which Formax presented as evidence of these procedures did not strongly support the claim of trade secret status as they did not apply to the relevant period (that of the defendant's period of employment with Formax). Furthermore, two of the agreements did not clearly designate the information contained in the blueprints as confidential.

In addition, evidence was provided by DSG that Formax did not restrict access to the blueprint information. The prints were kept in an unlocked cabinet, with no security guard keeping a record of who removed prints. Many vendors, potential vendors, suppliers and customers in fact possessed Formax prints. The ability of Formax competitors to learn the specifications of Formax parts from reverse engineering also weighed against treating the blueprints as trade secrets.

Formax presented evidence that blueprints and copies of blueprints were stamped with confidentiality and proprietary information notices, which raised with the court an "issue of material fact as to whether the blueprint information is a trade secret." The court further concluded:

> This is true, despite much of the parties' evidence, which suggest that (1) Formax did not take reasonable steps to maintain the confidentiality of the blueprint information and (2) the blueprint information did not in fact remain confidential. In short, while the evidence on the trade secret question favors defendants, it is not so strong as to allow the court to grant summary judgment in their favor.

The court denied Formax's requests for a temporary restraining order and a preliminary injunction because of Formax's failure to seek a preliminary injunction in the seven-year period from 1979 (when they first became aware that their former employee had "a complete set" of prints) to September 1986 (when the complaint was filed). This extended period of delay undercut the claim that irreparable harm or extensive loss of business would result from the lack of a preliminary injunction.

Even though the court grudgingly allowed Formax's trade secret misappropriation claim to survive, the case sounds a clear warning to computer firms regarding the steps which must be taken to protect proprietary information. First, confidentiality agreements must specifically and clearly define the particular information which a firm seeks to protect from disclosure. Second, trade secrets must be kept secret through the use of various security protections (e.g., locks, security guards, photocopying restrictions). Third, a computer firm must carefully monitor when it provides its trade secrets to outside parties, particularly vendors, customers and suppliers. Finally, if specifications for computer products are freely available and the products can be reverse engineered using the specifications, a court likely will not protect the alleged trade secrets underlying such products.

~~~

In conclusion, these cases demonstrate that merely calling confidential information a "trade secret" may not prevent such information from being disclosed. Rather a firm should (1) carefully draft employment agreements, particularly restrictive covenants; (2) monitor federal procurements to ensure that trade secrets are not inadvertently divulged; and (3) institute a trade secret program tailored to the firm's particular needs and concerns.

*Tobey B. Marzouk, Esq. practices law at the Washington, D.C. law firm of Marzouk & Parry. Specializing in all aspects of high technology law and litigation, he has represented data processing firms, independent software developers, software publishers, computer manufacturers and purchasers, ADP government contractors and other high technology enterprises. Mr. Marzouk is also Trade Secrets/Litigation Editor of the *Computer Law Reporter*. He has lectured extensively on various issues of computer law, and has published numerous articles in trade and legal journals.

PROTECTING YOUR PROPRIETARY RIGHTS

IN THE COMPUTER AND HIGH TECHNOLOGY INDUSTRIES

APPENDIX B

Computer Law Reporter

Suite 200, 1519 Connecticut Ave., N.W., Washington, D.C. 20036

CRUCIAL CONSIDERATIONS IN NEGOTIATING AND DRAFTING HIGH TECH EMPLOYMENT CONTRACTS

by

Tobey B. Marzouk*

Computer hardware and software firms often expend considerable time, resources and money in developing and marketing various computer products, including custom software, firmware, and integrated circuits. The contents of such products, as well as the methods for their production and utilization, are typically viewed as confidential and trade secret information by computer firms. In the normal course of computer product development and marketing, the employees of computer firms (and independent contractors) generate or must be provided with access to confidential and trade secret information regarding the products of their employers. Many computer and high technology firms, however, commit a crucial business error by failing to provide an employment contract that limits the employees' ability to divulge confidential and trade secret information and to compete with or otherwise damage the business of the employer.

Clearly, the absence of a carefully drafted employment contract can be devastating to a computer firm whose business survival depends on the protection of its proprietary rights. This article discusses the basic elements of employment contracts in the computer industry from the perspective of the employer seeking to protect his business interests. Specifically, the article addresses the negotiation, drafting, execution and enforcement of high technology employment contracts in light of recent case law, as well as the experience of employers in the computer industry.

NEGOTIATING THE EMPLOYMENT CONTRACT

Since the employment contract will ultimately govern relations between the employer and the employee, it is essential for a computer firm to establish careful procedures for negotiating the contract. Failure to comply with certain procedural and legal requirements before executing a contract may nullify its effect or preclude its enforcement. The following guidelines, therefore, should be followed by the computer firm engaged in contract negotiations with its prospective employees.

1. *Watch what you say during contract negotiations.*

During contract negotiations, company representatives should be extremely careful in what they say to the pros-

pective employee. Even though a contract may be drafted to prevent an employee from enforcing oral commitments not embodied in the contract,[1] a court may in certain circumstances rely on oral statements made by the employer to determine the meaning and intent of the parties.

In one recent case, for example, *Weiner v. McGraw-Hill, Inc.*,[2] a prospective employee was assured by a company representative that the firm's policy was to terminate employees only for "just cause" and that employment at the company had the advantage of job security.[3] The employment contract also referenced the employer's personnel handbook, which represented that "the company will resort to dismissal for just and sufficient cause only."[4] After several years of employment, the employee was dismissed for "lack of application."[5] He subsequently brought suit against his employer for wrongful dismissal. Under these facts, the New York Court of Appeals held that the employee could sue his former employer based on the oral representations and assurances made to him prior to his employment, as confirmed by the statement of policy set forth in the firm's personnel manual.[6]

Clearly, an employer should not make any gratuitous oral promises during contract negotiations. Such promises, if relied upon by the prospective employee, may come back to haunt the employer at a later date.

2. *Carefully draft personnel policy manuals.*

In addition to oral assurances made by the employer during contract negotiations, written statements in office handbooks or personnel manuals may be used to expand an employee's rights under a contract. In several recent court cases, for example, employees have been able to enforce personnel policy manuals as supplements to their employment contracts, and thereby bind their employers beyond the specific terms of the individual contracts.[7]

While a personnel manual serves the useful function of informing employees of company policies, the computer firm must exercise extreme caution in drafting such a manual. The manual, for example, should include a statement that it is not intended to constitute any type of contract between the company and the employees. The statement should include words to the effect that the policies set forth in the manual, particularly those involving

---

employee terminations, are meant only as guidelines, not rigid standards. This disclaimer should not, however, be used as a substitute for careful drafting of the manual's contents; where the disclaimer contradicts other expectations raised by the contents of the manual, the ambiguity in the manual will be construed against the employer. In addition, the manual should not include unnecessary detail about termination policies. The more specific the standards and procedures for termination, the more likely (i) an employee will claim substantive and procedural rights arising from the manual, and (ii) a particular termination will violate the standards set forth in the manual.

In short, a personnel or office manual may be used against an employer. The employer, therefore, should make every effort to limit the binding effect of the manual to avoid unforeseen liabilities to employees.

3. *Give the employee ample opportunity to review the contract.*

Often, computer firms present a proposed employment contract to a new employee on the first day of work, thereby giving the employee no meaningful opportunity to review the contract or negotiate specific terms. As a matter of policy, however, a computer firm should provide the prospective employee a copy of the employment contract before the start of employment. Following this procedure will guard against any allegation that the employee was placed at a disadvantage relative to the employer.

An employer who fails to provide a prospective employee the opportunity to review the proposed contract may be unable to enforce the contract, particularly if a court concludes that the employee was not given a fair chance to negotiate the terms of his employment. In *PEMCO Corp. v. Rose*,[1] for example, the defendant was offered and accepted employment with an engineering firm in West Virginia. Thereafter, the defendant cancelled his housing lease in Washington, D.C., signed a contract to purchase a home in West Virginia, and moved all his personal belongings to his new place of residence. When the defendant arrived at his employer's offices for the first day of work he was asked to sign an "agreement" restricting his right to compete with his employer should he leave the firm. Having already moved to West Virginia, the defendant had no choice but to sign the contract. In an action by the former employer to prevent the defendant from working for one of the employer's competitors, the court concluded:

> Under the circumstances in which the employee found himself, it is beyond cavil that his ability to negotiate with respect to the post-employment res-

traint was markedly diminished. At the very least, the employee was not as freely able to bargain concerning the provision as he was at the time he received the offer of employment!. The covenant not to compete was not a freely bargained for term or condition of employment, but rather was a term or condition of employment extracted from or imposed upon an employee under circumstances which deprived him of any fair ability to negotiate.[9]

A computer firm should therefore provide the prospective employee a copy of the contract prior to employment. Failure to do so may seriously undermine the validity and enforceability of the employment contract.

4. *Determine whether the prospective employee is bound by a prior employment contract.*

Given the frequency of job changes among professional employees at computer firms, an employer should know whether a prospective employee is bound by a contract with a former employer that restricts the scope of the employee's work. During contract negotiations, therefore, the employer should specifically ask the prospective employee whether the employee is still subject to a prior employment contract. If the employee is not bound, then the employer should obtain a written assurance to that effect. If, however, the employee is subject to a prior employment contract, the new employer should consult with counsel to determine (i) whether and to what extent the contract does in fact restrict the prospective employee's ability to work for the new employer, (ii) whether the restrictions are enforceable, and (iii) the manner in which the new employer should contact the old employer to discuss the scope and effect of the prior employment contract. Absent a careful review of prior contractual restrictions on the prospective employee, the new employer and employee may find themselves subject to a suit for injunctive relief and/or damages by the former employer.

DRAFTING THE EMPLOYMENT CONTRACT

The terms and conditions in any employment contract generally depend upon the particular needs of the computer firm, as well as the prospective employee's scope of employment. The computer firm should draft the employment contract so as to protect its business interests and proprietary rights, while giving the employee a clear understanding of his obligations under the contract. The following guidelines should be considered by a computer firm in drafting an employment contract.

1. *Protect trade secrets and confidential information through confidentiality and non-disclosure agreements.*

Perhaps the most important provision in any computer employment contract is a confidentiality and non-disclosure agreement. Under the terms of this agreement, the employee pledges to hold in confidence and not to disclose directly or indirectly trade secrets and confidential information obtained from the employer during the course of employment. Such trade secrets and confidential information may include (i) discoveries or inventions; (ii) ideas or concepts; (iii) software (object code and source code), regardless of the stage of development; (iv) software documentation, including flow charts and diagrams; (v) designs, drawings, and models; (vi) internal specifications and testing procedures; (vii) data and data bases; (viii) marketing, development and research plans; (ix) novel techniques and procedures; (x) certain kinds of customer lists; (xi) bidding policies and procedures; and (xii) miscellaneous marketing information concerning finances, pricing policies and price lists.

A confidentiality and non-disclosure agreement specifically restricts the employee from divulging to the public, particularly the employer's competitors, any information treated as secret or confidential by the employer. To qualify for trade secret protection, the information must fulfill three criteria. *First*, the information must be "used in one's business" and must give the employer an opportunity to obtain an advantage over competitors who do not know or use it."[10]

Second, the information must be unique or not commonly known.[11] "[M]atters of public knowledge or of general knowledge in the particular industry cannot be appropriated by one as his secret."[12] With respect to software, uniqueness requires the application of "new principles and concepts with unique engineering logic and coherence,"[13] and the expenditure of time and money for the development of new software features that provide the employer a competitive advantage.[14] As a practical matter, most software will be treated as unique, since any given program will involve numerous algorithms and programming decisions that vary with each programmer and result in differences in "speed, accuracy, cost and commercial feasibility . . . from system to system."[15]

Third, to acquire trade secret protection for business information imparted to an employee, the employer must treat such information as secret and must bind the employee, either expressly or implicitly, to preserve the trade secret status of the information.[16] This will require the employer to preserve confidentiality by instituting certain programs and policies which will be discussed in detail below.[17]

To ensure complete protection of its trade secrets, a computer firm should require its non-technical support personnel, as well as its technical employees, to sign confidentiality and non-disclosure agreements. Non-technical or lower-level employees often have access to considerable proprietary data. Absent a specific agreement, an employer may be unable to prevent such employees from divulging trade secrets or confidential business information.[18] Similarly, independent contractors and visitors may acquire or have access to a firm's trade secrets. To preserve the confidentiality of such information, the computer firm should also require these individuals to sign confidentiality and non-disclosure agreements.

Confidentiality and non-disclosure agreements, when carefully enforced, serve to place employees and other affected parties on notice that their jobs might involve trade secrets.[19] The employee is therefore more likely to be "secrecy conscious" and to exercise prudence with respect to confidential matters entrusted to him.[20] Confidentiality and non-disclosure agreements can also assist the computer firm in convincing its existing and potential clients that confidential information submitted to the firm will be protected from disclosure. The computer firm is therefore advised to require all prospective employees and independent contractors, as well as visitors with access to confidential information, to sign such agreements.

2. *Protect trade secrets and confidential information through covenants not to compete.*

In addition to demanding that employees, independent contractors, and visitors execute confidentiality and non-disclosure agreements, an employer should protect his confidential information and trade secrets by requiring professional employees to sign covenants not to compete. A covenant not to compete seeks to prevent an employee with access to sensitive proprietary information from competing with or working in the same line of business as his former employer within a given geographic area and for a given period of time. The practical effects of such a covenant are (i) to prevent the employee from directly or indirectly disclosing trade secrets to any new employer who might be in competition with the old employer, (ii) to prevent other firms from "buying" confidential information by hiring employees of a competitor, and (iii) to prevent the employee from appropriating confidential information to start his own business.

Because of their restrictions on worker mobility, covenants not to compete must be narrowly defined and carefully drafted. The enforceability of such covenants is discussed in detail below.[21]

3. Make sure the employment contract transfers to the employer the rights to all works by the employee.

Under the Copyright Act of 1976, a computer program or other work prepared by an employee within the scope of his employment is a "work made for hire,"[22] and "the employer or other person for whom the work was prepared is considered the author" and owns all rights in the copyright.[23] Accordingly, absent an employment contract that provides otherwise, copyright in all the works produced by an employee in fulfilling his duties vests with the employer. Some questions, however, might arise as to whether an individual is an "employee"—under the direct control and supervision of the employer—or an independent contractor,[24] and whether work performed by an employee is within the scope of his employment. To avert any misunderstanding or confusion between the employer and the employee on these questions, the employment contract should include the following provisions, tailored to fit each employer's needs:

(i) all work by the employee or independent contractor is deemed to be a "work made for hire" to which copyright vests with the employer;

(ii) to the extent any work performed by the employee or independent contractor is not a "work made for hire," copyright in the work is assigned and transferred to the employer;

(iii) copyright in any work performed during work hours (including lunch), on the employer's premises, or using the employer's facilities or money vests with and is transferred to the employer; and

(iv) the employee must disclose, assign and transfer to the employer all patent and trademark rights to any ideas or inventions developed during the course of employment that involve the employer's business and products.

4. Include family members in the employment contract.

Too often, computer firms fail to place any contractual restrictions on the employee's family. To prevent the improper or unauthorized use of trade secrets and confidential information by the employee and his family members, computer firms should include a provision in all employment contracts restricting the employee, directly or indirectly through a family member or other person acting on his behalf, from serving as an officer, director or employee of another company without prior approval of the employer, and from owning an interest in any competitor of the employer, if such interest is significant enough to interfere or conflict with the employee's responsibilities and obligations to the employer.

The courts have held that such contractual provisions are reasonable and not in violation of anti-discrimination laws.[25] In *Moore v. Honeywell Information Systems, Inc.*,[26] for example, a federal district court upheld a policy restricting employees and their family members from working for or owning an interest in a computer firm's competitors. The court reasoned that where one family member, a spouse, is engaged in a competing business "it would be perfectly reasonable to conclude that the interests of both parties will eventually intertwine, since the success of the spouse's competing business will be of a real and direct benefit to both spouses."[27]

The court went on to note that in the computer industry a company policy restricting family members is both reasonable and essential:

> Honeywell [the employer] is undoubtedly in possession of valuable trade secrets, such as software programs, marketing techniques, market studies, and other valuable information developed perhaps at great cost to the company. The employment policy here seems to be a reasonable means to prevent the improper and unauthorized use of such information by persons or businesses which may unjustly benefit themselves with such information.[28]

To avert any conflict of interest, therefore, a computer firm is well advised to place restrictions on family members of its employees.

5. Make sure the contract identifies a jurisdiction or forum whose law will govern.

The law governing employment and contractual relations varies from state to state. Accordingly, a computer firm should specify in the employment contract the jurisdiction or forum whose law will control the interpretation and enforceability of the contract. The selection of a jurisdiction should be made in consultation with counsel, based upon such factors as whether the employer and employee have sufficient contacts with the particular state, and whether the governing state law is favorable to the employer.

The contract should also require the employee to consent to jurisdiction in the appropriate state(s) most convenient to the employer. In this way, if legal action must be initiated against an employee to enforce the terms of an employment contract, the employer will not be required to litigate his case in a distant jurisdiction. Courts, however, will not enforce such provisions when they are so burdensome as to be unconscionable.[29]

Finally, the employer might wish to require employees to submit certain contractual disputes to an arbitration board pursuant to standards and guidelines set forth in the employment contract. The use of arbitration to resolve contract disputes between an employer and an employee is usually less expensive and more speedy than court litigation and should be considered seriously by the employer.

6. Include a severability clause in the employment contract.

A "severability clause" should be included in every employment contract. Such a clause states that every paragraph or condition in the contract is considered a separate entity and may be enforced separately, regardless of the validity of the remainder of the contract. If a contract lacks a severability clause, a decision by a court to strike one contract provision could void the entire contract.[30] A severability clause therefore insures that if one paragraph in the contract is declared invalid, the other paragraphs will remain enforceable.

7. Include an integration clause in the employment contract.

Another provision that should be in every employment contract is an "integration clause."[31] This clause reflects the intention of the parties that the written contract is an integration of the entire agreement and constitutes the sole evidence of such an agreement. A typical integration clause reads:

> The employee agrees that this contract is the complete and exclusive statement of the agreement between the parties, which supersedes all proposals or prior agreements, oral or written and all other communications between the parties relating to the subject matter of this agreement.

The purpose of an integration clause is to prevent both parties from relying upon statements made prior to, during, or after contract negotiations. In the absence of an integration clause, a court may be inclined to expand the contract terms by looking to the general subject matter of and the circumstances surrounding the contract,[32] particularly if the contract is fragmentary,[33] ambiguous or uncertain.[34] To guard against allegations by the employee that the employer made various promises and assurances not embodied in the contract, an integration clause should be included as a standard provision.

8. Remind the employee of the legally binding effect of the employment contract.

Every employment contract should end with a statement that the employee acknowledges that he has read the agreement and agrees to abide by its terms. In addition, the contract should state that it is legally binding and that the employee has the right to consult with legal counsel concerning the contract terms. Such a provision will (i) stress to the employee the importance of the contract and the employer's intent to enforce it, and (ii) place the employee on notice that an attorney may be necessary to review the contract.

EXECUTING THE EMPLOYMENT CONTRACT

Execution of the contract is largely a formal, uncomplicated procedure. The employer, however, should adhere to the following guidelines.

1. Have the employee sign each page and initial important paragraphs of the contract.

As a matter of policy, the employee should sign every page and initial all important paragraphs, particularly paragraphs involving confidentiality and non-disclosure agreements and covenants not to compete. Following this procedure will guard against any allegation that the pages of the contract were replaced. In addition, the procedure will highlight significant clauses of the contract, thereby undercutting any claim by the employee that he did not read or was told to ignore certain important paragraphs.

2. Be careful with employment contracts with existing employees.

Many computer firms begin as a small group effort with "technically-oriented" personnel who view attorneys as intruders in the firms' technical or business domain. This attitude has led to rude awakening when, several years into operations, the firms realize that they have no formal confidentiality agreements and covenants not to compete from their employees. The prime objective then becomes the securing of such agreements at the least possible cost.

Before executing employment contracts with an *existing* employee, computer firms should consult with legal counsel to determine whether the governing law requires that additional consideration be provided to the employee. Consideration is in effect something of value given in exchange for a promise.[35] For a prospective employee, the consideration is that he will be employed and will receive a given salary and certain benefits in exchange for signing the contract and agreeing to be bound by its terms.

An existing employee who executes an employment contract, however, already has a job. Some jurisdictions have held that continued employment alone is not adequate consideration for an existing employee who is required to sign an employment contract containing restrictive covenants.[36] If an employment contract with an existing employee is governed by a jurisdiction that requires additional consideration, the employer should provide some benefit to the employee in exchange for signing the contract. The benefit could be a small cash bonus, a salary increase, or a job change. To ensure that no additional sums are spent, the computer firm could require existing employees to execute contracts prior to annual salary adjustments and treat the increase in salary as consideration for the contract.

ENFORCING THE EMPLOYMENT CONTRACT

Most employees will abide by the restrictions in their employment contracts. In some instances, however, the computer firm will be required to enforce its contracts to ensure compliance by its employees. In this regard, a computer firm must be willing to take legal action when necessary and to implement certain "in-house" procedures to protect its interests.

1. *Make sure the departing employee submits to an exit interview.*

Whenever an employee terminates his employment, an exit interview should be held to remind the employee of his obligations under the contract. Specifically, the interview should stress the importance of maintaining the computer firm's confidential information and trade secrets, and remind the employee of any covenants not to compete against the employer.

The employer also should require the departing employee to execute a termination agreement acknowledging obligations and restrictions set forth in the employment contract. Naturally, an employee's unwillingness to sign such an agreement will cast serious doubt as to whether the employee will preserve the employer's trade secrets and otherwise comply with the employment contract.

2. *Establish "in-house" policies regarding the use and disclosure of trade secrets.*

As discussed above,[37] trade secret protection for business information is available only if the employer makes efforts to maintain such information as secret. Accordingly, the computer firm must implement stringent security procedures and monitor compliance with such procedures. The following suggestions may be helpful to the computer firm seeking to maintain the confidentiality of its business secrets:

(i) Limit access to computer programs and proprietary business data on a "need-to-know" basis.

(ii) Limit access to sensitive areas to approved personnel only.[38] Keep such areas segregated and locked securely.

(iii) Institute proper sign-out procedures in tape libraries. Restrict access to such libraries to designated individuals.

(iv) Place terminals with access to confidential data in segregated and safe areas. Use passwords or keys to limit access to highly sensitive files. Make sure passwords and keys are changed periodically.

(v) Monitor all copying of software, manuals and other confidential documents.

(vi) Dispose of paper, tapes, notes and other trash carefully.[39]

(vii) Periodically instruct all personnel regarding security precautions. Post warning signs and security notices when appropriate.

(viii) Exclude all terminated employees from access to confidential data. If an employee leaves on bad terms, take further precautions such as changing terminal passwords and keys.

(ix) Label all confidential information as "SECRET AND CONFIDENTIAL." Each page of proprietary computer printouts should also be labelled confidential.

(x) Instruct employees not to leave confidential data unattended.

(xi) Monitor and review all speeches and publications to ensure that employees do not divulge trade secrets and confidential data.[40]

(xii) Periodically review the security program in effect at the firm.

3. *Remember that covenants not to compete provide only limited protection.*

The computer firm should realize that covenants not to compete do not provide unlimited protection against former employees. Indeed, the courts have placed various restrictions on the enforceability of such covenants. As discussed earlier,[41] some courts require the employer to give additional consideration to an existing employee who agrees not to compete against the employer. In addition, covenants that place unduly restrictive limitations as to subject matter, geographic area or time period will not be enforced.[42] Courts either will revise such covenants so as to protect equitably the interests of both the employer and employee,[43] or will strike the covenants in their entirety.[44] Accordingly, the employer is well advised not to be overly greedy in efforts to restrict an employee's job mobility.

Finally, in some jurisdictions, all covenants not to compete are deemed to be void as a matter of public policy.[45] The employer should therefore consult legal counsel to determine the law governing such covenants with his employees.

4. *Be willing to enforce employment contracts to let the*

Computer Law Reporter

Suite 200, 1519 Connecticut Ave., N.W., Washington, D.C. 20036

employees know you mean business.

The computer firm should be willing and able to enforce its employment contracts for two reasons. First, active enforcement will alert other employees that their employer fully intends to hold them to their employment contracts. Second, selective enforcement or non-enforcement of restrictive covenants may undermine their effect. A court may conclude that the employer is not entitled to protection since other employees were allowed to violate their restrictive covenants. The employer should therefore initiate a policy of regularly enforcing restrictive covenants in employment contracts.

CONCLUSION

Employment contracts are essential to computer firms, regardless of size. Carefully drafted employment contracts will protect the business interests and confidential data of the firm, while informing employees of their obligations to their employer. The computer firm, however, must follow proper procedures in negotiating, drafting, executing and enforcing its employment contracts. Only then will the firm receive the necessary protection under law.

FOOTNOTES

* Tobey B. Marzouk is an attorney at the law firm of Spriggs, Bode & Hollingsworth in Washington, D.C., where he specializes in computer law and federal court litigation. He is currently a member of the Board of Advisors of the Computer Law Reporter and has authored several articles in the area of computer law. Mr. Marzouk received his legal education at Harvard Law School (J.D. *cum laude*) and his Bachelor of Arts degree at Princeton University (A.B. *magna cum laude*).

1. Most employment contracts will include an "integration clause" which states that the written contract is an integration of the entire agreement and constitutes the sole evidence of the agreement. The use and application of integration clauses are discussed in greater detail below. *See* section of this article entitled "Drafting the Employment Contract," Item 7, *infra.*

2. 443 N.E.2d 441 (N.Y. 1982).

3. *Id.* at 442.

4. *Id.*

5. *Id.* at 443.

6. *Id.* at 445.

7. *See, e.g., Murphy v. American Home Products Corp.*, 448 N.E.2d 86, 91 (N.Y. 1983); *Weiner v. McGraw-Hill, Inc., supra,* note 2 at 445-6; *Speciale v. Tektronix, Inc.*, 590 P.2d 734, 736 (Or. Ct. App. 1979); *Piper v. Board of Trustees of Community College District No. 514*, 426 N.E.2d 262, 267 (Ill. App. Ct. 1981), *Carter v. Kaskaskia Community Action Agency*, 322 N.E.2d 574, 576 (Ill. App. Ct. 1974).

8. 257 S.E.2d 885 (W. Va. 1979).

9. *Id.* at 890.

10. Restatement of Torts (1939), ¶ 757, Comment b.

11. *Id.*

12. *Sperry Rand Corp. v. Pentronix*, 311 F. Supp. 910, 913 (E.D. Pa. 1970). *See also Kewanee Oil Co. v. Bicron*, 416 U.S. 470, 475 (1973) ("subject of trade secret must be secret, and must not be of public knowledge or of a general knowledge in the trade or business").

13. *Com-Share v. Computer Complex, Inc.*, 338 F. Supp. 1229, 1234 (E.D. Mich. 1971).

14. Restatement of Torts (1939), ¶ 757, Comment b.

15. *Com-Share v. Computer Complex, Inc., supra* note 12 at 1234.

16. Restatement of Torts (1939), ¶ 757, Comment b.

17. *See* section of this article entitled "Enforcing the Employment Contract," Item 2, *infra.*

18. *Shatterproof Glass Corp. v. Guardian Glass Co.*, 322 F. Supp. 854, 865, *aff'd*, 462 F.2d 1115 (6th Cir. 1972).

19.
A written agreement clearly and unequivocally puts an employee or an independent contractor on notice of the trade secret owner's claims. . . . In a sense, standard use of a written employment agreement will create a rebuttable presumption that an employee was on notice of its terms even where the employee may claim to have forgotten signing the agreement. Care should be taken, however, to regularly acquaint an employee with the fact that he is being asked to sign a restrictive covenant and its meaning.
12 Business Organizations, MILGRIM, TRADE SECRETS, 3.02[1][C] (1977).

20. *Id.*

21. *See* section of this article entitled "Enforcing the Employment Contract," Item 3, *infra.*

22. 17 U.S.C. §101.

23. 17 U.S.C. §201(b).

24. *See, e.g., Epoch Producing Corp. v. Killiam Shows, Inc.*, 522 F.2d 737, 744 (2d Cir. 1975).

25. *See, e.g., Moore v. Honeywell Information Systems, Inc.*, 558 F. Supp. 1229, 1231 (D. Hawaii 1983); *Klanseck v. Prudential Ins. Co. of America*, 509 F. Supp. 13, 17 (E.D. Mich. 1980); *Thomson v. Sanborn's Motor Express, Inc.*, 382 A.2d 53, 56 (N.J. Super. Ct. App. Div. 1977).

26. 558 F. Supp. 1229 (D. Hawaii 1983).

27. Id. at 1233.

28. Id.

29. *See Horning v. Sycom*, 556 F. Supp. 819 (E.D. Ky. 1983). *See* also Marzouk, *Unconscionability in Computer Contracts With Small Businesses*, 2 Comp. L. Rptr. 214 (1983).

30. *See, e.g., Naseef v. Cord, Inc.*, 216 A.2d 413, 418 (N.J. Super. Ct. App. Div. 1966).

31. Restatement, Second, Contracts §209.

32. *St. Clair v. Exeter Exploration Co.*, 671 F.2d 1091, 1095-96 (8th Cir. 1982); *American Fletcher Mortgage Co., Inc. v. Cousins Mortgage and Equity Investments*, 623 F.2d 1228, 1237 (9th Cir. 1980).

33. *See, e.g., William H. Waters, Inc. v. March*, 269 NYS 420, 424 (N.Y. App. Div. 1934).

34. *See, e.g., Stoffel v. Stoffel*, 41 N.W.2d 16, 18-19 (Iowa 1950).

35. CALAMARI and PERILLO *The Law of Contracts* 2d ed. West Pub., 1976 §53.

36. *See, e.g. PEMCO Corp. v. Rose*, 257 S.E.2d 885, 890 (W. Va. 1979); *Maintenance Specialties, Inc. v. Gottus*, 314 A.2d 279, 281 (Pa. 1974). But see *Puritan-Bennet Corp. v. Richter*, 657 P.2d 589, 592 (Kan. Ct. App. 1983); *Matlock v. Data Processing Sec., Inc.*, 607 S.W.2d 946, 948 (Tex. Civ. App. 1980), *aff'd as modified*, 618 S.W.2d 327 (Tex. 1981); *Davies & Davies Agency, Inc. v. Davies*, 298 N.W.2d 127, 130-1 (Minn. 1980).

37. *See* section of this article entitled "Drafting the Employment Contract," Item 1, *supra.*

38. Sign-in procedures and identification badges may be helpful in limiting access.

39. Depending on the size of the computer firm, a paper shredder may be necessary.

40. *See, Jostens, Inc. v. National Computer Systems, Inc.*, 318 N.W.2d 691, 700 (Minn. 1982) (court finds "particularly damaging" fact that former employee wrote article and gave speech describing CAD/CAM system that employer regarded as trade secret).

41. *See* section of this article entitled "Executing the Employment Contract," Item 2, *supra.*

42. *See, e.g., Trilog Associates Inc. v. Famularo*, 314 A.2d 287, 294 (Pa. 1974) (covenants, unrestricted in territorial application are unreasonable restraints on trade and cannot be upheld); *Reading Aviation Service, Inc. v. Bertolet*, 311 A.2d 628, 629, 630 (Pa. 1973) (covenant void as unreasonable restraint of trade "since it was without limitation as to time or space"; "open-ended restrictions . . . impose an unconscionable burden on [an employee's] ability to pursue his chosen occupation").

43. *See, e.g., U.S.Achem, Inc. v. Goldstein*, 512 F.2d 163, 167 (2d Cir. 1975) (covenant barring employee from competing with former employer will be enforced only to the extent necessary to prevent former employee's use or disclosure of former employer's trade secrets); *Fidelity Union Life Insurance Co. v. Protective Life Insurance Co.*, 356 F. Supp. 1199, 1203 (N.D. Tex. 1972), *aff'd*, 477 F.2d 594 (5th Cir. 1973) ("if the covenant is adjudged unreasonable, it does not follow that the entire covenant is void; rather, contract may in effect be reformed to aid in enforcement thereof").

44. *See, e.g., Trilog Associates, Inc. v. Famularo*, *supra* note 40 at 294 ("such a failure to limit the territorial application of the covenant . . . renders the [entire] covenant invalid).

45. *See, e.g.*, Cal. Bus. Prof. Code §16600.

PROTECTING YOUR PROPRIETARY RIGHTS

IN THE COMPUTER AND HIGH TECHNOLOGY INDUSTRIES

APPENDIX C

Computer Law Reporter

Suite 200, 1519 Connecticut Ave., N.W., Washington, D.C. 20036

UNCONSCIONABILITY IN COMPUTER CONTRACTS
WITH SMALL BUSINESSES*

by

Tobey B. Marzouk,** Gary R. Rinkerman***
and Scott R. Porter****

I.   INTRODUCTION

In recent years, small businesses with no prior experience in the use of computers have become the targets of computer vendors offering services and products designed to automate various record-keeping functions. Computer vendors generally have much greater knowledge of and experience with computers than small businesses, which are oftentimes technologically unsophisticated and unaware of their computer needs. As a consequence, small businesses are placed at a decided disadvantage when negotiating contracts for computer products and services.

**/ Tobey B. Marzouk is an attorney at the law firm of Spriggs, Bode & Hollingsworth in Washington, D.C., where he specializes in computer law and federal court litigation. He is currently a member of the Board of Advisers of the Computer Law Reporter and has authored several articles in the area of computer law. Mr. Marzouk received his legal education at Harvard Law School (J.D. cum laude) and his Bachelor of Arts degree at Princeton University (A.B. magna cum laude).

***/ Gary R. Rinkerman is currently Co-Managing Editor of the Computer Law Reporter. He received his law degree from Georgetown Law Center and his Bachelor of Arts degree from Rutgers University.

****/ Scott R. Porter is currently enrolled in University of Santa Clara Law School. He received his Bachelor of Arts degree from the University of California at Berkeley.

Recognizing this imbalance in bargaining positions, computer vendors have sought to insulate themselves from liability to small businesses by requiring computer purchasers to consent to various contractual provisions disclaiming all express and implied warranties and waiving all rights to damages. These contractual provisions, however, are increasingly being contested by small businesses which, as first-time computer users, had relied on the knowledge and expertise of computer vendors in contracting for data processing equipment and services. Although few courts have directly ruled on the validity of contractual provisions that seek to limit the liability of computer vendors, such provisions, when applied to small businesses, may well be regarded as "unconscionable," and therefore, unenforceable.

This article explores the viability of the doctrine of unconscionability in the context of computer contracts with small businesses. Based on recent case law, there appears to be a growing tendency to impose a higher standard of care on computer vendors dealing with small businesses. Under this higher standard, courts may well consider contractual limitations on liability to be unconscionable when applied to small businesses that lack sufficient knowledge of computer technology.

II.   THE NATURE AND APPLICATION OF THE
      UNCONSCIONABILITY DOCTRINE

Under the doctrine of unconscionability, a contracting party may avoid the enforcement of a contract or its severable provisions1/ if consent to the contract was obtained in an inequitable manner2/ or the contract itself contains unreasonable or onerous terms so as to

---

1/ Under the doctrine of unconscionability, which is embodied in Uniform Commercial Code ("UCC") § 2-302, "courts have the power to refuse to enforce any contract or limit the application of any clause therein to avoid an unconscionable result." Bank of Indiana, Nat'l Ass'n. v. Holyfield, 476 F. Supp. 104, 109 (S.D. Miss. 1979).

2/ Bargaining unfairness is commonly referred to as "procedural unconscionability." Courts look to whether the bargaining involved unscrupulous or deceptive practices, use of fine print and incomprehensible language, or inequality of bargaining power. Procedural unconscionability is largely dependent upon the sophistication of the contracting parties. For the origin of this term see Leff, Unconscionability and the Code -- The Emperor's New Clause, 115 U. Pa L. Rev. 485, 487 (1967).

render the contract void as a matter of public policy.3/ This equitable4/ doctrine is predicated on a finding of unacceptable behavior or "overreaching"5/ on the part of the party seeking to enforce the contract. Unlike tort claims for fraud and misrepresentation, which may be used affirmatively as grounds for compensatory and punitive damages,6/ the doctrine of unconscionability may be used only to obtain a modification or rescission of a contract7/ for the purpose of avoiding an unconscionable result. When used to circumvent or

---

3/ Unreasonable contract terms that are void for public policy have been termed "substantively unconscionable." Computer contracts often involve remedy limitations, warranty disclaimers, and choice of forum clauses which may be substantively unconscionable. In determining substantive unconscionability, courts look for such factors as general imbalance in contract terms, unfair price, and unreasonably high liquidated damages. For the origin of this term see, Leff, supra note 2, at 487.

4/ The doctrine of unconscionability originally arose in the courts of equity, but is now also recognized in courts of law. See generally J. White and R. Summers, Handbook of the Law Under the Uniform Commercial Code, § 4-2, at 149 (1980) [hereinafter cited as White and Summers].

5/ "Overreaching" generally involves both unfair bargaining and unreasonable contract terms. "UCC 2-302 mandates a finding of unconscionability only where there is an absence of meaningful choice for one party plus contract terms which unreasonably favor another party." Fleischmann Distilling Corp. v. Distillers Co. Ltd., 395 F. Supp. 221, 232 (S.D.N.Y. 1975).

6/ See Glovatorium v. N.C.R. Corp., No. C-79-3393 (N.D. Cal. May 1, 1981) (unreported oral decision), reprinted in 1 Computer Law Reporter 141 (July 1982), aff'd, 684 F.2d 658 (9th Cir. 1982).

7/ The court may refuse to enforce the entire contract, it may refuse to enforce unconscionable terms, or it may limit application of the terms of a contract so as to avoid an unconscionable result. White and Summers, supra note 4, § 4-8, at 167.

---

modify contractual limitations on liability, however, the unconscionability doctrine serves as an indirect, yet affirmative method of securing damages under a contract.8/

Courts have generally been extremely reluctant to afford relief based on claims of unconscionability, particularly where the party seeking protection is a business rather than a consumer.9/ The difficulty experienced by businesses in obtaining redress from unconscionable contracts arises from a judicial presumption that businesses are generally experienced in the marketplace and knowledgeable about

---

8/ Although the doctrine of unconscionability embodied in UCC § 2-302 governs only transactions in goods, the doctrine has been applied to other kinds of contracts by analogy. For example, the doctrine has been applied to service contracts as well as leases. See Zapatha v. Dairy Mart, Inc., 381 Mass. 284, 291, 408 N.E.2d 1370, 1375 (1980) ("We view the legislative statements of policy concerning . . . unconscionability as fairly applicable to all aspects of the franchise agreement, not by subjecting the franchise relationship to the provisions of the sales article but rather by applying the stated principles by analogy.") See also Earman Oil Co., Inc. v. Burroughs Corp., 625 F.2d 1291 (5th Cir. 1980) (unconscionability applied to computer lease contract). Where one party to the contract has limited his liability through a disclaimer of warranty, and the disclaimer is found to be unconscionable, the court may strike the disclaimer, thus leaving the party liable for incidental and consequential damages. See Henningsen v. Bloomfield Motors, Inc., 32 N.J. 358, 161 A.2d 69 (1960).

9/ The unconscionability doctrine has generally been used where the party seeking relief is a consumer who has fallen victim to the sharp practices of unscrupulous businesses. Accordingly, courts have generally been unenthusiastic about granting relief under the doctrine of unconscionability when the contracting parties are both businesses. Indeed, "it is the exceptional commercial setting where a claim of unconscionability will be allowed. . . ." County Asphalt, Inc. v. Lewis Welding & Eng'g Corp., 323 F. Supp. 1300, 1308 (S.D.N.Y. 1970). See also White and Summers, supra note 4, § 4-2, at 149.

the terms of the contract.10/ In essence, courts assume that parties with business experience, sophistication and expertise are capable of protecting themselves against the coercion and "sharp dealing" which give rise to unconscionable contract provisions. A determination of unconscionability, however, is based on a given court's application of equitable considerations to the particular facts of the case.11/ Indeed, there are some contracts that are unusually complex, such as insurance agreements,12/ where courts have been less hesitant to protect businesses, particularly small businesses. As shown below, the willingness of courts to protect small businesses in complicated contracts, has become increasingly evident in the context of computer contracts.13/

10/ See, e.g., Bakal v. Burroughs Corp., 74 Misc. 2d 202, 343 N.Y.S.2d 541 (1972) (In action against computer vendor for breach of implied warranties and for recovery of incidental and consequential damages, court upholds contractual provisions disclaiming all warranties and limitations of liabilities: "This court finds nothing unusual in this limitation of damages, it being common in these types of commercial agreements, and therefore finds nothing unconscionable as far as the agreement between the parties."). Accord, Office Supply Co., Inc. v. Basic/Four Corp., 538 F. Supp. 776 (E.D. Wis. 1982); Earman Oil Co., Inc. v. Burroughs Corp., 625 F.2d 1291 (5th Cir. 1980); Badger Bearing Co. v. Burroughs Corp., 444 F. Supp. 919 (E.D. Wis. 1977), aff'd without opinion, 588 F.2d 838 (7th Cir. 1978).

11/ "The term 'unconscionable' is . . . flexible, to be applied within the framework of the transaction under scrutiny, and considered in the light of the commercial climate then existing and the common law." Industralease Automated & Scientific Equipment Corp. v. R.M.E. Enterprises, Inc., 396 N.Y.S.2d 427, 431, 58 A.D.2d 482, 488 (1977).

12/ See generally R. Keeton, Insurance Law, 358 (1971).

13/ See Chesapeake Petroleum & Supply Co. v. Burroughs Corp., 6 Computer L. Serv. Rep. 768, (Cir. Ct. Md. March 18, 1977), aff'd, 282 Md. 406, 384 A.2d 734, 6 Computer L. Serv. Rep. 782 (Ct. App. 1978). See also Glovatorium, supra note 6.

III. THE NATURE OF COMPUTER CONTRACTS
WITH SMALL BUSINESSES

Although valid in most situations, the judicial presumption of
equal knowledge and bargaining power among parties to a commercial
contract is often not applicable to the sale of computer products and
services to small businesses. Many business purchasers and end-
users who seek to take advantage of computer technology lack the
basic knowledge necessary to gauge the amount of computerization
that would produce optimum benefits for their business.14/ Such
purchasers may not even have the ability to understand and compare
the capabilities and limitations of particular computer systems.15/
As a consequence, small business purchasers are frequently forced
to rely exclusively on the knowledge and expertise of the computer
vendor, who in turn must assume the dual, oftentimes conflicting,
roles of business automation consultant and computer salesman. As
the computer vendor's goal is to sell as much of its own product as
possible, the vendor is hardly in a position to evaluate objectively a
potential purchaser's need, or lack thereof, for the vendor's products. Indeed, the almost complete reliance of many computer purchasers and the assistance of vendors before and after the sale of
computer products, has been acknowledged and used by computer
manufacturers in antitrust cases to justify vertical non-price
restraints.16/

Presumably, a lack of sophistication as to the subject matter of
an agreement should make a purchaser more attentive to contractual
provisions, such as disclaimers of warranties and limitations on liability, that abridge common law rights. A first-time computer purchaser, however, may argue that the experienced computer vendor
controls the contracting process by inducing the novice purchaser to

---

14/ Businesses, the main purchasers of computers, often lack
"computer literacy," since they are usually purchasing data processing equipment for the first time. The purchase of a computer is a
major business change which creates a dependancy on the computer
and on the computer vendor. Furthermore, most businesses fail adequately to negotiate and bargain for the sale of a computer. This
often forces the buyer to rely upon the vendor and elevates the
vendor to a position of consultant, as well as salesman. See generally C. Tapper, Computer Law, 42 (2d ed. 1982).

15/ Id. at 42-43.

16/ O.S.C. v. Apple, No. CV-81-6132 CBM (GX) (N.D. Cal.
March 14, 1983) (prohibition against mail order sales), reprinted in 1
Computer Law Reporter 984 (May 1983).

rely completely on the vendor's expertise and his representations as to the lack of need for warranty, remedy and other contractual provisions that would protect the purchaser.[17] Nevertheless, where the dissatisfied purchaser has some degree of business sophistication and the resources to afford competent counsel, a court may conclude that, in the absence of any clear wrongdoing by the vendor, the contract should not be disturbed.[18]

In addition to, or as a consequence of, the technological naivete of first-time computer users, computer transactions are potentially unconscionable because vendors typically offer prospective purchasers of mini and microcomputer systems standard form sale and service agreements on a "take it or leave it" basis.[19] Often referred to as contracts of adhesion,[20] these form contracts invariably contain

---

[17] See C. Tapper, supra note 14, at 44.

[18] See, e.g., F.M.C. Finance Corp. v. Murphree, 632 F.2d 413, 420 (1980) ("While Illinois courts will readily apply the unconscionability doctrine to contracts between consumers and skilled corporate sellers, they are reluctant to re-write the terms of a negotiated contract between businessmen.").

[19] "Typically, Data Processing Contracts bear little or no reasonable relationship to reality. This is so because these contracts are generally preprinted affairs and are remarkably similar from vendor to vendor; there is generally little room for negotiation or modification of the preprinted language, at least when you're dealing with a major vendor; and the preprinted language in the contract typically contains a plethara of exculpatory language and disclaimers of liability of any sort." T. Christo, DP Contracts Don't Leave Users Defenseless (Reader Commentary), Computerworld, June 13, 1983, at 73.

[20] A contract of adhesion is a standardized contract form offered to a contracting party on a take it or leave it basis, without affording the party a realistic opportunity to bargain and under such conditions that the party cannot obtain the desired product or services except by agreeing to the form contract. See Wheeler v. St. Joseph Hospital, 63 Cal. App. 3d 345, 356, 133 Cal. Rptr. 775, 783 (1976); Standard Oil Co. of Cal. v. Perkins, 347 F.2d 379, 383 (9th Cir. 1965).

---

clauses limiting remedies and disclaiming all warranties.21/ These limitations presumably reflect the parties' informed and deliberate allocation of the risks associated with the transfer and operation of computer products and services. Where the vendor serves in the dual and not necessarily complimentary roles of consultant and product supplier, however, the opportunity for meaningful negotiation may be remote at best.22/ Even if such an opportunity did exist, it is doubtful that a small, first-time computer purchaser would have the sophistication or economic leverage to effect worthwhile changes to the terms of the contract. Indeed, by the time the purchaser has decided the data processing equipment and services he wishes to buy, he is often in a position where he must move rapidly to procure the computer system and simply has no time or desire to negotiate meaningful changes to the vendor's standard form adhesion contract.23/

IV. JUDICIAL RECEPTIVITY TO CLAIMS OF
     UNCONSCIONABILITY IN COMPUTER CONTRACTS

Although the question of unconscionability has been raised in many cases involving computer contract provisions that disclaim warranties or limit rights to damages, courts have only recently been willing to grant relief based on a finding of unconscionability. Three recent decisions have addressed the doctrine of unconscionability as it applies to small businesses which are first-time computer purchasers. In Chesapeake Petroleum & Supply Co. v. Burroughs Corp.24/ and Glovatorium v. N.C.R. Corp.,25/ the trial courts

---

21/ T. Christo, supra note 19, at 73.

22/ J. Zammit, Contracting For Computer Products, 1 Computer Law Reporter 728, 732 (March 1983).

23/ See J. Aver and C. Harris, Computer Contract Negotiations 17 (1981).

24/ Chesapeake, supra note 13.

25/ Glovatorium, supra note 6.

specifically held that limitations on liability in computer contracts with small businesses were unconscionable under the factual circumstances of the cases.[26] Similarly, in Horning v. Sycom,[27] the court ruled that a choice of forum provision in a computer contract was unconscionable, given the disparity in bargaining power between the vendor and the small business purchaser. Each of these cases demonstrates the principles underlying the unconscionability doctrine in the context of small businesses purchasing computer products and services for the first time.

> A. Chesapeake Petroleum & Supply Co. v.
> Burroughs Corp.

In 1971, Chesapeake Petroleum & Supply Co., a small, first-time computer purchaser, entered into a sales contract for the purchase of a Burroughs L-5000 computer, as well as application software for various record-keeping functions, including billing, accounts receivable and inventory control. On the reverse side of the contract were fourteen paragraphs in fine print, one of which provided: "Purchaser hereby expressly waives all damages, whether direct, incidental or consequential."[28]

Burroughs delivered the computer system a month later than agreed. For over two years the system failed to perform the functions required under the contract, despite Burroughs' attempts to correct defects in the programs. Chesapeake subsequently stopped using the Burroughs computer, purchased a new computer from a different vendor, and brought suit against Burroughs for breach of contract, negligence, and misrepresentation.[29]

The circuit court for Montgomery County, Maryland found that Burroughs had breached its contract, and awarded Chesapeake $30,000 in damages, representing the cost of a new computer (less the salvage value for the Burroughs computer), fees paid to a computer systems analyst, and the cost of wasted labor and materials

---

[26] The decisions in Chesapeake and Glovatorium were both upheld on appeal on other grounds, without consideration of the question of unconscionability. See supra notes 6, 13.

[27] Horning v. Sycom, 556 F. Supp. 819 (E.D.Ky. 1983).

[28] Contract reprinted in 6 Computer L. Serv. Rep., at 776-781.

[29] Chesapeake, supra note 13, 6 Computer L. Serv. Rep. at 768.

arising from Burroughs' failure to perform under the contract.30/ In awarding these damages, the court held that the waiver of damages provision printed on the reverse side of the contract was unconscionable and therefore unenforceable.

The court observed that Chesapeake "is a small corporation and none of its employees had any familiarity with computers, nor had any type of computer machinery, theretofore, been in the office of this company."31/ Given the technological naivete of Chesapeake, the court placed the burden on Burroughs to justify what seemed on its face to be an overreaching contract provision:

> The court finds that this provision under the situation revealed before the court would be unconscionable to enforce. Extensive testimony was received to determine all the surrounding circumstances and to afford the defendants a reasonable opportunity to present evidence as to commercial setting, purpose and effect of the contract. . . . No evidence was received to justify the waiver and additionally it has been often held that such waivers are looked upon with disfavor.32/

The court went on to hold in the alternative that the waiver of damages provision on the reverse side of the contract was inoperative because of a drafting defect:

> [O]n the first page of the equipment sale contract it states: "Terms and conditions on reverse side are part of this security agreement", when in fact there was no such security agreement involved.33/

30/ Id. at 776.

31/ Id. at 769.

32/ Id.

33/ Id.

Thus, when faced with a harsh contract provision, the court found it appropriate to construe strictly the mistake in wording on the front page of the contract so as to exclude the provisions on the reverse side of the agreement.

On appeal, the appellate court affirmed the decision of the lower court and allowed Chesapeake to recover damages against Burroughs. The appellate court, however, never reached the question of unconscionability, but limited its holding to the drafting defect in the contract.34/ Nevertheless, the result was the same and the court signalled a subtle message that if a computer vendor overreaches with small, technologically unsophisticated businesses, the court will not hesitate to use rules of construction to overcome unfairness in the contract.

B.   Glovatorium, Inc. v. N.C.R. Corp.

Like Chesapeake, Glovatorium involved a small, first-time computer user. In that case, Glovatorium had purchased an NCR SPIRIT/8200 computer system for performing routine accounting functions.35/ The system, however, never performed properly and Glovatorium eventually sued NCR on a variety of contract and tort theories.36/

After a jury trial, Glovatorium was awarded compensatory damages of approximately $225,000 on its claim of intentional misrepresentation and approximately $50,000 on its breach of warranty claim. In addition, Glovatorium was awarded over $2 million in punitive damages, roughly three days of NCR's net profit.37/

34/ Burroughs Corp. v. Chesapeake Petroleum and Supply Co., Inc., 282 Md. 406, 412, 384 A.2d 734, 737, 6 Computer L. Serv. Rep. 782, 787 (Ct. App. 1978).

35/ Glovatorium, supra note 6, 684 F.2d at 660-61.

36/ Glovatorium brought suit for breach of contract, intentional and negligent misrepresentation, breach of warranty, and fraud for conversion of equipment. Id. at 659.

37/ Glovatorium, supra note 6, Unreported Oral Decision at 168.

In obtaining this substantial award, Glovatorium had to convince the court to strike certain provisions in the computer contract whereby NCR disclaimed all warranties and sought to limit its liability. The court ultimately ruled in favor of Glovatorium and held that the warranty disclaimer and limitations on liability in the sales contract were unconscionable.38/

In reaching this decision, the court noted that NCR's "product . . . was targeted at the first-time computer user, that is, people who didn't know . . . anything about computers, [and] had no experience with them, and didn't know what the consequences would be of an inadequate product."39/ Accordingly, the court held, "NCR was under a special obligation in dealing with the first-time computer user."40/

The court also observed that "we're not talking here about customers like General Motors or AT&T, who can take care of themselves, but small businesses that cannot."41/ When buying a mini-computer, the Court concluded, a small business relies upon and "puts itself into the hands of its supplier."42/ As the court stated:

> [the first-time user] relies on the reputation of NCR, and its experience, its competence, the fact that it's been making computers for a long time and surely knows what it's doing and has substantial organization to back it up. All of those things would lead a purchaser to put his trust in NCR, and certainly in this case, the purchaser was induced to do that.43/

38/ The court noted that "if there was ever a case of unconscionability, this is the classic case." Id. at 146.

39/ Id. at 147. The court further stated that "a purchaser who has no experience in computers doesn't have any inkling of . . . how wrong these things can go." Id. at 150.

40/ Id. at 147. Even counsel for NCR readily admitted that Glovatorium "was unsophisticated in the art of computer sciences, being a first time user." Id. at 149. The court cited this factor as "a very important element in this case." Id. at 147.

41/ Id. at 167.

42/ Id.

43/ Id. at 150.

In essence the court indicated that sophisticated computer vendors such as NCR have a heightened duty of candor and fairness when contracting with first-time purchasers who have little or no knowledge of computers. When a vendor breaches that duty, however, the doctrine of unconscionability may limit the enforceability of unreasonable contract provisions.

NCR appealed the court's decision to the United States Court of Appeals for the Ninth Circuit. The Court of Appeals affirmed the lower court's finding of fraud and the award of compensatory and punitive damages.[44] Even though the jury in Glovatorium awarded separate damages for fraud and contract violations, the Court of Appeals felt that its affirmance of the finding of fraud obviated the need to consider the contractual theory of liability under the doctrine of unconscionability.[45]

C. Horning v. Sycom

Although primarily used against contractual provisions disclaiming warranties and waiving rights to damages, the unconscionability doctrine can be asserted against any agreement that imposes an onerous burden upon the party.[46] For example, in Horning v. Sycom,[47] a forum selection clause in a computer sales agreement was challenged as unconscionable. That case involved a sole practitioner dentist in Kentucky who had purchased a computer system from the defendants to assist in compiling financial data, tax records and patient information. After the system failed to perform satisfactorily and the defendants proved unresponsive to the purchaser's complaints, the purchaser instituted a suit in Kentucky for breach of contract, breach of warranties, negligence, and fraud. Defendants unsuccessfully attempted to transfer the case to Wisconsin, the forum

---

[44] Glovatorium, supra note 6, 684 F.2d at 663.

[45] Id. at 662.

[46] See   Bank of Indiana, Nat'l Ass'n v. Holyfield,   supra note 1.

[47] Horning v. Sycom, supra note 27.

which the purchase contract designated as "the exclusive jurisdiction for any legal proceedings regarding this Purchase Agreement. . . ."[48]

In denying defendants' motion, the court stated:

> While the court cannot say that the defendant has engaged in overreaching, it does regard the clause as bordering on unconscionability as applied to the sale of an important piece of office machinery to a small businessman for the substantial purchase price involved.[49]

The court further noted: "The forum selection clause is only one of many clauses in the sales contract that together represent the best job of boiler-plating since the building of the Monitor."[50]

Clearly, the court in Horning felt that it would be seriously inconvenient for a small business to be required to litigate a computer contract case in Wisconsin. Recognizing the disparity in size, expertise, and bargaining power between the purchaser and the vendor, the Court concluded that the forum selection clause bordered on unconscionable and should not be enforced.

V. CONCLUSION

The findings of unconscionability in all three of the above cases are predicated on several factors. First, a small business that has never used a computer is technologically unsophisticated and cannot be expected to deal knowledgeably with computer vendors. Second, the small business purchaser will often be forced to rely on the knowledge and expertise of the vendor. Third, the computer vendor under these circumstances is obligated to deal with small businesses in a candid, fair manner. Finally, the difference in bargaining power between the small business purchaser and the computer vendor may cause the court to question the terms of a computer contract, particularly when the vendor has taken advantage of the buyer's technological naivete by including clauses that limit the purchaser's judicial recourses.

---

[48] Id. at 820-21.

[49] Id. at 821.

[50] Id.

The computer vendor who markets data processing equipment and services to small businesses, therefore, must be aware of the potential disparity in bargaining power and computer knowledge and experience between himself and small purchasers. As more computers are sold to first-time business users, and as computer vendors attempt to insulate themselves from liability by requiring first-time purchasers to agree to contractual provisions that disclaim all warranties or waive rights to damages, the courts may be more inclined to look at the particular facts of each case and strike such provisions as unconscionable.

PROTECTING YOUR PROPRIETARY RIGHTS

IN THE COMPUTER AND HIGH TECHNOLOGY INDUSTRIES

APPENDIX D

Computer Law Reporter

Suite 200, 1519 Connecticut Ave., N.W., Washington, D.C. 20036

High Technology Litigation
Before The International Trade Commission:
A Respondent's Guide

By

Tobey B. Marzouk* and Val D. Hornstein**

I. INTRODUCTION

The American high technology electronics and software industry has available to it an increasing number of legal weapons to combat unfair methods of competition from foreign imports. Least known and most misunderstood, but highly effective and increasingly employed by sophisticated American businesses, are the relief measures provided by the United States International Trade Commission ("ITC") under Section 337 of the Tariff Act of 1933 ("Section 337").

Long considered only a method to remedy international patent infringements, Section 337 as administered by the ITC is, because of its speed and effectiveness, becoming a favored device to halt the importation of infringing high technology products which have flooded the United States market in recent years! Section 337 litigation, however, is often unfamiliar to both foreign and domestic respondents, and can offer significant strategic advantages to the experienced practitioner. The attractiveness of the ITC as a forum for domestic complainants is further augmented by the fact that the rapidity of Section 337 proceedings can be used as a tactical weapon against a respondent whose counsel is not fully aware of, or experienced in, the unique aspects of Section 337 practice.

A significant part of the attractiveness of Section 337 to complainants, as well as the unattractiveness to foreign businesses, is that Section 337 actions are *in rem* proceedings and, thus, the Commission's remedies extend to all imports found to be violative of the complainant's rights, irrespective of who manufactured or imported the products. The case of the infringing Apple-compatible computers from the Far East is a recent example of the use of Section 337 as a remedy against unfair imports. In January 1983, Apple Computer, Inc. filed a Section 337 complaint with the ITC alleging patent, copyright and trade dress infringement of

its microcomputers—the Apple II, II+, IIe and III. *In re Certain Personal Computers and Components Thereof*, Inv. No. 337-TA-140 (Mar. 1984). Complainant Apple named 20 respondents, mostly Taiwanese manufacturers and exporters, who had been producing infringing microcomputers and shipping them to the United States under brand names such as "Golden II," "Orange," "Orange +," and "AP II." The products were exact copies of the patented Apple hardware circuitry, housed in look-alike cases; some were fitted with read-only-memory (ROM) chips which contained pirated copies of the Apple operating system and BASIC interpreter. Those units which did not contain infringing ROMs—including "ROM-less" or "ROM deficient" circuit boards—were designed to be fitted with ROM chips after their arrival in the United States.

The ITC undertook the investigation and, on March 9, 1984, found for the complainant on all counts. All of the respondents were judged guilty of infringing Apple's patents. In addition, the ITC concluded that (i) the "knock-offs," which contained ROM, directly infringed Apple's copyrights; and (ii) the microcomputers and circuit boards, which did not contain infringing ROMs, contributorily infringed the same copyrights.[2] (Apple had dropped its trade dress allegations during the course of the investigation.) The Commission ordered a total exclusion of all infringing microcomputers from entry into the United States.

This article seeks to provide an overview of how the ITC handles Section 337 cases, with a special emphasis on the unique considerations facing respondents in such actions. The article begins with a review of the relevant law which the ITC administers and then proceeds to a discussion of the sequence of a Section 337 investigation. The last half of the article highlights the problems which a respondent to such a proceeding faces and what steps the respondent should take to protect its interests.

PROTECTING YOUR PROPRIETARY RIGHTS

II. THE LAW

The ITC is responsible for administering various trade statutes. One of these, the Tariff Act of 1930, includes sections on anti-dumping, countervailing duty, and unfair practices in import trade. The principal purpose of the latter section on unfair imports—Section 337—is to curtail unfair trade practices by foreign manufacturers and importers, which substantially injure or tend to injure economically and efficiently operated American industries.

Section 337 of the Tariff Act of 1930, as amended, states:

Unfair methods of competition and unfair acts in the importation of articles into the United States, or in their sale by the owner, importer, consignee, or agent of either, the effect or tendency of which is to destroy or substantially injure an industry, efficiently and economically operated, in the United States, or to prevent the establishment of such an industry, or to restrain or monopolize trade and commerce in the United States, are declared unlawful, and when found by the Commission to exist shall be dealt with, in addition to any other provisions of law, as provided in this section.[3]

The ITC is empowered to conduct investigations into alleged unfair import trade practices, and, if it has reason to believe that such practices exist, must undertake an investigation. The remedies that the ITC can provide include temporary or permanent exclusion orders, as well as cease and desist orders. Further, the federal courts can impose civil penalties for violations of ITC orders.

Section 337 investigative proceedings are conducted in a hearing format guided by the due process requirements of the Administrative Procedures Act.[4] The investigative arm of the ITC, the Unfair Imports Investigations Division, is an independent third party to the hearing that conducts an impartial investigation of all allegations. The Unfair Imports Investigation Division must consider the public policy effects of its decision—including the effects on public welfare, competitive conditions in the market, and the economy in general—and must recommend appropriate action.[5] The subsequent hearing is adjudicative, with all parties given full rights to have counsel, conduct discovery, introduce evidence, and present witnesses.

This procedure is distinguished from federal court litigation in that the Tariff Act requires investigations to be completed within twelve months, or eighteen months for "more complicated" investigations.[6] If the Commission issues an exclusion order, the President has sixty days to review the order, which becomes effective and enforceable absent his veto. (During this sixty-day review period, the infringing items may enter the United States under a bond, which for all practical purposes is usually prohibitive.) If the Commission determination survives Presidential review, the adversely affected party may then seek judicial review in the Court of Appeals for the Federal Circuit.

III. ITC PROCEDURE

A. Complaint

A domestic company which believes it has suffered or may suffer substantial injury from an unfair act in connection with an imported product may file a complaint with the ITC. Also, the Commission may initiate an investigation *sua sponte*.[7] The fact that other similar or related legal actions have been filed in other forums prior to, concurrent with, or subsequent to the ITC action will not, under most circumstances, prevent the investigation from proceeding.[8]

B. Informal Inquiry

Upon receipt of the complaint, the ITC may conduct an informal inquiry to collect data, judge the scope of the problem, and consolidate proceedings before it. Under the Trade Act of 1974,[9] such an investigation will conclude with the decision to commence a formal investigation or to drop the matter entirely.[10] During the pendency of this informal inquiry, the Commission will not order any formal discovery or issue exclusion orders.

C. Formal Investigation

Once the Commission receives a complaint, irrespective of whether an informal inquiry has been conducted, the Commission has thirty days within which to decide whether to institute a formal investigative proceeding.[11] If the Commission decides to proceed with a formal investigation, the twelve-month (or eighteen-month) time limit on the term of the investigation begins to run after a notice of the proceeding is published in the *Federal Register*.[12] Thereafter, all named respondents are served with a notice of the investigation and the complaint,[13] and a presiding Administrative Law Judge is appointed.

Each respondent then has twenty days within which to

file a response[14] Failure to comply with this time limit may result in a default judgment being entered against the respondent[15] with appropriate statutory remedies applied accordingly.

Prior to the hearing, both parties may amend their pleadings[16] supplement their prior submissions[17] and file appropriate motions[18] The party opponent must answer all motions within ten days, or else be deemed to have consented to them[19] (At least one Administrative Law Judge at the ITC routinely shortens the response time to five days.)

The parties to the proceeding may use the discovery process to "flesh-out" their positions. The parties may take depositions, serve interrogatories, and seek stipulations of admissions for all non-privileged relevant information.[20] The Administrative Law Judge will determine the limitations on discovery and is empowered to issue protective orders limiting disclosure of certain confidential, proprietary or trade secret information.[21] In addition, the Commission investigative staff is also authorized to propound discovery requests and otherwise participate as a full party in the litigation.[22] Failure to comply with discovery requests may result in adverse *ex parte* rulings against the non-complying party.[23] Such rulings will apply to foreign respondent parties who have not subjected themselves to the personal jurisdiction of the ITC forum, because the ITC has full authority to impose appropriate relief on the basis of *in rem* jurisdiction over the imported articles.

In a complex federal court trial, the parties might take years to discover all relevant documents and data. In an ITC proceeding, however, due to the extremely short time limit involved, most evidence-gathering must be completed within five to six months after the commencement of the proceeding.

D. Hearing

The statute provides for a public evidentiary hearing, which generally takes two weeks, with full rights of notice, cross-examination, presentation of evidence, objection, motion, and argument.[24] At the end of the hearing the parties file post hearing briefs and the Administrative Law Judge must issue an initial determination, based on findings of fact and conclusions of law. The initial determination must be filed within nine months—fourteen months for cases designated "more complicated" by the Commission—from the

date of commencement of the investigation.[25] The parties, including the ITC investigative staff, may then request the Commission's reversal of all or part of the initial determination.[26]

E. Commission Review

The Administrative Law Judge's initial determination is then reviewed by the full Commission, composed entirely of Presidential appointees. The Commission decides whether to adopt, modify or reject the judge's initial determination[27] and what remedy, if any, to apply. The Commission reviews the initial determination for legal and evidentiary soundness and then makes its decision in light of "public policy" considerations. In reaching its conclusion, the Commission may consult with other administrative agencies—at a minimum, the Department of Health and Human Services, the Department of Justice and the Federal Trade Commission[28]—and hear arguments from other private parties including parties to the action.[29]

If the Commission finds a violation, or reason to believe that there is a violation, it will, within ten months of the commencement of the proceeding, publish its order in the *Federal Register* and send a copy to the President for review in light of executive policy considerations.[30] Unless the President, within sixty days, disapproves of the Commission's decision for policy reasons, the decision and order become final.[31] During the course of Presidential review, the infringing articles may be imported under bond.

If the Commission finds a violation of Section 337, it must—absent public policy considerations—direct that the foreign articles be excluded from entry into the United States.[32] In appropriate circumstances, the Commission may issue interim Temporary Exclusion Orders whereby entry is permitted under bond while the investigation proceeds.[33] In lieu of or in addition to a temporary or permanent exclusion order, the Commission may issue an appropriate cease and desist order.[34]

Any party that violates a Commission order is subject to a federal court-imposed civil penalty of $10,000 per day or an amount equal to the domestic value of the articles imported or sold on each day in violation of the order, whichever is greater.[35] Adversely affected parties may petition the Commission for reconsideration within fourteen days[36] or seek review in the United States Court of Appeals for the Federal Circuit.[37]

F. Current Developments

The remedies available to the prevailing complainant involve the exclusion of infringing products from entry into the United States. In recent years, due to the alarming increase in counterfeit goods entering the United States, as well as the concern over American economic productivity in general, Congress has considered stronger remedies. Among the additional remedies which have been suggested during recent Congressional hearings are: (i) creating a conclusive presumption of injury;[38] (ii) allowing Section 337 actions even when the products have not yet entered the marketplace and no industry has been damaged;[39] (iii) extending the life of an infringed patent for a new seventeen year term as to any foreign firm adjudicated an infringer by the ITC;[40] (iv) requiring importers to certify that their products do not infringe American intellectual property rights before such products are allowed into the United States stream of commerce;[41] and (v) imposing stiffer monetary and product exclusion penalties on infringing foreign firms,[42] including forfeiture and/or destruction of illicit merchandise, instead of mere exclusion from entry.[43]

The 98th Congress has reacted to these suggestions by recreating the Senate Subcommittee on Patents, Copyrights and Trademarks,[44] and by proposing legislation which has reached the subcommittee hearing level in both Houses.[45] In recent years, moreover, the United States Customs Service, one of the bodies charged with enforcing ITC exclusion orders, has increased its technical capability to identify infringing high technology goods at American ports of entry. The Customs Service now has seven major laboratory facilities to test for infringing electronics products, such as computer chips, and a nationwide automated data processing system which contains extensive information on infringing importers and their goods.[46] The Customs Service also conducts continuous seminar programs to keep enforcement personnel aware of the different products entering the United States.[47]

With respect to copyright violations, Customs officials may sieze articles that infringe copyrights registered with the Customs Service.[48] Although a recent Customs ruling made clear that ROM-less computers will *not* be subject to seizure and forfeiture under applicable law,[49] the Customs Service may effect the exclusion of ROM-less computers if ordered to do so under the independent authority of an ITC Section 337 order.[50]

Another enforcement agency, the Federal Bureau of Investigation, has similarly taken a more active role in preventing the infringement of intellectual property rights. Recently, the Bureau has authorized computer chip manufacturers to affix to their products warning labels which have the initials "FBI" and the Bureau logo in bold print, in addition to the following:

Warning
Federal law provides severe civil and criminal penalties for the unauthorized reproduction, distribution, or exhibition of copyrighted audiovisual works and video games.

The Federal Bureau of Investigation investigates allegations of criminal copyright infringement.[51]

IV. RESPONDENT'S STRATEGY

A. Introduction

In the fast-paced procedure of a Section 337 investigation, the best prepared party has a clear advantage over those who are caught by surprise. Because the complainant has knowledge of the proceeding well in advance of the commencement of the investigation, which is when the public first becomes aware of the proceeding, the complainant can prepare its entire case before the action has even been instituted. Therefore, the complainant can control the sequence of events during the proceeding by having its discovery requests and motions substantially researched and ready for filing before the respondents even learn of the complaint. In addition, respondents often have the burden of overcoming the presumed validity of complainant's intellectual property rights.[52] Thus, the complainant may have a distinct advantage in the course of the proceeding if respondents fail to secure adequate representation.

When the respondent receives service of process, it must answer each specifically pleaded allegation with a point-by-point admission, denial or explanation. Unfair acts alleged under Section 337 typically include (i) patent infringement; (ii) copyright violations; (iii) misappropriation of trade secrets, trademarks or trade dress (passing off or palming off); (iv) false designation of origin; (v) false marking, advertising or labeling; and (vi) a range of antitrust violations. The complainant must also allege that the act complained of has the tendency to injure or destroy an efficiently operating domestic industry, to prevent the establishment of such an industry, or to violate the antitrust laws.

In general, all legal and equitable defenses which are available to a defendant in federal court civil proceedings are available to ITC respondents.[53] If a respondent is ill-prepared or ill-advised, it may be confronted with potential default or adverse judgments after a hearing. The respondent, therefore, should retain experienced and competent legal counsel as early in the process as possible.

While counsel for respondent prepares its legal defenses, he should simultaneously begin preparing his client's discovery requests and prepare to respond to complainant's discovery demands. The following is a primer of tactical maneuvers which can assist the respondent.

B. Denial of Statutory Grounds of Complaint

Section 337 requires specific pleadings in the complaint. In addition, the Commission Rules require that the grounds of the unfair act be explained in detail and substantiated with specific facts and data to a degree not found in federal court notice pleading practice.[54] In opposing a complaint, therefore, the respondent can attempt to show that the imported articles in question do not fall within the statutory grounds or that the pleading is insufficiently precise.

1. Importation by or for the use of the United States

Section 337(i) specifically exempts from the statute "any articles ... imported for, and to be used for, the United States." If the respondent affirms in its answer, therefore, that the allegedly infringing goods are for the eventual use of, or will be integrated into a final product specifically produced for the Federal Government, the complainant's cause of action may be nullified or summarily dismissed. Whether such an approach can be used for articles imported for use by, or for integration into products for use by, state agencies under federal grant programs, has not yet been addressed, but might prove to be a valid defense.

2. Importation

The complainant will often name as many respondents as it can identify. (Indeed, the number of respondents has varied from one to forty-eight.)[55] Each of the named respondents bears the same legal burden of answering the complaint or facing an *ex parte* judgment against it. A named respondent may argue that it is not the source of the imported items or that such items are not sufficiently related to the alleged unfair act to provide a sufficient nexus between the importation and the injury. In other circumstances, the alleged infringer might assert that it is no longer importing the items or that importations have been made pursuant to license, thus allowing for early termination of the proceeding with respect to that party.[56]

3. Lack of domestic industry

The definition of what constitutes a domestic industry for Section 337 purposes has undergone radical changes in recent years. In both patent[57] and non-patent[58] cases, the term "domestic industry" historically has referred to domestic facilities which manufacture the article or use the patented method. Mere ownership or licensing of patent rights did not constitute an industry.[59] In a recent case,[60] however, the Commission has expanded the definition of "domestic industry" to include domestic industries which do not actually produce goods, but which add significant value domestically to imported goods through, for example, domestic assembly, quality control, or sales and repair service. In addition, in some cases, the Commission has extended the definition of domestic industry beyond the actual product in question to include similar products, thereby allowing complainant to measure injury against a more broadly defined market.[61]

In either event, the respondent should try to allege and show that the complainant fails to meet the statutory "domestic industry" requirement or is not in the process of establishing such an industry. The ITC defines "establishing" an industry as "a readiness to commence production" and an "indication that management has decided to produce or has made any overt acts toward commencing production.[62] To demonstrate that the complainant has not attempted to establish a domestic industry, the respondent can show that the complainant has made no preliminary estimates of production costs or rates of production or has performed no studies relative to the industry.[63]

A recent defensive strategy of respondents is to argue that the complainant has failed to meet the domestic industry requirement because it uses foreign-made components in its domestically produced goods. In today's world of global trade and multinational corporations, however, it is difficult to find a product which is comprised exclusively of domestic components and completely manufactured and assembled domestically. One of two scenarios is more than likely to occur: (i) the complainant assembles its products domestically using some foreign-produced components, or (ii) the complainant, a foreign-owned domestic subsidiary, manufactures and sells domestically produced items. Either scenario arguably falls outside the scope of the Tariff Act of 1930, and a respondent could argue convincingly that the ITC has no jurisdiction because of the lack of a "domestic industry." Such an argument was made in *In re Certain Miniature, Battery Operated, All-Terrain, Wheeled Vehicles*, Inv. No. 337-TA-122, USITC Pub. No. 1300, *aff'd sub nom, Schaper Mfg. Co. v. USITC*, 717 F.2d 1368 (Fed. Cir. 1983), where the ITC denied relief to a domestic importer and patent licensee because the complainant's domestic activity was insufficient to constitute an "industry in the United States."

4. Lack of efficient and economic operation

Assuming the complainant can prove that there is a domestic industry, the respondent may then attempt to show that the existing industry is not efficiently and economically operated. This defense requires extensive discovery of complainant's proprietary business records (which complainant most likely will be ordered to produce under a protective order). Case law indicates that the Commission will make its determination of whether an industry is efficiently and economically operated after weighing various factors, such as (i) increase in production by the complainant as compared to other domestic producers; (ii) improvements in the products; (iii) possession and use of well-equipped facilities and modern procedures, including the use of automated data processing equipment; (iv) favorable current profit ratio; (v) relatively low debt-to-equity ratio; and (vi) promotional campaigns for the product.[64]

5. Lack of substantial injury or tendency to injure substantially

The respondent also can argue that its actions do not substantially injure or tend to injure the complainant's operations. Like the information needed to challenge the efficiency or economic operation of the complainant's industry, data to support this defense will only be available after extensive discovery of the complainant's business records, viewed in light of the relevant domestic market. For example, if the complainant has a large share of the relevant market and the respondent's alleged unfair imports comprise a *de minimus* fraction of that market and have no likely impact on complainant's business, the Commission may dismiss the action under its "public policy" jurisdiction. Indeed, the respondent's actions may have a favorable pro-competitive influence on the domestic market, in which case, absent other countervailing negative factors, the complainant would most likely drop its complaint.[65]

In evaluating the extent of injury, the Commission has traditionally considered such factors as loss or potential loss of sales, lost royalties and/or lost profits, decline in production and/or rate of employment, underselling by the respondent, the volume of imports, and the relative abilities of the complainant and the respondent to increase their respective market shares.[66]

6. Lack of unfair methods of competition

The respondent can further argue that the complainant has failed to prove unfair methods of competition or unfair acts. For example, if the alleged unfair act is a patent infringement, the respondent might argue that complainant's patent is statutorily invalid (due to obviousness or lack of novelty) or that it should be held unenforceable on equitable grounds (such as unclean hands or misuse of the patent). Such challenges, if substantiated, may result in a negotiated settlement, such as a licensing agreement[67] or a consent order,[68] which terminates the formal proceeding at a cost savings to all parties, without either side admitting liability or suffering an adverse judgment.

7. Public Policy Considerations

As a catchall defense, the respondent may admit its technical violation of Section 337 but attempt to persuade the Commission of the potentially harmful public policy effects of an adverse decision. For example, one respondent in the Apple Computer case sought to persuade the Commission not to exclude its products because exclusion would (i) "deprive [the American public of] access to a unique model personal computer, at a retail price significantly lower than that of the Apple IIe;" (ii) "deprive the [American] public of the well-established advantages of competition by leaving Apple more secure in its ability to command high premium prices within its 'niche' in the market place;" and (iii) "have an adverse effect on the production of like or directly competitive articles in the United States."[69] Although creative—like the child who murders his parents and begs the court for mercy because he is an orphan—the respondent's arguments were unequivocally rejected by the Commission.

C. Default

A defensive strategy of last resort is default. A Section 337 complainant must present a *prima facie* case, before the Commission will grant any remedy. The Administrative Procedures Act[70] requires that an affirmative Commission determination be supported by "reliable probative, or substantial evidence" on the record.[71] "The effect of a finding of default is to authorize the presiding officer to create certain procedural disabilities for the defaulting party and to entertain, without opposition, proposed findings and conclusions, based upon substantial, reliable and probative evidence, which would support a ... determination."[72] It is noteworthy, however, that even if a respondent fails to defend against a complaint, the Commission's investigative attorney, as a full party to the investigation, may still propound discovery and force the complainant to present adequate evidence to support its allegations of unfair imports.

As a matter of strategy, therefore, a respondent who feels that the complaint is spurious, weak, or very difficult to prove, or that the complainant might not or could not prosecute its case, might find default an appropriate course action.

D. Motions Strategy

In addition to relying on statutory grounds for opposing a complaint, the respondent can employ certain procedural motions to achieve favorable results. These motions are based on ITC practices and procedures as outlined in 19 C.F.R. 210, *et seq.*, and closely resemble, but are not identical to, federal court civil motions.

In general, prehearing motions are addressed to the presiding officer and simultaneously presented to the other parties to the action. A motion must contain particulars of the ruling or action desired, supported by adequate legal arguments.[73] In keeping with the swift pace of the proceeding as a whole, the non-moving party has a maximum of ten days within which to respond or be deemed to have consented to the motion.[74] In practice, however, the length of time within which parties must respond to motions is often

restricted to only three days.[75]

1. Motion for summary determination[76]

The moving party may use a motion for summary determination to allege that all or part of the issues raised by the investigation are ripe for determination.[77] A respondent may allege, for example, that it should not be a party to the action for the same reasons set out in its statutory defenses, or, more generally, that there are no genuine issues of material fact to be resolved.[78] A respondent also may assert that dismissal is appropriate on public policy grounds. An argument that dismissal is warranted to conserve ITC resources because a similar suit is pending in federal court will not meet with success, since Section 337 expressly provides that its remedies are in addition to other remedies available at law or equity.[79]

2. Motion for termination[80]

A motion for termination differs from a motion for summary determination in that the latter seeks dismissal or modification of a portion of complainant's cause of action against a particular respondent, whereas the former requests a complete end to the investigation of all parties. The same supporting arguments used for a motion for summary determination may be used for a motion to terminate.

A motion to terminate is often appropriate when the private parties to the investigation reach a settlement, such as a licensing agreement or consent order.[81] It is noteworthy that any settlement agreement must be approved by the ITC in light of public policy considerations and that the investigative attorney may oppose a settlement.

3. Motion to suspend[82]

A motion to suspend may be brought to suspend the investigation temporarily pending the outcome of a collateral judicial or administrative proceeding. As noted previously, an ITC investigation generally will not be held in abeyance pending a similar federal court action. Under some circumstances, however, the Administrative Law Judge might grant a motion to suspend. In *In re Certain Microprocessors, Related Parts and Systems from Japan*, Inv. No. 337-TA-153 (Feb. 1984), for example, the judge indicated that a proceeding might be suspended if a parallel federal court patent infringement case were nearing a verdict. Patent Office proceedings that may bear on issues raised in an investigation could also justify suspension.

The basis for a temporary suspension is a clear and convincing showing that substantial judicial economy, expedience, and a savings of time and expense could be achieved without prejudicing the rights of the parties.[83] During the term of suspension, all investigative activities are halted and the twelve-month (or eighteen-month) clock is tolled. This is not to say, however, that a party should suspend its case preparation.

4. Motion to make more complicated[84]

Assuming that the proceeding will not be dropped, a respondent's major concern may be to obtain additional time within which to prepare its case. A motion to make more complicated, if accepted by the Administrative Law Judge and approved by the Commission, will extend the duration of the investigation from twelve to eighteen months. For this argument to succeed, however, respondent must point to specific reasons justifying an extension of time—such as complex patent and/or antitrust issues, the problem of securing discovery from all (foreign) parties to the proceeding, or other hardships.

5. Motion for extension[85]

If the entire proceeding is not extended, the respondent may find it necessary to seek extensions of time in which to respond to certain of complainant's specific discovery requests. By statute, each party must respond to the moving party's requests within ten days. Because its case is generally prepared in advance of filing, the complainant can quickly propound specific requests for documents and other information; therefore, a respondent might find it necessary to move for time extensions to respond to these requests.

6. Discovery motions

In contrast to the complainant, a respondent generally will not be prepared to file discovery requests for complainant's documents, nor will it be able to determine which requested documents it can produce immediately to the complainant. If a respondent cannot satisfy complainant's discovery requests, it may simply decide to oppose these requests on various procedural and substantive grounds.[86]

The respondent also may seek a protective order[87] or an *in camera* inspection order,[88] which shields secret or proprietary records and information from certain parties to the proceedings. Generally, protective orders, which are issued as a matter of course in Section 337 investigations, allow only opposing counsel to view the documents, while *in camera* orders limit the review of documents to the Administrative Law Judge. Under a protective order, all outside counsel sign affidavits stating that they will keep the information confidential. As a matter of precedent,[89] inhouse legal counsel will generally not be allowed to view information under a protective order. The rationale behind this policy is that such counsel are presumed to be too closely tied to the business operations of their company, whereas independent outside counsel have no presumed conflict of interest.

In conjunction with complainant's requests for discovery, the respondent should file its own discovery requests. Each party has ten days within which to produce discovery documents,[90] but this time limit is often routinely shortened to three to five days as the discovery phase of the investigation draws to a close.

7. Request for admissions[91]

After the respondent reviews the relevant documents obtained from the complainant in discovery, it should move to request admissions on all facts that are not in dispute. Obtaining such admissions will expedite the entire proceeding by eliminating admitted facts as points of contention at trial. Admissions by either party on any fact are limited to the ITC investigation and have no collateral legal effect.

V. CONCLUSION

Clearly, a named respondent cannot afford to ignore Section 337 proceedings before the ITC. The Commission conducts a rigorous adjudicative investigation on very complex matters, all within a compressed twelve-month (or eighteen-month) time period.

The complainant has the distinct advantage of being able to research and prepare its legal arguments, evidence, and discovery requests well in advance of the respondent's knowledge of the complaint. Once the proceeding commences, the respondent must defend its interests vigorously or else suffer the legal sanctions of the Commission's *ex parte* decision(s).

The ITC was formerly considered a sleepy tribunal, concerned only with patent infringement cases; however, it is now an aggressive forum which, in recent years, has seen an exponential growth in litigated cases. It therefore behooves high technology importers immediately to obtain expert advice from competent legal counsel.

FOOTNOTES

*Tobey B. Marzouk is an attorney at the law firm of Spriggs, Bode & Hollingsworth in Washington, D.C., where he specializes in computer law and high technology litigation. He is currently the Trade Secrets/Litigation Editor of the *Computer Law Reporter* and has authored several articles in the area of computer law. Mr. Marzouk received his legal education at Harvard Law School (J.D. *cum laude*) and his Bachelor of Arts degree at Princeton University (A.B. *magna cum laude*).

**Val D. Hornstein attended Colgate University and will graduate this fall from George Washington University, National Law Center. He has spent five years as a computer and telecommunications software consultant and intends to practice in the fields of intellectual property and trade law.

The authors gratefully acknowledge the invaluable advice and assistance of Gary Rinkerman, Editor-in-Chief of the *Computer Law Reporter* and an Investigative Attorney with the Unfair Import Investigations Division of the International Trade Commission.

¹According to a recent survey by the ITC, United States industry lost during 1982 approximately $8 billion in sales due to infringing imports. This represents a 57.3 percent increase for lost domestic sales and a 14.3 percent increase for lost export sales since 1980. *The Effects of Foreign Product Counterfeiting On U.S. Industry: Final Report on Investigation No. 332-158 Under Section 332(b) of the Tariff Act 1930*, ITC Pub. 1479 at 24 (Jan. 1984). These losses are in addition to (i) lost product goodwill, (ii) lost employment in the domestic industries, and arguably (iii) lost productivity (including research and development) due to lack of capital and/or entrepreneurial incentive, and the increased costs associated with the prevention, detection and prosecution of infringing imported goods. *See Unfair Foreign Trade Practices: Hearings before the Subcomm. on Oversight and Investigations*, 98th Cong., 1st Sess., Part I, at 52 *et seq.* (1983) (testimony of Stanford R. Ovshinsky).

²The Commission relied on *Universal City Studios, Inc. v. Sony Corporation of America*, 659 F.2d 963, 975 (9th Cir. 1981), *rev'd on other grounds*, _____ U.S. _____, 104 S. Ct. 774 (1984) (the "Betamax" case), for authority here.

³19 U.S.C. § 1337(a) (1983).

⁴5 U.S.C. § 706 *et seq.* (1983).

⁵The ITC, however, cannot be swayed by any desire to protect *individual* competitors.

⁶19 U.S.C. § 1337(b)(1) (1983) and 19 C.F.R. § 210.15 (1983).

⁷19 U.S.C. § 210.10(b) (1983). One of the first instances of the Commission's use of this power was in *Certain Airtight Cast Iron Stoves*, Inv. No. 337-TA-106 (Sept. 1981).

⁸In rejecting arguments against duplicative proceedings, the ITC and the federal courts have relied on 19 U.S.C. § 1337(a) (1983), which states that Section 337 remedies "are in addition to any other provision of law . . ." *See Pfizer, Inc. v. International Rectifier Corp.*, 545 F. Supp. 486 (C.D. Cal. 1980), *aff'd* 685 F.2d 357 (9th Cir. 1982), *cert denied*, _____ U.S. _____, 103 Sup. Ct. 818 (1983); *Dennison Manufacturing Co. v. Ben Clements & Sons, Inc.*, 467 F. Supp. 391 (S.D.N.Y. 1979) (cost of hiring additional counsel for overlapping proceedings in federal court is not such injury as would support injunction of ITC investigations). *Accord, In re Von Clemm*, 229 F.2d 441 (C.C.P.A. 1955) (concurrent investigation). Nevertheless, the Commission agreed to stay the investigation in *Certain High Voltage Circuit Interrupters*, Inv. No. 337-TA-64 (1979), pending the completion of certain Patent and Trademark Office proceedings.

⁹19 U.S.C. § 2482 (1983) and 19 C.F.R. § 210.11(b) (1983).

¹⁰*See, e.g.*, ITC Informal Inquiry, Eastern Airbus Lease (June-Dec. 1977) (informal inquiry into financing terms under which European A300 Airbus was leased to Eastern Airlines led to decision not to institute formal investigation).

¹¹19 C.F.R. § 210.12 (1983).

¹²*Id.*

¹³19 C.F.R. § 210.13 (1983).

¹⁴19 C.F.R. § 210.21(a) (1983).

¹⁵19 C.F.R. § 210 21(d) (1983). *See* Section IV.C., *infra*.

¹⁶19 C.F.R. § 210.22 (1983).

¹⁷19 C.F.R. § 210.23 (1983).

¹⁸19 C.F.R. § 210.24 (1983). *See* Section IV.D., *infra*.

¹⁹19 C.F.R. § 210.24(c) (1983).

²⁰19 C.F.R. § 210.30 (1983).

²¹19 C.F.R. § 210.30(c),(d), 210.44 (1983).

²²19 U.S.C. § 1333 (1983).

²³19 C.F.R. § 210.36(b). *See, e.g., Certain Multicellular Plastic Film*, Inv. No. 337-TA-54 (June 1979) (manufacturer/exporter did not comply with discovery and was subjected to exclusion order for its products, based

upon inferences drawn against it).

[24]19 C.F.R. § 210.41 (1983).

[25]19 C.F.R. § 210.53 (1983).

[26]19 C.F.R. § 210.54 (1983).

[27]19 C.F.R. § 210.56(c) (1983).

[28]19 C.F.R. § 210.14(a)(2) (1983).

[29]19 C.F.R. § 210.56(a) (1983). *See* Section IV.C.7., *infra*.

[30]19 C.F.R. § 210.57(b) (1983).

[31]19 C.F.R. § 210.57(d) (1983).

[32]19 U.S.C. § 1337(d) (1983) and 19 C.F.R. § 211.56 (1983).

[33]19 U.S.C. § 1337(e) (1983) and 19 C.F.R. § 211.58 (1983).

[34]19 U.S.C. § 1337(f)(1) (1983) and 19 C.F.R. § 211.56 (1983).

[35]19 U.S.C. § 1337(f)(2) (1983).

[36]19 C.F.R. § 210.58 (1983).

[37]19 C.F.R. § 210.61 (1983).

[38]*Unfair Foreign Trade Practices: Hearings before the Subcomm. on Oversight and Investigations*, 98th Cong., 1st Sess., Part II, 11 (1983).

[39]*Id.* Part I at 66.

[40]*Id.*

[41]*Id.* Part II at 6-7.

[42]*Id.* Part I at 66.

[43]*Id.* at 164.

[44]*Id.* Part II at 51.

[45]The Trademark Counterfeiting Act of 1983 was originally introduced in the Senate (97th Cong.) as S.2428 in April 1982, by Senator Charles Mathias (R-Md.), Chairman of the Senate Judiciary Subcommittee on Criminal Law. An identical version, H.R. 6175, was introduced in the House by Judiciary Committee Chairman Peter Rodino (D-N.J.). Both bills died in committee, but the Senate bill was reintroduced as S. 875 in the present (98th) Congress; the House bill was reintroduced as H.R. 2447. The legislation would amend Title 18, United States Code, by adding Section 2320 to provide that anyone who knowingly traffics or attempts to traffic in a counterfeit mark in foreign or domestic commerce shall, if an individual, be fined not more than $250,000 and/or imprisoned for up to 5 years, and, if a firm, be fined not more than $1 million. The proposed law would apply only to marks registered on the Principal Register or otherwise specifically protected by statute. The owner of such a mark may also bring a civil action in the United States District Court to obtain injunctive relief and recover treble damages or profits, and costs,

including attorney fees. Prejudgment interest on actual damages may be awarded in the discretion of the court. A final judgment or decree rendered in favor of the United States in the criminal proceeding would estop the defendant from denying its criminal violations in a civil action. The court may ultimately order destruction of the counterfeit products or—after obliteration of the mark — disposal to the United States, the trademark owner, a charitable institution, or any other party, except the defendant. *Ex parte* search and seizure orders are also authorized for both criminal and civil actions. *The Effects of Foreign Product Counterfeiting On U.S. Industry, supra,* note 1 at 23.

[46]*Unfair Foreign Trade Practices, supra,* note 38 at 352-53.

[47]*Id.* at 170.

[48]17 U.S.C. § 509, 602 (1983).

[49]U.S. Customs Service Ruling RE: COP-2-03:R:E:E 724225 KP (Mar. 30, 1984).

[50]*See, e.g., In re Certain Personal Computers and Components Thereof,* Inv. No. 337-TA-140 (Mar. 1984).

[51]*Unfair Foreign Trade Practices, supra,* note 38 at 127.

[52]*Solder Removal Co. v. ITC,* 582 F.2d 628 (C.C.P.A. 1978). *See* 35 U.S.C. § 282 (1983).

[53]19 U.S.C. § 1337(c) (1983).

[54]19 C.F.R. § 210.20 (1983).

[55]Duvall, *Adjudication Under Statutory Time Limits: The ITC Experience,* 32 Ad. L.R. 733, 736 (1980).

[56]19 C.F.R. § 210.50 (1983).

[57]In *Certain Inclined-Field Acceleration Tubes and Components Thereof,* Inv. No. 337-TA-67 (1979) (Recommended Determination), the presiding officer stated that for purposes of Section 337, the domestic industry is "that part of [complainants'] business devoted to the development, production, design, rebuilding, servicing and sale" of the product in question.

[58]*Steel Toy Vehicles,* Inv. No. 337-TA-31 USITC Pub. No. 880 (April 1978).

[59]*Certain Miniature, Battery-Operated All Terrain, Wheeled Vehicles,* Inv. No. 337-TA-122 (Oct. 1982); *Certain Ultra-Microtone Freezing Attachments,* Inv. No. 337-TA-10, USITC Pub. No. 771 (April 1976).

[60]*Certain Airtight Cast-Iron Stoves,* Inv. No. 337-TA-69 (July 1979). For an excellent discussion of this case and its potential ramifications, *see* Sirilla, *A View of the USITC As a Forum For Suit by Domestic Importers of Products Made Abroad,* 65 J. Pat. Office Soc'y 46 (Jan. 1983). *See also, Certain Cube Puzzles,* USITC Pub. 1334 (Jan. 1983).

[61]*Certain Surveying Devices,* Inv. No. 337-TA-68, USITC Pub. No. 1085 at 29-30, (July 1980); *Expanded, Unsintered Polytetrafluoroethylene in Tape Form,* Inv. No. 337-TA-4, USITC Pub. No. 769 at 18-19 (April 1976).

[62]*Certain Ultra Microtone Freezing Attachments, supra,* note 59 at 10.

⁶³*Id.*

⁶⁴*Exercising Devices*, Inv. No. 337-TA-24, USITC Pub. No. 813, note 39 at 25-7 (April 1977); *In-The Ear Hearing Aids*, USITC Pub. No. 182, at 20-1 (July 1966). *See generally Certain Centrifugal Trash Pumps, Inv. No. 337-TA-43* at 22-3 (Feb. 1979).

⁶⁵For a list of factors considered in determining "material injury" under the Act, *see* 19 C.F.R. § 207.26 (1983).

⁶⁶Brunsvold, Ellsworth and Schmitt, *Injury Standards in Section 337 Investigations*, 4 N.W.J. In'tl L. & Bus. 75, 86 (Spring 1982).

⁶⁷*In re Certain Microprocessors, Related Parts and Systems From Japan*, Inv. No. 337-TA-153 (Feb. 1984) and 19 C.F.R. § 210.51(c) (1983).

⁶⁸*Certain Cattle Whips*, Inv. No. 337-TA-57 (Aug. 1979) and 19 C.F.R. § 210.51(d) (1983).

⁶⁹In re *Certain Personal Computers and Components Thereof, supra*, note 50.

⁷⁰U.S.C. § 556(d).

⁷¹*In re Certain Electric Slow Cookers*, Inv. No. 337-TA-42 (1979).

⁷²*Id. See also Coin Operated Video Games and Components Thereof*, Inv. No. 337-TA-87 (Nov. 1980) (ALJ's Order No. 17).

⁷³19 C.F.R. § 210.24(b) (1983).

⁷⁴19 C.F.R. § 210.24(c) (1983).

⁷⁵Kaye, Lupo and Lipman, *The Jurisdictional Paradigm Between the United States International Trade Commission and the Federal District Courts*, 64 J. Pat. Office Soc'y 118, 127 (March 1982).

⁷⁶19 C.F.R. § 210.50 (1983).

⁷⁷*See, e.g., Certain Apparatus for the Continuous Production of Copper Rod*, Inv. No. 337-TA-52 (March 1979).

⁷⁸*Doxycycline*, Inv. No. 337-TA-3 (May 1982).

⁷⁹*See, e.g., Certain Microprocessors, Related Parts and Systems from Japan, supra*, note 67; *Certain Electronic Printing Calculators*, Inv. No. 337-TA-11 (Jan. 1976) (patent cases terminated upon request of parties after negotiation of license agreements); *Piezoelectric Ceramic 10.7 MHz Electric Wave Filters*, Inv. No. 337-TA-8 (Dec. 1975).

⁸⁰19 C.F.R. § 210.15 (1983).

⁸¹For a list of other factors the Commission will consider, *see Certain Color Television Receiving Sets*, Inv. No. 337-TA-23 (Aug. 1981).

⁸²19 C.F.R. § 210.15 (1983).

⁸³19 C.F.R. § 210.24(d) (1983).

⁸⁴*See, e.g., In re Certain Personal Computers and Components Thereof, supra*, note 50.

⁸⁵19 C.F.R. § 210.30(d), 210.44 (1983).

⁸⁶19 C.F.R. § 210.44 (1983).

⁸⁷*See, e.g., Certain Rotary Wheel Printing Systems*, 337-TA-185 (Pending).

⁸⁸C.F.R. § 210.24(c) (1983).

⁸⁹19 C.F.R. § 210.34 (1983).

PROTECTING YOUR PROPRIETARY RIGHTS

IN THE COMPUTER AND HIGH TECHNOLOGY INDUSTRIES

APPENDIX E

Computer Law Reporter

Suite 200, 1519 Connecticut Ave., N.W., Washington, D.C. 20036

FEDERAL DATA PROCESSING CONTRACTS *

By

Dennis J. Riley P.C. ** and Tobey B. Marzouk ***

I. INTRODUCTION

The large volume of paperwork and records generated by the federal bureaucracy compels the federal government to acquire extensive data processing facilities. The government obtains much of its automatic data processing support from private industry. To benefit from this growing trend, however, private data processing suppliers must understand the policies and procedures governing the federal acquisition of data processing equipment and services. Litigation results from the juxtaposition of huge expenditures of public funds and controversial or ineffective control over competition for federal data processing contracts.

---

* Copyright 1983 by Dennis J. Riley, P.C. and Tobey B. Marzouk. This is the first of two articles on federal data processing acquisition. This article discusses the statutory and regulatory procedures and standards for procurement and testing of automatic data processing equipment. The second article will discuss federal contract specifications for data processing hardware and software.

** Dennis J. Riley has practiced law for ten years and is a partner at Spriggs, Bode & Hollingsworth in Washington, D. C., where he specializes in public contract law. He was validictorian of his graduating class at LaSalle College in Philadelphia, Pennsylvania (B.A. 1970), and received his legal training in Ithaca, New York at the Cornell Law School (J.D. 1973). Mr. Riley has published and lectured extensively on a number of public contract topics, including federal procurement of automatic data processing equipment. Mr. Riley is an officer of the American Bar Association's Public Contracts Law Section and the Federal Bar Association Government Contracts Council. In 1983, Mr. Riley will publish a treatise on federal contracts and grants for the McGraw Hill Publishing Company.

*** Tobey B. Marzouk is an associate at the law firm of Spriggs, Bode & Hollingsworth, where he specializes in federal court and computer related litigation. Mr. Marzouk received his legal education at Harvard Law School (J.D. 1977 cum laude) and his Bachelor of Arts Degree at Princeton University (A.B. 1974 magna cum laude).

PROTECTING YOUR PROPRIETARY RIGHTS

II. THE BROOKS ACT

The General Services Administration (GSA) nominally coordinates data processing activities of the federal government, pursuant to the Brooks Act of 1965. 1/ Enacted as an amendment to the Federal Property and Administrative Services Act of 1949, the Brooks Act established special contracting procedures and policies for automatic data processing equipment purchased by the federal government. 2/ The major objectives of the Brooks Act are:

      (1) to centralize the acquisition of automatic data processing systems,

      (2) to coordinate utilization through joint use and sharing of equipment, and

      (3) to allow the federal government to maintain an automatic data processing inventory. 3/

Under the Brooks Act, GSA exercises overall operational responsibility for automatic data processing equipment contracts. 4/ This authority is implemented through the Federal Property Management Regulations 5/ and the Federal Procurement Regulations. 6/

In addition to conferring direct control of federal data processing to the GSA, the Brooks Act authorizes the Department of Commerce, through the National Bureau of Standards, to provide "scientific and technological advisory services" for data processing needs of the federal government, and to establish uniform standards for automatic data processing equipment. 7/ Finally, the Brooks Act

---

1/   40 U.S.C. § 759.

2/   40 U.S.C. § 759(a).

3/   S. Rep. No. 938, 89th Cong., 1st Sess. (1965), reprinted in 1965 U.S. Code Cong. and Ad. News 3859.

4/   40 U.S.C. § 759(b).

5/   FPMR Part 101-32; 41 C.F.R. § 101-35.

6/   FPR Subpart 1-4.11; 41 C.F.R. § 1-4.11.

7/   40 U.S.C. §. 759(f).

gives the Office of Management and Budget (OMB) ultimate supervisory responsibility over the activities of the General Services Administration and the Department of Commerce and authorizes OMB to issue fiscal and policy directives concerning data processing by the federal government.

GSA's authority under the Brooks Act applies to only "general purpose, commercially available, mass-produced automatic data processing devices" which are not designed to perform a specific series of computations for a single purpose. 8/ Thus, purchase of a word processing system by the Department of Housing and Urban Development would be subject to the Brooks Act, while a computer for use by the National Aeronautics and Space Administration for tracking space flights probably would be outside GSA's contracting jurisdiction.

Considerable question has been raised as to whether the term "automatic data processing equipment" as used in the Brooks Act encompasses computer software or firmware. On the one hand, the Office of Management and Budget has stated that the Brooks Act applies to only the purchase, lease or maintenance of automatic data processing equipment, and not to data processing software or services. 9/ The General Services Administration, on the other hand, has concluded that "commercially available software, maintenance services and related supplies" are within the scope of the Brooks Act and subject to GSA's authority. 10/

Generally, GSA's authority under the Brooks Act applies to all federal agencies, including any "establishment in the legislative or judicial branch." 11/ GSA, however, does not have authority "to impair or interfere with the determination by agencies of their individual automatic data processing equipment requirements," including the specifications for and the selection of the equipment needed. 12/ Nor does GSA have the authority to "interfere with or

---

8/ FPR 4.1102-1.

9/ This interpretation of the Brooks Act is based in part on a report of the Committee on Government Operations of the House of Representatives. See Letter from Paul H. O'Neill, Deputy Director of the Office of Management and Budget, to Jack Eckert, Administrator of the General Services Administration, December 9, 1976.

10/ FPR 4.1100.

11/ FPR 4.1102-18. See Federal Judicial Center, 58 Comp. Gen. 350 (1979).

12/ 40 U.S.C. § 759(g).

---

attempt to control in any way the use made of automatic data processing equipment or components thereof by any agency." 13/

To discharge its responsibilities under the Brooks Act, GSA has established the Automatic Data and Telecommunication Service (ADTS), which has "Government-wide responsibility for the development and implementation of management policies and procedures concerned with the effective and efficient acquisition and use of the [data processing] resources of the Federal government." 14/ ADTS is the main branch of GSA that coordinates all data processing activities of the federal government, including software and hardware acquisition, telecommunications, time-sharing and other federal data processing services.

Although GSA has the theoretical power to purchase all general purpose, commercially available data processing equipment for the federal government, the Brooks Act recognizes inter-agency jealousies and allows GSA to delegate its procurement authority when it determines that such action is "necessary for the economy and efficiency of operations." 15/ As a practical matter, GSA allows most acquisitions to be made by the user agency. Before purchasing any hardware, software, or maintenance services, however, the contracting agency generally must submit to ADTS an Agency Procurement Request setting forth the proposed solicitation and other facts necessary for GSA to determine if the acquisition is economical and efficient under the Brooks Act. 16/

The Brooks Act also allows GSA to delegate its procurement authority when it determines that such action is essential to "national defense or national security." 17/ Under this provision, automatic data processing equipment or software specially designed with unique scientific, cryptologic or military applications to national defense are exempt from the Brooks Act, while general purpose, commercially available automatic data processing components used in conjunction

---

13/ Id.

14/ FPMR 36.400-1.

15/ 40 U.S.C. § 759(b)(2).

16/ See FPR 4.1105.

17/ 40 U.S.C. § 759(b)(2).

with such specially designed systems or for routine administrative and business applications remain under GSA's control. 18/

III. HARDWARE ACQUISITION STANDARDS AND PROCEDURES

The primary method of system validation of major 19/ procurements of automatic data processing hardware by the federal government is "benchmarking." Oftentimes referred to as "live test demonstration," benchmarking is nothing more than "user-witnessed running of a [mixed] group . . . of programs representative of the user's predicted workload on a vendor's proposed computer system in order to validate system performance."20/ The Department of Commerce, which establishes uniform technical standards for data processing equipment under the Brooks Act, has published "Guidelines for Benchmarking ADP Systems in the Competitive Procurement Environment," that set forth standards and procedures for proper benchmarking. 21/ Briefly, the guidelines discuss the various steps in the benchmarking process, including workload definition and analysis; construction, validation and documentation of benchmarks; procedural documentation and preparation for vendors; vendor construction of required demonstrations; and conduct of benchmark tests. Under the guidelines, the primary factors affecting the validity of benchmarks are the estimation of workload and the selection of programs and data processing requirements that are representative of the user's actual minimum needs. 22/

18/ S. Rep. No. 938, 89th Cong., 1st Sess. (1965), reprinted in 1965 U.S. Code Cong. & Ad. News 3859, 3863.

19/ FPR 4.1109-22 generally excludes benchmarks in solicitations involving low dollar value procurements when performance can be validated by other means.

20/ Federal Information Processing Standards Publication (FIPS PUB) 42-1, Guidelines For Benchmarking ADP Systems in the Competitive Procurement Environment, May 15, 1977.

21/ Id.

22/ When live test demonstrations are unfeasible, GSA has allowed the use of "remote terminal emulation." See FPR 4.1109-23. Remote terminal emulation is a benchmarking technique:

> for conducting tests of teleprocessing computer systems and services when it is impractical to

(Footnote Continued)

The General Accounting Office (GAO), in the context of protests, reviews federal data processing practices and has upheld
benchmarking as "a legitimate means to ensure that a prospective
contractor has the technical capability" to provide data processing
services to the federal government. 23/ While the contracting
agency has the authority to establish benchmarks and pre-award
testing procedures, 24/ the GAO places some limitations on the
agency's discretion. In Sperry Univac Computer Systems, 25/ for
example, the GAO held that the contracting agency could not establish benchmark instructions that contradicted the announced objective
evaluation criteria in the contracting agency's Request for Proposal
(RFP). In that case, the RFP allowed the offerors to redesign an
existing system; however, the contracting agency interpreted the
benchmark instructions to preclude any system redesign or program
conversion. One offeror that failed the benchmark test protested
because it had redesigned the agency's system. The GAO ruled that

---

(Footnote 22 Continued)

> configure for a test the total planned network of
> computer, teleprocessing devices, and data
> communication facilities. Remote terminal emula-
> tion uses an external driver computer and com-
> puter programs to imitate the teleprocessing
> devices to be supplied by, and to impose the
> workload demands on, the actual computer
> system or service being tested . . .

See General Services Administration Handbook, Use and Specifications of Remote Terminal Emulation in ADP System Acquisition 1
(Aug. 1979), which describes when and how agencies should use
remote terminal emulation and specifies the remote terminal emulation
capabilities that an agency may require offerors to provide for
testing automatic data processing systems.

23/ Informatics, Inc., B-190203, March 20, 1978, 781 CPD 215, aff'd
Aug. 2, 1978, 78-2 CPD 84. The GAO in Informatics, Inc. went on
to state that "there is no better way to determine a prospective
contractor's technical capability than through" benchmarking. See
also Aeronautical Instrument and Radio Company, B-190920, Oct. 13,
1978, 78-2 CPD 276; Burroughs Corporation, B-187769, July 12,
1977, 77-2 CPD 16.

24/ Informatics, Inc., supra, n. 23.

25/ B-194003, Oc. 29, 1979, 79-2 CPD 300.

either the offeror should be deemed to have passed the benchmark test, or the contracting agency should amend its RFP to reflect its actual minimum needs and require all offerors to submit revised proposals.

Similarly, in ADP Network Services, Inc., 26/ the GAO rejected the contracting agency's benchmarks on the grounds that the benchmark narrative did not fully describe the functions to be performed, failed to identify system-controlled variables and define program command functions, and required the conversion of large amounts of undocumented proprietary code. The GAO held under these circumstances that the benchmark instructions should be revised to provide more detailed information to the offerors. 27/

To permit meaningful competition once the government establishes consistent benchmark requirements, the contracting agency must allow some flexibility in administering the benchmark tests. In Sycor, Inc., 28/ for example, the GAO ruled that in the absence of prejudice to other offerors, a contracting agency could delay the benchmark test of the low offeror to allow it to make minor adjustments to its proposed equipment. The GAO also has held that an offeror may use another company's personnel to perform a benchmark test, given the flexibility inherent in competitive negotiations and the ambiguity of the RFP. 29/

Agencies may in their discretion allow a second benchmark test when an offeror would otherwise be rejected due to unforeseen failures, such as machine-dependent conversion errors, power failures, and equipment, communication line, or system software failures. 30/ In Tymshare, Inc., 31/ the contracting agency was allowed to run a second benchmark test for an unsuccessful offeror

---

26/ B-196286, May 12, 1980, 80-1 CPD 339.

27/ See also Information International, Inc., B-191013, Aug. 8, 1980, 80-2 CPD 100, which held that benchmarks must be precise and unambiguous to be used in comparing cost data.

28/ B-180310, April 22, 1974, 74-1 CPD 207.

29/ Linolex Systems, Inc., 53 Comp. Gen. 895 (1974), 74-1 CPD 296, modified, 54 Comp. Gen. 483, 74-2 CPD 344.

30/ FIPS PUB 42-1, supra, n. 20.

31/ B-192987, August 28, 1979, 79-2 CPD 158.

---

after the deadline for such tests had expired. The GAO concluded that the second test was justified for two reasons. First, the other vendors were not prejudiced since the RFP gave everyone a second opportunity to pass the benchmark and all other vendors had successfully passed the initial benchmark or failed the second benchmark. Second, in the second benchmark test, the unsuccessful offeror made only machine dependent changes necessary to complete the test on the vendor's proposed equipment, and did not "optimize" the benchmark program by adjusting the program logic or method of processing function to improve performance.

Similarly, in The Computer Company, 32/ the GAO recommended that the contracting agency allow the unsuccessful offeror that had met all other technical requirements to conduct a second benchmark test when its initial failure could have been averted had agency personnel immediately notified the offeror of the performance deficiency. In Burroughs Corporation, 33/ however, the GAO distinguished this ruling and upheld a decision not to grant a second benchmark on the grounds that the agency in the RFP had notified offerors of the importance and impact of failing the benchmark test and had communicated adequately the nature, scope and specific requirements of the benchmark. In that case, the GAO also noted that the second benchmark would have permitted the unsuccessful offeror unfairly to optimize system performance, thereby prejudicing the offerors who had successfully completed the benchmark.

When an agency is permitted to exercise its discretion in applying benchmark requirements, the GAO may require the agency to amend its RFP to afford other offerors a similar opportunity. 34/ In addition, the GAO has held that a contracting agency may not exclude an offeror from the "competitive range" solely because of its failure to pass a benchmark test. 35/ Thus, contracting agencies do not have unfettered discretion to establish and apply benchmark tests. Oftentimes the contracting agency's benchmark instructions or tests unfairly restrict competitive bidding on automatic data processing contracts. Under these circumstances, the unsuccessful

32/ B-198876, October 3, 1980, 80-2 CPD 240.

33/ B-202316, June 8, 1981, 81-1 CPD 460.

34/ Sperry Rand Corporation, 56 Comp. Gen. 312 (1977), 77-1 CPD 77.

35/ Honeywell Incorporated, 47 Comp. Gen. 29 (1976).

offeror can lodge a formal and timely protest to prevent the award of the contract and to require the agency to change its benchmarks or testing procedures.

V. SOFTWARE ACQUISITION STANDARDS AND PROCEDURES

Even though there remains some question as to whether the Brooks Act covers computer software, GSA has exercised some control over the procurement of commercially available software by federal agencies. While agencies generally must obtain GSA approval of commercially available software, 36/ GSA does not require prior approval of special types of software, including software provided with and not separately priced from the data processing hardware, and software acquired through the Federal Software Exchange, which collects, maintains and disseminates common-use software. 37/

GSA has set forth specific goals and policy guidelines for agencies procuring software services. 38/ When acquiring commercially available software, agencies must "[a]void restrictive clauses that limit the use of the software to a specific computer system installation, or organization." 39/ Agencies are also urged to incorporate contract provisions that would permit other federal agencies to obtain the software under the same contract. 40/ Furthermore, procuring agencies are asked to obtain quantity discounts should other agencies acquire the same software under the contract in question. 41/ Finally, GSA urges all agencies to make sure that "the vendor is contractually obligated to support and maintain the software in subsequent years." 42/ The maintenance obligation may

---

36/ FPMR 36.203-2.

37/ See FPR 4.1104-2; FPMR 36.16.

38/ FPR 4.1109-16.

39/ FPR 4.1109-16(a).

40/ FPR 4.1109-16(b).

41/ FPR 4.1109-16(c).

42/ FPR 4.1109-16(d).

---

last five to ten years, given GSA's estimate of the useful life of applications software, without redesign or reprogramming. 43/

The Department of Commerce has published mandatory standards for software contracts awarded by the federal government. These standards include instructions regarding the use of COBOL programming language, 44/ standards for flowchart symbols, 45/ and instructions for describing computer programs and automatic data systems. 46/ Yet despite these guidelines and directives, GSA has failed to provide mandatory standards for the control and validation of software development contracts similar to those applicable to computer hardware procurements. Consequently, software development contracts often are characterized by unexpected costs and delays arising from lack of specific performance requirements in contracts, uncertainty concerning the state of the art at the time the contracts are awarded, lack of federal control over contract performance, failure to manage software development during contract performance, uncertainty of software testing requirements, lack of communication between the government and the contractor, and failure of contractors to provide adequate software performance documentation. 47/

To eliminate the purchase of inappropriate software, GSA has issued informal policy guidelines for software contracts. 48/ These voluntary guidelines suggest that the contracting agency define its software requirements specifically and describe in detail the environment in which the software must operate, the area of applications, and the needs and functions that the software must satisfy. In addition, the agencies are urged to retain the integrity of current systems by determining whether incremental improvement of all or part of the systems (e.g. transfer from sequential file to direct access processing, from batch to on-line processing, from low level languages to high level languages) would meet the needs of the agency. GSA also has asked agencies to plan all design, production

---

43/ FPMR 35.206-1(c).

44/ FPMR 36.1305-1, FIPS PUB 21-1.

45/ FPMR 36.1305-2, FIPS PUB 24.

46/ FPMR 36.1305-3, FIPS PUB 30.

47/ GSA, Bulletin FPMR F-131, May 19, 1981.

48/ Id.

---

and implementation phases of a software development contract, including systems analysis, requirements definition, systems design, detailed design, programming, debugging, program testing, systems integration, documentation, operational use, final testing and acceptance, and post-implementation evaluation. Finally, GSA has given some guidance to agencies to insure the quality of software procured by the government. Specifically, GSA has recommended that the contracting agency define precisely the quality expected, and describe the criteria for acceptance of each phase and the methodology for applying the acceptance criteria. 49/

Since most of GSA's guidelines applicable to software procurement are voluntary, substantial uncertainty exists among agencies and within private industry as to the standards for evaluating and validating software systems. In the absence of more specific and mandatory standards and procedures governing the procurement of software services, the federal government is likely to continue experiencing inefficiencies and delays in procuring software services.

V.   CONCLUSION

One cannot overestimate the ever-increasing demands of the federal government for computer services. Since government operations cannot meet many of these demands, private industry has assumed a greater role in the procurement process. By understanding the procedures and standards used in the procurement of computer hardware and software, private industry will be able to respond to, and ultimately profit from, the automatic data processing needs of the federal government.

49/   Id.

MARZOUK

PROTECTING YOUR PROPRIETARY RIGHTS

IN THE COMPUTER AND HIGH TECHNOLOGY INDUSTRIES

APPENDIX F

Federal Contract Specifications
for ADP Hardware and Software

By Tobey B. Marzouk

When the Government purchases ADP hardware and software, the responsibility for technical matters, including the preparation of contract specifications, rests with technical personnel in the contracting agency, the Federal Telecommunications Service, and the National Bureau of Standards. The agency must tailor specifications so as to document and provide for the satisfaction of minimum agency needs while maximizing competition among potential suppliers. Even though certain ADP hardware and software are not always compatible with existing computer systems owned or operated by the Federal Government, agencies still must adhere to the requirements of "nonrestrictive" specifications and maximum competition. With the advancing technology in ADP equipment and services, special regulations have been promulgated to address unique aspects of ADP procurement.

Methods of Procurement

The Government buys ADP hardware and software in a number of ways which range in complexity from a simple order from a supplier who already has a contract with the General Services Administration (GSA) to a complex competitive procurement for an extensive ADP system. The method of contracting depends upon the type of ADP equipment and services to be purchased, the approximate value of the purchase, the number of potential suppliers, and the uniqueness of the contracting agency's needs.

Prior to developing a contract solicitation, a contracting agency must prepare a comprehensive requirements analysis to determine its needs and how best to meet them. This analysis must address whether any alternatives exist to purchasing the ADP equipment or services. For example, GSA maintains an inventory list of excess ADP hardware and software that can be transferred among Federal agencies. If excess data processing equipment or services fit a contracting agency's needs, GSA transfers them to the contracting agency, rather than allow the agency to purchase new products. In general, the policy is not to purchase new ADP hardware or software when other, less costly alternatives are available.

When an agency needs software or specialized hardware that will cost less than $10,000, the agency may use a simplified small purchase procedure. In this case, many of the required reviews and procedures applicable to more costly procurements are waived.

An agency can usually purchase standard "off-the-shelf" computer products by ordering from one of the many requirements contracts maintained by the Automated Data and Telecommunications Service of GSA. Initially negotiated by GSA, these contracts establish price, payment, and delivery terms and a maximum order limitation for various "common" items such as memory devices, disk packs, and tape and disk drives. If an agency determines that it needs one of the items offered by a requirements contract, purchase under such contract at the prenegotiated terms is mandatory and no other source may be used.

GSA also maintains nonmandatory contracts on the ADP Schedule. This group of

PROTECTING YOUR PROPRIETARY RIGHTS

contracts is available for use at the agency's option, and includes such items as word processing equipment, personal computers, and ADP maintenance services. The ADP Schedule makes purchase of computer hardware and software easier for an agency by prenegotiating prices, terms, and clauses. If the agency can get a better price or more favorable terms through the competitive procurement process, however, it need not purchase the item from the ADP Schedule.

In any ADP supply or service contract to which the Government is a party, a supplier must offer its "most-favored-customer" price reduction to the Government at least equal to the best price offered by the supplier to any of its customers.

Mandatory requirements contracts and the ADP Schedule require less time and effort by the contracting agency than a competitive procurement. If, however, the agency cannot meet its needs by the above methods, it must resort to competitive procurement.

Preparation of Specifications: Standardized Solicitation Requirements

The standardization of Government ADP procurements assists agencies unskilled in such procurements and helps reduce the purchase of incompatible computer hardware and software. It assists a potential bidder on an ADP contract by assuring that inexperienced Government personnel will draft comprehensible and reasonable specifications. Standardization also allows the bidder to offer a product to different agencies without significant modification.

To standardize competitive procurements, GSA provides an agency with a model solicitation document. The National Bureau of Standards publishes Federal information processing standards, referred to as FIPS PUBS, which establish standard terminology for Government ADP procurement.

Drafting Specifications to Meet Minimum Needs

Aside from the standardized solicitation requirements, procurement officials and technical personnel have broad discretion, notes the General Accounting Office, in "drafting proper specifications reflective of the needs of [the] Government." The procuring agency's specified needs must be the product of informed and critical judgment. Agency specifications, however, are presumed material and essential to Government needs, and GSA will not question agency determinations so long as they are within the bounds of reasonableness.

Because the Government bears the risk that specified items will be insufficient to meet its needs, it cannot allow contractors to determine agency needs or write specifications representing those needs. The contracting agency, on the othr hand, must be careful not to place unnecessary restrictive specifications for computer equipment and services.

In a case involving SMS Data Products Group, for example, the Comptroller General, who is empowered to declare specifications unduly restrictive and in excess of government needs, reviewed a solicitation to lease an IBM computer. The solicitation included, as one of the evaluation factors, membership in an IBM user group. Many of the publications distributed to members of the IBM user group, however, were publicly available. The Comptroller General held that "absent a clear showing that the direct, identifiable, and quantifiable benefits of membership . . . outweigh the attendant costs, such membership may not be considered as an evaluation factor." But it may be accorded a minimal weight in distinguishing "between otherwise essentially equal proposals."

The Comptroller General usually accepts the agency's version of the facts in protests of restrictive specifications, largely because the office is not staffed to handle technical fact investigations. As long as it is possible for professional technical opinions to honestly differ, and the agency determination is not clearly unreasonable or in error, the Comptroller General will accept the agency's determination.

In addition, to the mandatory requirements, the solicitation for ADP equipment and services may set forth "evaluated optional" features that can be included in the offeror's proposal. These features are generally items that the Government is not sure are technically feasible or that the Government would like to have but can only afford at the right price. An agency may also deem a feature to be an evaluated optional feature if making it mandatory would unduly restrict competition. The Government must indicate the relative value of each evaluated optional feature and an offeror includes it at his own discretion.

All specifications for ADP equipment are restrictive in some form, because not everyone is willing or able to provide the Government the computer products it needs. Potential bidders, for example, may not be able to provide the features requested in a solicitation because they do not possess the required technology or because the features are prohibitively expensive.

An improperly restrictive specification contains additional requirements that are not necessary to meet legitimate Government needs. Yet a specification that restricts competition is not unduly restrictive if the specification is necessary to meet the Government's ADP needs. For example the 1964 case of *Champion Machinery*, the Comptroller General upheld an award of a contract to a higher bidder, because the successful bidder was able to produce a necessary proprietary item, while the low bidder was not.

Minimum needs are not an absolute, objective standard, because agencies may specify different requirements for a particular procurement item if the requirements are reasonable. The term "minimum needs" should not suggest that the Government must only purchase the cheapest items available. The Government may procure a more expensive item will in fact satisfy those needs. This is especially true in the procurement of ADP equipment and services, where hardware components are often not compatible with existing systems and different software packages are not always interchangeable. ■

Mr. Marzouk is an attorney at the law firm of Marzouk & Parry in Washington, D.C.

PROTECTING YOUR PROPRIETARY RIGHTS

IN THE COMPUTER AND HIGH TECHNOLOGY INDUSTRIES

APPENDIX G

Agencies Can Enhance Competition in Procurements

By Tobey B. Marzouk

Although the primary purpose of contract specifications is to document government needs, full and open competition is a basic procurement objective of the government, under the Federal Procurement Regulations (FPR). Competition is desirable to promote the efficient use of resources, and thereby to lower government procurement costs. The desire to promote competitive procurement is so strong that competitive, advertised solicitation is considered proper, even when a product is produced by only one firm, as long as other firms can supply that product. The FPR requires that agencies design specifications and purchase descriptions to promote competition to the maximum practicable extent among manufacturers, leasing companies, third party vendors and ADP service contractors.

Maximizing Competition in Hardware Procurement

An agency can enhance competition by using functional specifications for ADP equipment that explain generally the agency's objectives and intended use of the ADP system. The FPR defines functional specifications as a "delineation of the program objectives based on mission needs in a form that ADP system is intended to accomplish and the data processing requirements underlying that accomplishment." Using functional specifications gives potential vendors a chance to offer the lowest priced computer hardware configurations that the vendors already have available and that would do the job, without being limited to specific equipment or technologies.

If functional specifications are inappropriate, an agency may use equipment specifications that state minimum user output requirements, such as the amount of data to be stored or the required processing time. Other specifications that are less preferred because of their limitation on competition are software compatibility, plug-to-plug compatibility, brand name or equal purchase descriptions, or specific make or model purchase descriptions.

Although make or model descriptions are the most restrictive of competition, the comptroller general has upheld their use on several occasions. In a case involving Amdahl Corp., for example, the comptroller general found a make or model restriction permissible when the agency determined that the incumbent contractor running the existing operating system software would not support the operating system on non-IBM machines.

Maximizing Competition In Software Procurement

When an agency purchases software, the FPR establishes additional requirements. Software procurements are made on the basis of the stated specifications, which, in turn, must be based on the agency's minimum needs. The comptroller general's policy is not to substitute his judgment for that of the contracting officer unless the protester can prove that the contracting officer's evaluation was arbitrary or unreasonable.

In some cases, restrictions are necessary because of the need for software compatibility with existing hardware. Any specification that requires the purchase of

ADP equipment or software to be compatible with an installed system must be supported by a software conversion study. It must also be justified on the basis or agency mission, essential data processing requirements, and economy and efficiency. Because a compatibility requirement is so restrictive, mere economy or efficiency is an inadequate justification.

The FPR considers the following to be adequate justifications for limiting the compatibility of ADP software:

- The essentiality of existing software, without redesign, to meet agency critical mission needs.
- The additional risk associated with conversion.
- The additional adverse impact of factors such as delay, lost economic opportunity, and less than optimum utilization of skilled professionals if compatibility specifications are not used.
- The steps being taken to foster competitive conditions.

The right of a contracting agency to restrict software specifications, however, is not unlimited. The comptroller general has struck down as unreasonable an agency rejection of a software proposal in which the offeror used two programs rather than a single program, as suggested by the solicitation. In the case, CompuServe Data Systems otherwise met the stated performance requirements and mandatory technical specifications. The comptroller general sustained the protest of the unsuccessful offerer on the grounds that the two programs were machine-integrated and no additional user input was necessary.

In order to determine the actual cost of software that is not compatible with an existing system, the contracting agency must perform a software conversion study. If the agency's technical personnel are not sufficiently qualified or would prefer outside assistance, the Federal Conversion Support Center may perform the software conversion study on behalf of the agency.

To maximize the utility of federal acquired software, the contracting agency attempts to avoid restrictive clauses that limit use of the software to a specific system currently in operation at the agency or to a single government installation or organization. The FPR suggests inserting contractual clauses that will permit other agencies to obtain software under the contract being negotiated and to provide for quantity discounts for purchases by other agencies.

Procuring agencies also evaluate potential suppliers of software and software services on the basis of both the qualifications of a supplier's employees and the supplier's past experience with software contracts. When replying to a government solicitation, the supplier must specifically set forth his experience and those of his employees. The case of Science Information Services, involving the procurement of computer input services, illustrates the importance of identifying prior experience when replying to ADP contract solicitations. In that case, the evaluator for the National Institute for Occupational Safety and health gave the bid poster's project manager high marks for his knowledge of occupational safety and health but gave the company low marks for its experience with computer input services, even though the project manager was also the president of the company. The comptroller general dismissed the protest, stating that it was the agency's task to evaluate the proposal. Because it did not clearly offer the requested experience, the proposal was properly rejected.

Bid Protests of Specifications

Bid protests of indefinite or ambiguous specifications, as opposed to unduly restrictive specifications, may be made after the bid opening, but must be made prior to the contract award. After bids have been opened, the award must be made to the lowest responsible bidder unless there is a compelling reason to reject all bids. Compelling reasons for cancellation include (1) inadequate or ambiguous specifications, (2) the revision of specifications, and (3) receipt of bids indicating that the needs of the Government can be satisfied by less expensive ADP equipment or services differing from that which the solicitation specified. Solicitations may be canceled when a bidder is prejudiced by misleading specifications, when the specifications fail to meet the government's legitimate needs, and when the specifications confuse a majority of bidders.

Industry Review of Specifications

In order for government requirements to reflect the current state of the art and existing technology, an agency may release the proposed specifications to industry prior to issuance of the solicitation. An agency is acting within its discretion in deciding whether or not prior release is appropriate. Interested parties are generally given 30 days (60 days if the procurement is complex) in which to review and submit comments on the proposed specifications. If, after issuance of the solicitation, the agency deems a specification inappropriate, the solicitation can be amended to reflect the change.

Conclusion

Specifications for ADP equipment and software purchased by the federal government represent a delicate balance between the needs of the contracting agency and the requirement of maximum practicable competition. In the future, as technology advances and computer hardware and software become generally more compatible, the procurement of ADP equipment and services may become more routine. In the meantime, government contractors should carefully monitor agency requirements and specifications and spot any arrangements that may unduly restrict competition without providing any additional technical benefit. This will open the realm of federal ADP procurement to a greater number of participants with increasingly superior products. ■

Marzouk is an attorney at the law firm of Marzouk & Parry in Washington, D.C., where he specializes in computer law and federal court litigation.

PROTECTING YOUR PROPRIETARY RIGHTS

IN THE COMPUTER AND HIGH TECHNOLOGY INDUSTRIES

AUTHOR BIOGRAPHY

Author Biography

Tobey B. Marzouk, a leading computer law expert specializes in all aspects of high technology law and computer litigation. He has represented data processing firms, independent software developers, software publishers, computer manufacturers and purchasers, ADP. government contractors, and other high technology enterprises. Mr. Marzouk is also Trade Secrets/Litigation Editor of the *Computer Law Reporter*, the leading legal journal of the high technology industry, and a Founder and General Editor of the *International Business and Trade Law Reporter*. He has lectured extensively on various issues of computer law and has published numerous articles in trade and legal journals. Mr. Marzouk received his Bachelors Degree from Princeton University and his law degree from Harvard Law School. His law offices are located in Washington, D.C. (telephone: 202-463-7293).

Other Computer Society Press Texts

Ada Programming Language
Edited by S.H. Saib and R.E. Fritz
(ISBN 0-8186-0456-5); 548 pages

Advanced Computer Architecture
Edited by D.P. Agrawal
(ISBN 0-8186-0667-3); 400 pages

Advanced Microprocessors and High-Level Language Computer Architectures
Edited by V. Milutinovic
(ISBN 0-8186-0623-1); 608 pages

Communication and Networking Protocols
Edited by S.S. Lam
(ISBN 0-8186-0582-0); 500 pages

Computer Architecture
Edited by D.D. Gajski, V.M. Milutinovic,
H.J. Siegel, and B.P. Furht
(ISBN 0-8186-0704-1); 602 pages

Computer Communications: Architectures, Protocols, and Standards (2nd Edition)
Edited by William Stallings
(ISBN 0-8186-0790-4); 448 pages

Computer Graphics (2nd Edition)
Edited by J.C. Beatty and K.S. Booth
(ISBN 0-8186-0425-5); 576 pages

Computer and Network Security
Edited by M.D. Abrams and H.J. Podell
(ISBN 0-8186-0756-4); 448 pages

Computer Networks (4th Edition)
Edited by M.D. Abrams and I.W. Cotton
(ISBN 0-8186-0568-5); 512 pages

Computer Text Recognition and Error Correction
Edited by S.N. Srihari
(ISBN 0-8186-0579-0); 364 pages

Computers for Artificial Intelligence Applications
Edited by B. Wah and G.-J. Li
(ISBN 0-8186-0706-8); 656 pages

Database Management
Edited by J.A. Larson
(ISBN 0-8186-0714-9); 448 pages

Digital Image Processing and Analysis: Volume 1: Digital Image Processing
Edited by R. Chellappa and A.A. Sawchuk
(ISBN 0-8186-0665-7); 736 pages

Digital Image Processing and Analysis: Volume 2: Digital Image Analysis
Edited by R. Chellappa and A.A. Sawchuk
(ISBN 0-8186-0666-5); 670 pages

Distributed Control (2nd Edition)
Edited by R.E. Larson, P.L. McEntire, and J.G. O'Reilly
(ISBN 0-8186-0451-4); 382 pages

Distributed Database Management
Edited by J.A. Larson and S. Rahimi
(ISBN 0-8186-0575-8); 580 pages

Distributed Processor Communication Architecture
Edited by K.J. Thurber
(ISBN 0-8186-0258-9); 526 pages

DSP-Based Testing of Analog and Mixed-Signal Circuits
Edited by M. Mahoney
(ISBN 0-8186-0785-8); 272 pages

End User Facilities in the 1980's
Edited by J.A. Larson
(ISBN 0-8186-0449-2); 526 pages

Fault-Tolerant Computing
Edited by V.P. Nelson and B.D. Carroll
(ISBN 0-8186-0677-0 (paper) 0-8186-8667-4 (case)); 432 pages

Gallium Arsenide Computer Design
Edited by V.M. Milutinovic and D.A. Fura
(ISBN 0-8184-0795-5); 368 pages

Human Factors in Software Development (2nd Edition)
Edited by B. Curtis
(ISBN 0-8186-0577-4); 736 pages

Integrated Services Digital Networks (ISDN)
Edited by W. Stallings
(ISBN 0-8186-0625-8); 332 pages

Integrating Design and Test: Using CAE Tools for ATE Programming: Monograph
Written by K.P. Parker
(ISBN 0-8186-8788-6 (case)); 160 pages

Interactive Computer Graphics
Edited by H. Freeman
(ISBN 0-8186-0266-X); 420 pages

Interconnection Networks for Parallel and Distributed Processing
Edited by C.-l. Wu and T.-. Feng
(ISBN 0-8186-0574-X); 500 pages

JSP and JSD: The Jackson Approach to Software Development
Edited by J.R. Cameron
(ISBN 0-8186-8516-6); 264 pages

Local Computer Networks (2nd Edition)
Edited by K.J. Thurber and H.A. Freeman
(ISBN 0-8186-0368-2); 372 pages

Local Network Equipment
Edited by H.A. Freeman and K.J. Thurber
(ISBN 0-8186-0605-3); 384 pages

Local Network Technology (3rd Edition)
Edited by W. Stallings
(ISBN-0-8186-0825-0); 512 pages

Microcomputer Networks
Edited by H.A. Freeman and K.J. Thurber
(ISBN 0-8186-0395-X); 288 pages

Models and Metrics for Software Management and Engineering
Edited by V.R. Basili
(ISBN 0-8186-0310-0); 352 pages

Modern Design and Analysis of Discrete-Event Computer Simulations
Edited by E.J. Dudewicz and Z. Karian
(ISBN 0-8186-0597-9); 486 pages

National Computer Policies: Monograph
Written by Ben G. Matley and Thomas A. McDannold
(ISBN 0-8186-8784-3); 192 pages

For Further Information:

Computer Society of the IEEE, 10662 Los Vaqueros Circle, Los Alamitos, CA 90720

Computer Society of the IEEE, Avenue de la Tanche, 2, B-1160 Brussels, BELGIUM